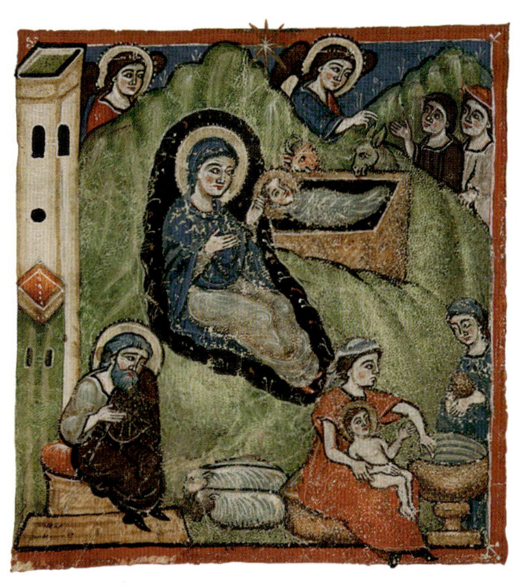

ILLUSTRIOUS ILLUMINATIONS
輝煌的啟示

From the McCarthy Collection
麥卡錫蒐藏

ILLUSTRIOUS ILLUMINATIONS

CHRISTIAN MANUSCRIPTS

FROM THE HIGH GOTHIC TO THE HIGH RENAISSANCE

(1250–1540)

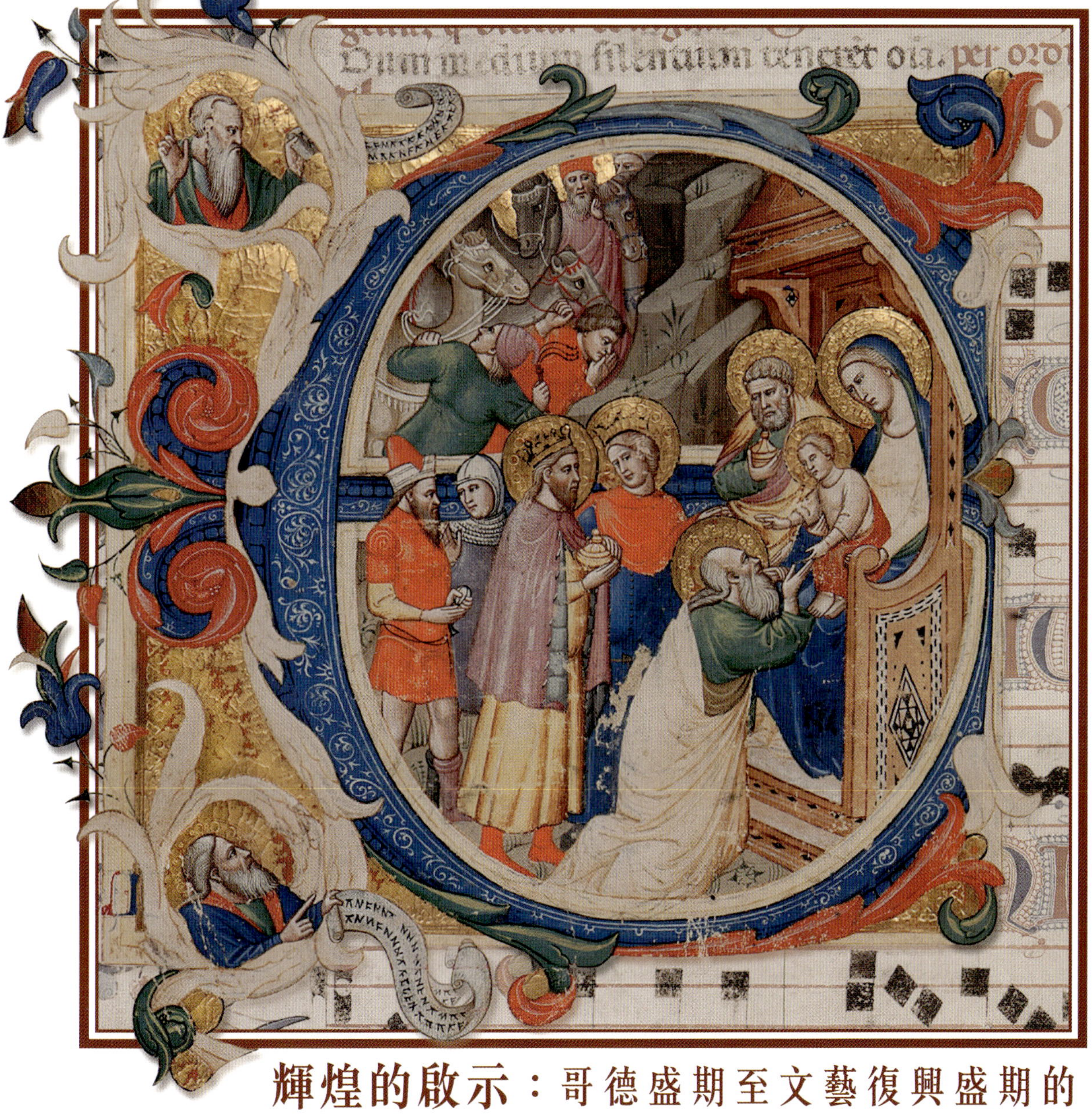

輝煌的啟示：哥德盛期至文藝復興盛期的

基 督 宗 教 手 稿

〔一 二 五 零 年 至 一 五 四 零 年〕

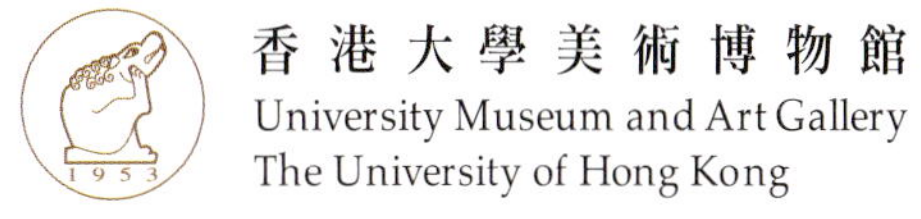

ILLUSTRIOUS ILLUMINATIONS: CHRISTIAN MANUSCRIPTS FROM THE HIGH GOTHIC TO THE HIGH RENAISSANCE (1250-1540)

輝煌的啟示：哥德盛期至文藝復興盛期的基督宗教手稿〔一二五零年至一五四零年〕

CURATOR 策展人

DR FLORIAN KNOTHE 羅諾德博士

AUTHOR 作者

DR FLORIAN KNOTHE 羅諾德博士, ROBERT MCCARTHY 羅伯特 · 麥卡錫

PUBLISHER 出版

CHRISTOPHER MATTISON 馬德松

（UNIVERSITY MUSEUM AND ART GALLERY,

THE UNIVERSITY OF HONG KONG 香港大學美術博物館）

CHINESE TRANSLATION 中文翻譯

ANDREA CHEN 陳劍, EDWARD ZHOU 周政

DESIGN 設計

PAULINE HO 何寶妮

PHOTOGRAPHY 攝影

RICKY POON 潘榮健

EDITION 版次

December 2015 二零一五年十二月

ISBN 國際標準書號

978-988-19023-4-4

UNIVERSITY MUSEUM AND ART GALLERY, THE UNIVERSITY OF HONG KONG

90 Bonham Road, Hong Kong

香港大學美術博物館

香港般咸道九十號

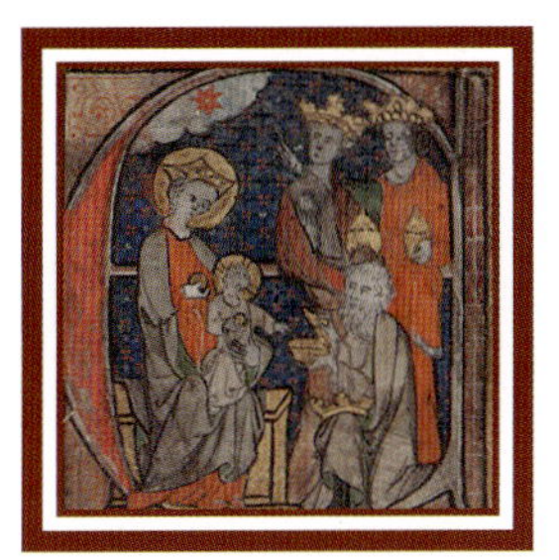

CONTENTS 目次

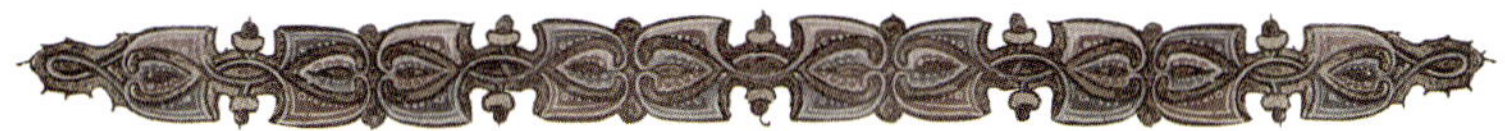

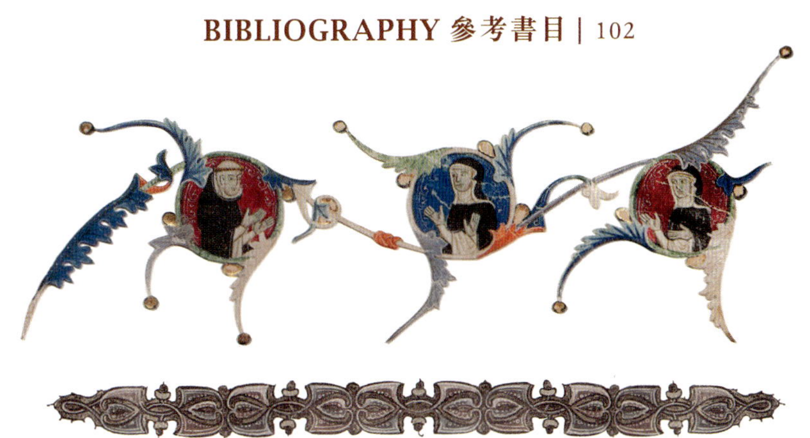

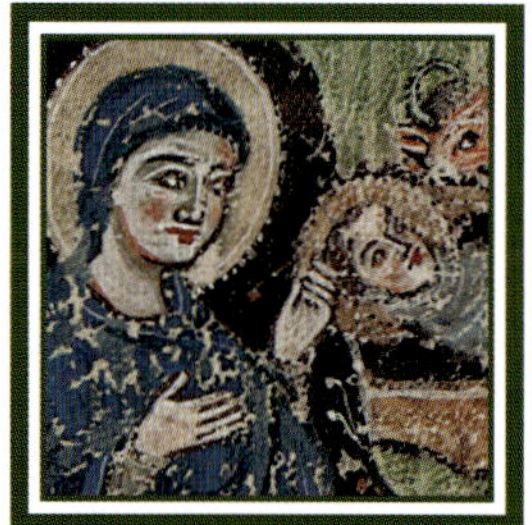

Foreword 前言

Dr Florian Knothe
Director
University Museum and Art Gallery
The University of Hong Kong
羅諾德博士
香港大學美術博物館總監

The University Museum and Art Gallery is honoured to be working with the McCarthy Collection to display, for the first time in Hong Kong, an exquisite selection of Gothic and Renaissance illuminated manuscripts. Long treasured as visual representations of the Christian Gospel, these miniature paintings give evidence of the talent and culture connected to the art of book illustration. At a time when large parts of society remained illiterate, both text and images in rare books—such as Bibles and books of hours—created an art form to which few community members had access. Within today's flood of visual information, these exceptional documents highlight the important historic and cultural contexts from which they emerged.

Our focus on the time period 1250–1540 is twofold: it is worth noting, primarily, that the art of the book in Europe reached unprecedented heights during the late Gothic and Renaissance eras. Many of these vibrant, hand-copied volumes contain some of the finest illustrations ever produced across Europe, well before Johannes Gutenberg introduced the printing press in Mainz around 1454. Secondly, the detailed and often highly colourful illustrations exemplify a shift in style, from Gothic to Renaissance lines, which likewise was apparent in the architecture and paintings produced under the auspices of the Church. As a patron, the Catholic Church employed the best, and often most celebrated, architects and artists of the time. Based on this influence, it is not surprising that the illustrated books produced to communicate the Christian faith and culture are often, even in their smaller formats, as impressive as the church buildings and altar paintings that served the devout community.

香港大學美術博物館很高興與麥卡錫蒐藏合作，首次於香港展出一系列精心挑選的哥德及文藝復興時期的泥金插畫手繪本。此類微繪手稿長期以來作為基督宗教福音書的圖像化表述而被珍藏，她們體現著插畫藝術的才華與文化。在那個文字尚未普及的時代，古籍善本例如聖經和時禱書中的文字和圖像，皆體現了一種被少數社群成員所獨享的藝術形式。今時今日，於視覺信息的洪流之中，這些難得一見的珍貴文本集中呈現了其所誕生的那個世代的重要歷史和文化處境。

此次展覽對一二五零年至一五四零年這一時間段的關注是雙重的。首先值得一提的是，在哥德後期及文藝復興時代，歐洲的書籍裝幀藝術達到了史無前例的水平；而且，在一四五四年左右約翰內斯·古騰堡於美茵茨引入印刷機之前，配有最優秀插畫的手抄卷本早已遍佈歐洲。其次，這些精細且豐富多彩的插圖例證了一種風格轉變，即由哥德式轉向文藝復興式的線條，這種轉變在建築與繪畫中亦表現明顯，並同樣深受教會的支持與影響。作為這些藝術品的需求者與推動者，天主教會總會聘請最優秀且最著名的建築師與藝術家，故而製作出的教堂建築與祭壇畫乃是華麗無比；而相比之下，這些同樣蘊涵基督宗教信仰與文化的插畫書籍，儘管局限於較小的版式中，卻依然能綻放出奪目的藝術光彩，令人讚歎不已。

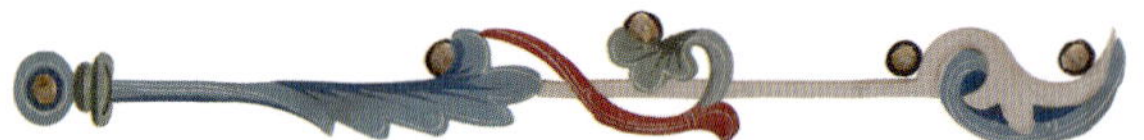
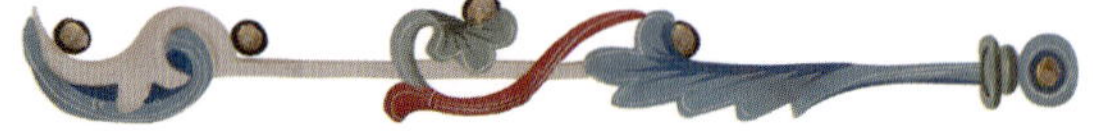

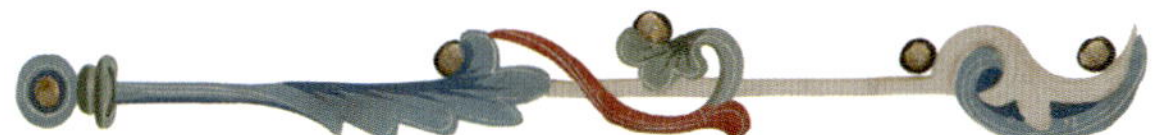

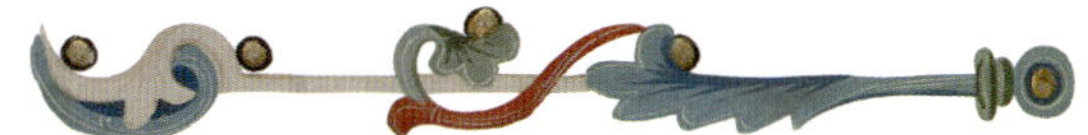

Further parallels between religious imagery and symbolism—within the fields of book illustration, sculpture and stained glass work—are found in the carefully chosen and highly detailed biblical scenes. Whereas large polychrome windows, paintings and sculpture were often created to introduce the illiterate to the Gospel, as well as to reinforce key episodes from the Bible, illuminated manuscripts served a sophisticated role for a more educated readership.

Illustrious Illuminations exemplifies the crucial developments in style and representation. The often harder, more contrasting, lines of the Gothic give way to the Renaissance's altogether natural contours, as well as to softer and increasingly personal facial features. Expressions, personal attire and the background details shift in ever-repeated depictions. Quite simply, these artistic evolutions and stylistic developments mark the beginning of our modern era. We would like to thank Robert McCarthy for allowing us to share his collection, which certainly will provide a wealth of knowledge about this time period for our museum visitors and students.

在書籍插畫、雕塑與彩繪玻璃作品等藝術形式中，通過對《聖經》場景的精心挑選與明確描畫，宗教意象與象徵愈發統一。大型彩飾窗、繪畫與雕塑，通常被看作是在向缺乏閱讀能力的人傳播福音，亦是在加深其對《聖經》中一些關鍵情節的認識；而泥金插畫手繪本則比之扮演了較為複雜的角色，其讀者群往往受過良好教育。

《輝煌的啟示》展覽完美印證了這些在風格與表現中的關鍵發展。哥德式風格中通常更硬朗且更具對比度的線條，讓位於文藝復興風格中完全自然的輪廓，以及更柔和且愈發個人化的面部特徵。表情、服飾與環境細節在不斷重複的描繪中變化。簡單而言，這些藝術流變與風格發展標誌著現代藝術時期的開始。本人謹代表香港大學美術博物館感謝羅伯特・麥卡錫先生慷慨分享其收藏，為我們提供了關於這一獨特時期的豐富知識，相信博物館的參觀者與學生定能從中獲益良多。

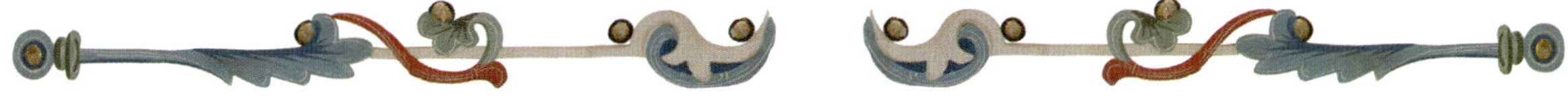

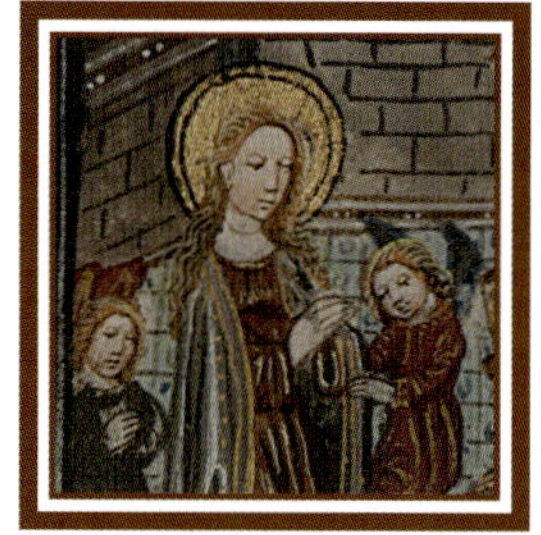

A Passion for Medieval Art:
The Genesis of the McCarthy Collection
一生所愛——中世紀藝術：
麥卡錫蒐藏之創世紀

Robert McCarthy
Collector of the McCarthy Collection
羅伯特·麥卡錫
展品藏家

I first came to appreciate medieval art as a teenager during a bicycle trip around Europe in July 1971. This included a visit to Chartres, which has one of the world's best preserved Gothic cathedrals, complete with the original stained glass and sculptures. Malcolm Miller, the English-language guide at the cathedral, who I believe is still active there to this day, described the history of the cathedral and the meaning behind the art. As with many who enter Chartres cathedral, I found it awe-inspiring and I immediately wanted to understand more about the culture that had created such beauty. Accordingly, I studied medieval history at university, and later completed a Master's Degree in medieval history while working in New York. On regular trips to Europe I visited many of the major surviving churches and monasteries from the medieval period. These included the early primitive monastery of St Martin du Canigou, the nearby red marble carving at Serrabone, St Michel de Cuxa (the source of the central cloister in the Cloisters Museum in New York), as well as the great high Romanesque church at Vezelay in Burgundy. Over the years, I also have visited the major Gothic cathedrals of Reims, Amiens, Bourges, Strasbourg and Cologne, along with numerous other medieval sites.

About 20 years ago I discovered that it was possible to own exquisite objects of medieval art. Over the centuries, a market has grown steadily for the numerous disassembled manuscripts, with particular interest in the images cut from the books. Likewise, as churches are closed or renovated, the artwork is often preserved and then sold.

一九七一年七月，在一次歐洲的騎行中，尚且年少的我第一次領略到中世紀藝術之美。這包括了對沙特爾的造訪，其中的沙特爾主教座堂乃是世界現存最完好的哥德式教堂建築之一，仍保存有原始的彩繪玻璃與雕塑。沙特爾主教座堂的英語導遊——馬爾科姆·米拿(我相信他至今依然從事這工作)，細述了教堂的歷史及其藝術的真諦。同許多初次進入沙特爾主教座堂的人一樣，我也油然而生敬畏之感，不由得立刻想要深入認識創造出此番壯美景象的文化；因此，我在大學時代修習了中世紀史，之後又在紐約工作時繼續深造並獲得了碩士學位。我會定期到訪歐洲，參觀許多現存的主要中世紀教堂與修道院，欣賞中世紀藝術精髓，包括早期的原始修道院——卡尼古山聖馬丁修道院，位於塞拉波涅修道院與聖米舍居扎修道院(紐約的修道院博物館分館的原型)的紅色大理石雕刻，位於勃艮第大區弗澤萊的羅曼式大教堂，以及位於蘭斯、亞眠、布爾日、史特拉斯堡、科隆的主要哥德式教堂與其他不計其數的中世紀景觀。

大約二十年前，我突然意識到我也能夠擁有屬於自己的中世紀藝術精品。數世紀以來，針對許多拆散的手繪卷本的交易市場不斷穩步發展，並以裁自這些書籍的插圖為熱點；而且，由於許多教堂被關閉或整修，其中的藝術品通常會先被保存並進而出售。

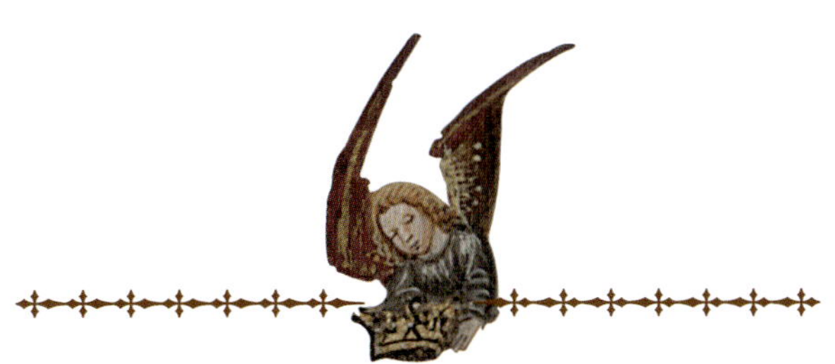

One of the first miniatures that I ever purchased was a Parisian psalter leaf depicting *The Circumcision* and *The Three Kings* (cat. no. 1a). It was painted around 1250, approximately the same time as Saint-Chapelle was being constructed on the Ile de Cite in Paris, not far from Notre Dame. The roundels displaying the scenes in this miniature and its sister leaves are reminiscent of the panels in the stained glass windows of Saint-Chapelle. Another early acquisition was the scene of *The Nativity* that was cut from a manuscript created in Monza, near Milan, around 1285 (cat. no. 5). This was strongly influenced by the tradition of Byzantine illumination. One can find similar patterns in a nativity in the mosaics from the late 13th century at Chora, in Constantinople (until A.D. 1453), present-day Istanbul.

I am delighted to be able to offer the opportunity for Hong Kong to view examples of medieval art from Western Europe. These particular items were chosen from my collection for their depictions of scenes from the Christmas story, including *The Annunciation*, *The Nativity*, *The Presentation in the Temple*, *The Adoration of the Magi* and *Mary with the Christ Child*. The works range in date from the 12th to the 16th century, and originate from France, Belgium, the Netherlands, Italy and Germany.

Christmas in medieval Europe was not as we experience it today in Hong Kong. Religion dominated medieval society and the annual calendar was based on the cycle of Church holidays. In fact, the word holiday derives from the term Holy Day; that is, a day sacred to the cycle of the Church calendar. The medieval period in Europe after the year 1000 was an extremely vibrant and creative

我購得的第一批微繪包括了這張描繪「基督割禮」與「三博士來朝」的《聖詠經》書頁（圖錄編號1a），約製作於一二五零年，幾乎是建造聖禮拜堂（位於巴黎西堤島，毗鄰巴黎聖母院）的同一時間。此幅微繪中用以展現故事場景的圓形圖版與其姊妹書頁一同令人聯想到聖禮拜堂中的彩繪玻璃窗。我的另一件早期藏品則是一幅關於「耶穌降生」的微繪（圖錄編號5），裁自一二八五年左右製作於蒙扎（米蘭附近）的手抄本。這幅作品深受拜占庭彩繪藝術的影響，人們可以在今日的伊斯坦堡、其前身君士坦丁堡（直到公元一四五三年）以及十三世紀晚期的科拉，找到馬賽克拼貼畫的「耶穌降生」作品。

我非常高興有此機會，同香港公眾分享這些來自西歐的麥卡錫蒐藏的中世紀藝術精品。這些展品之所以被挑選，皆因他們描繪了「聖誕故事」中的場景，包括「聖母領報」、「耶穌降生」、「獻主於聖殿」、「博士來朝」以及「聖母與聖嬰」等，起訖自十二世紀至十六世紀，起源於法國、比利時、尼德蘭、意大利與德國。

中世紀歐洲的聖誕節與今日於香港體驗的節日有所不同。那時的社會由宗教支配，而且年曆以教會禮儀的週期為基礎。事實上，單詞「Holiday」（假日），便是起源於詞組「Holy Day」（聖日），即教會禮儀年中的神聖日子。第一個千禧年之後的歐洲中世紀是一段充滿生機和創造力的時期，對此則有諸多解釋，比如此時期氣候較為溫暖，與此同時技術的發展促進了農業生

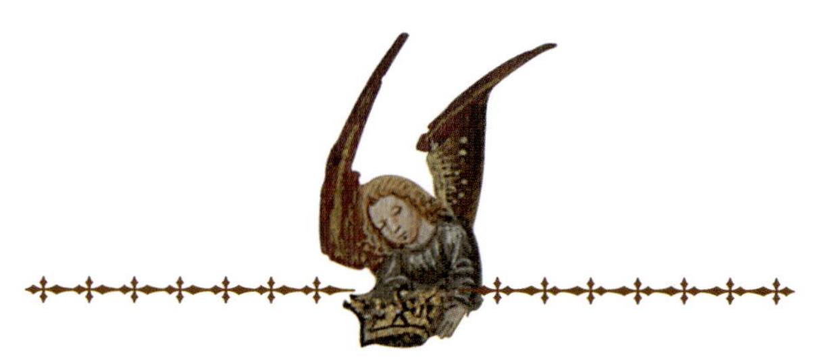

time. Numerous explanations have been put forward for this phenomenon, including the fact that the climate was considerably warmer in this era, coupled with the technological advances that allowed for increased agricultural production. A psychological explanation also has been put forward, positing that because the widespread belief that the world would end 1000 years after Christ did not materialize, Europe was able to redirect its energy towards building a better world upon this earthly realm. This is perhaps reflected in the chronicler Raoul Glaber's statement, found in his chronicle that likely dates to the 1020s: "the whole world . . .was clothed in a mantle of white churches" in the years after the Millennium. Developments in this era laid the foundation for modern Europe, and this time was witness to: the emergence of many of the nation states that exist today, significant population increases, the development of urban centers, the growth of trade and banking, the invention of double entry bookkeeping, the beginning of European expansion and the conquest of distant lands. The First Crusade was preached in 1095, the slow campaign to reconquer the Iberian Peninsula from the Moorish invaders was well underway at this time, and by the 15th century, Portuguese sailors were exploring the coast of Africa. Virtually every European town or city has a medieval core, which attests to its origins from this period; and if the church located at a city's center is not a medieval construction, it is only because it was renovated at some point over the centuries.

Accompanying these lively economic and political changes was the development of a sophisticated form of artistic expression. This is seen almost exclusively in the context of decorating religious buildings and providing objects for private devotion. In this exhibit, the sculptures originated as church decorations. Some of the miniatures, such as the large Italian leaves from choral books, were used as part of the church service. The book would have been propped up on a stand in the choir of the church for the benefit of the monks or canons participating in the service. Other miniatures, such as the small Parisian psalter leaves (cat. nos. 1a–c) or the Simon Bening paintings (cat. nos. 26a–b), come from

產，而在心理層面則有一種解釋，即當時相信主後一千年基督再臨的這種普遍信念沒有兑現，故而歐洲才得以重新調整去努力建立一個塵世領土之上的更好世界。編年史家拉夫·葛拉波在其一本約成書於一零二零年代的史書中寫道，千禧年之後的這一年，「整個世界……披上了白教堂的長幔」。這時期許多方面的發展均奠定了現代歐洲的基礎，也見證了：許多今日之國家的形成、迅猛的人口增長、城市中心的發展、貿易與銀行業的成長、複式記賬法的發明、歐洲擴張以及征服遙遠國土的開始。一零九五年，第一次十字軍東征的遊説開始，一場從摩爾人入侵者手中重新奪取伊比利亞半島的緩慢戰爭已然進行，直到十五世紀葡萄牙航海家對非洲海岸的探索為止，此時期才告結束。今日幾乎所有的歐洲市鎮皆有一個中世紀風格的中心，它們都源於這個時期；且如果一座建於市鎮中心的教堂並非中世紀風格，則只是因為它在過去數世紀的某個時刻經過翻修。

伴隨這些活躍的的經濟政治變化而來的是一種老練的藝術表現形式的發展，這幾乎只能從宗教建築裝飾與私人虔修物件的製作中得到體現。在是次展覽中，所有雕刻品最初皆用作教堂裝飾。其中一些微繪，比如來自聖詩集中的意大利文大型書頁，即是教堂司禮的一部分，此書用於教堂唱詩班的譜架上，以方便僧侶或教士們在禮拜中使用。其他微繪，比如小型的《聖詠經》書頁（圖錄編號1a–c），或施蒙·貝寧的繪畫作品（圖錄編號26a–b），則皆是用於私人虔修的小型書籍。「聖詠經」（包含聖經中的《詩篇》）逐漸發展為「時禱書」，自十四世紀起被上層社會的平信徒廣泛應用於日常禱文中。這四組佛萊明語跨頁提供了私人使用「時禱書」的絕佳例證（圖錄編號24a–d），而貝寧的微繪則來自於十六世紀早期一本奢華的《時禱書》。

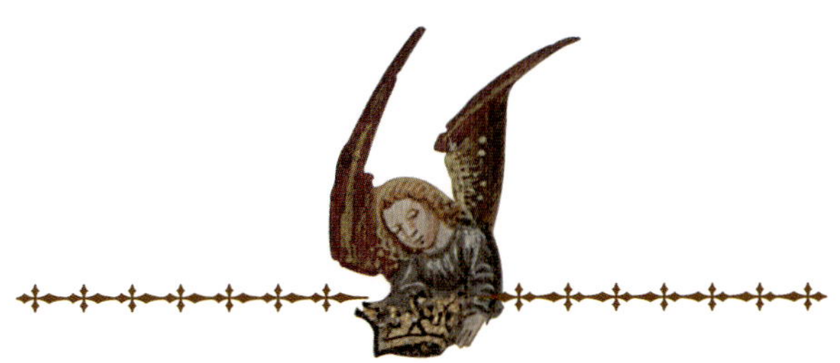

smaller books that were used in private devotion. The psalter (that includes psalms from the Bible) gradually evolved to become books of hours, which were used widely by the lay upper classes from the 14th century on as part of daily prayers. The set of four Flemish bifolia (double leaves) provide a good example of a book of hours (cat. nos. 24a–d) for private use, and the Bening miniatures were from a particularly lavish Book of Hours painted in the early 16th century.

I appreciate the fact that medieval work is seemingly less self-conscious than contemporary art. There is no need for an artist's statement of intent to accompany the work in order to explain to the audience what is being viewed. The art's purpose is extremely transparent. Thus, it was not art created purely for art's sake, but rather art to encourage religious devotion that accompanied a church service or daily prayers. This is not to say that this less conscious approach contains a lack of awareness of quality—quite the opposite. It is clear that the finest artists were engaged by those most able to pay—the high nobility and the richest churches—and their talent was greatly appreciated. However, the artists in the medieval period did not dissect, or have their work dissected, in the same theoretical way as much of 20th century art.

Although miniatures and sculpture such as these are not uncommon in collections found in Europe and North America, this is a rare opportunity to view medieval art in Hong Kong. Therefore, I am delighted to be able to share my collection, and I hope that there will be future opportunities to display further works of art for the benefit of my fellow Hong Kongers.

I would like to express my gratitude to Dr Romana Schuler, a professor at Vienna's University of Applied Arts, for her introduction to the concept of this exhibit, and for bringing me together with the University Museum; to Dr Florian Knothe, the Director of the University Museum for organizing the exhibit, and to the UMAG staff for producing this beautiful catalogue and for mounting the display.

我非常欣慰於中世紀藝術品似乎並不像當代藝術品那樣強調創作主體意識。也就是說不需要再附上作者的創作意圖來向觀者解釋映入眼簾的一切。眼見既是真相。因此，這並非一種純藝術形態，而是激發宗教情感並伴隨教堂禮儀和每日禱告的藝術。但這並非是說該項較少關注創作主體意識的藝術就缺乏對於品質的要求，事實恰恰相反。那些最優秀的藝術家往往受僱於極具購買力的主顧——上層貴族與最富有的教會——他們的藝術天分因此得到了充分的賞識。然而，中世紀藝術家並不像二十世紀的藝術家那樣會以理論為基礎來剖白自己的創作。

雖然像此類微繪與雕塑收藏在歐洲與北美的收藏界並非罕有，但對香港來說卻的確機會難得。我十分高興能與眾位分享我的收藏，亦希望未來能有更多機會，向香港的同道中人全面展示我的藏品。

在此，我要感謝維也納大學應用藝術專業教授，羅曼娜．舒樂博士，是她引入此展覽概念並引薦我同香港大學美術博物館結識；也要感謝香港大學美術博物館總監羅諾德博士及其團隊，他們的出色工作保證了展覽的順利組織與開展，以及此本精美圖錄的面世。

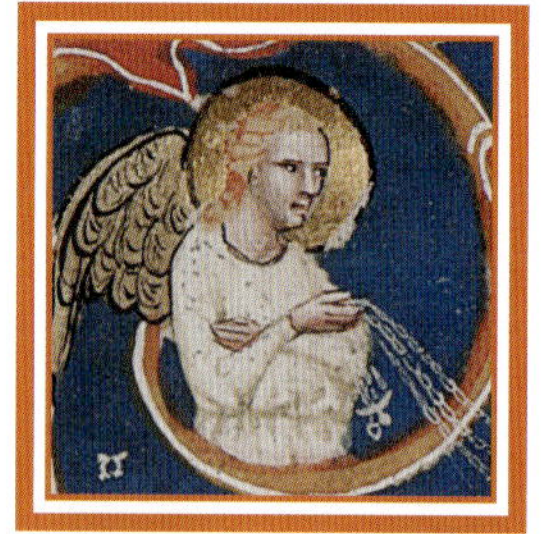

Illustrated Bibles, Psalters and Books of Hours: A Medieval Art Form Perfected in the Renaissance

Dr Florian Knothe

Illuminated manuscripts are a form of miniature painting.[1] Devised to both clarify and beautify, European manuscripts are typically Christian works in which the images illustrate and further explain the text. Related to the comprehensive visual references executed for church buildings in paint and stone, book illuminations differ in that they accompany a text—paintings and sculptures in Churches primarily replaced the text for illiterate community members—and show, often in a systematic form of repetition, key scenes from the Bible.

There is no single canonical script, as many Bibles have evolved over the past two millennia with corresponding and deviating contents. Various religious traditions have led to the creation of different, though largely related, churches that have produced diverse editions with different selections of texts; all of which share, however, a common core.[2] Essential to the daily practice and religious studies throughout the Christian and Judaic worlds, copies of the Bible were rare hand copied—and sometimes illustrated—books, until the distribution of the so-called Gutenberg Bible, printed by Johannes Gutenberg (c.1398–1468) in Mainz, Germany, in 1454. However, despite an increasing number of printed books since the fifteenth century, many of Europe's rulers and aristocrats continued to commission handwritten and often personalized books of hours for private devotion.

插圖裝飾的《聖經》、《聖詠經》和《時禱書》：文藝復興時期爐火純青的中世紀藝術形式

羅諾德博士

泥金裝飾手抄本是微繪的一種。[1] 歐洲手抄本是典型的基督教作品，設計理念既著重釋義又在乎形美，其中的圖畫為文本作出闡釋和澄明。相對於教堂建築之中那浩如煙海的以繪畫或石藝來表現的視覺創作，泥金裝飾手抄本的不同之處在於其與文本的相生相伴，並常常以一種系統化的重複來展現《聖經》中的重要場景，此情況下教堂之中的繪畫和雕刻則主要是為不識字的群體成員提供文字的替代品。

在過去的兩千年中，聖經文本在不同的處境之下經歷著演變，因而其並沒有簡單化一的正典可言。不同的宗教傳統造就了雖然彼此相聯卻迥然相異的教會，而這些教會又基於對不同文本的選擇而創造了多樣化的版本；儘管如此，這些版本依然擁抱同一個核心。[2] 基本來說，《聖經》貫穿了基督教和猶太世界的日常習俗和宗教研習，當時的聖經文本是時而以插圖裝飾的珍稀手抄本，此情況延續到所謂《古騰堡聖經》的出現。《古騰堡聖經》由約翰內斯．古騰堡（一三九八年至一四六八年）於一四五四年在德國美茵茨印製。然而，印刷書籍的數量雖自十五世紀以來不斷上升，但是許多歐洲領主和貴族們仍繼續定制手抄本的插圖裝飾《時禱書》用於私人虔修。

---

1 The word miniature, derived from the Latin *minium* ("red lead"), is a picture in an ancient or medieval illuminated manuscript. The simple decoration of the early codices having been miniated or delineated with that pigment.
單詞「Miniature」（「細密畫」或稱為「微繪」），來源於拉丁文「Minium」（紅鉛），是古代或中世紀時代的手抄本泥金插畫中的一種。早期抄本中的裝飾即用此種「紅鉛」顏料修飾上色。

2 Riches 2000, pp. 7–8.

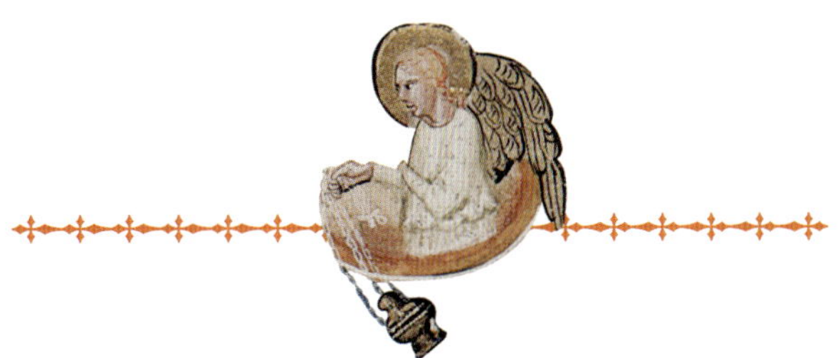

Like the Bible, psalters and books of hours also contain miniature illustration of, generally the same, religious contents. A psalter is a volume containing the book of psalms, which often includes supplementary devotional material, such as a liturgical calendar and the Litany of the Saints.[3] Until the later medieval emergence of books of hours, psalters were the books most widely owned by wealthy laypersons, and they were commonly used for learning to read. Many psalters are richly illuminated and include some of the most spectacular surviving examples of medieval book art. The book of hours is a Christian devotional book popular in the Middle Ages (5th–14th centuries). It is the most common type of surviving medieval illuminated manuscript. Like every manuscript, each illustrated book of hours is unique, although most contain a similar collection of texts, prayers and psalms, often with appropriate imagery for Christian devotion. Illuminations are often restricted to decorated capital letters at the start of psalms and other prayers, but books made for wealthy patrons could be extremely lavish, with full-page miniatures. Books of hours were usually written in Latin, although, over time, many copies entirely or partially written in vernacular European languages, such as French or Dutch, were produced for wider circulation.

In the early Middle Ages, manuscripts were either created as display editions with very full illuminations, or manuscripts for study with at most a few decorated initials and flourishes. By the Romanesque period, many

與《聖經》相同，同類宗教內容的微繪插圖也被用於《聖詠經》和《時禱書》的裝飾。《聖詠經》是讚美詩的集冊，通常還補充以其他敬拜資料，比如教會禮儀年與諸聖禱文。[3]中世紀末湧現出的《時禱書》及《聖詠經》，往往被富有的平信徒擁有，同時也可被用作識讀習字的書本。許多《聖詠經》都以繁複的插圖作為裝飾，其中有不少是中世紀書籍裝飾藝術中最為燦爛輝煌的存世典範。「時禱書」是中世紀（五到十四世紀）廣為流行的基督教敬拜書籍，是中世紀泥金裝飾手抄本現存於世的最典型類別。如同所有手抄本一樣，每本插圖版《時禱書》都是獨一無二的，伴隨著適合基督徒虔修的圖畫，其中的大多數都載有集合文本、禱告與讚美詩。插圖通常限定於讚美詩或者其他禱文的首字母裝飾方面，但是為富有主顧定制的書本則會竭盡繁奢之能事，常常有著整頁的微繪。《時禱書》大多以拉丁文撰寫，而同時，部分或全部的以歐洲地區語言如法語或荷蘭語撰寫的抄本也逐漸變得流行。

中世紀早期的手抄本只有兩種用途，一是被製作成為擁有相當完備插圖裝飾的展示品，二則是製作成為僅擁有首字母變體和簡略紋飾的學習用書。在羅曼藝術時期，更多的抄本採用了首字母變體或首字母花體紋飾的式樣，而主要為學習而製的抄本

[3] The Book of Psalms contains the texts of the Divine Office of the Roman Catholic Church. Other books associated with the Book of Psalms were the Lectionary, the Antiphonary and Responsoriale, and the Hymnary.
聖詠包括了羅馬天主教會的日課文本。與聖詠相關的書籍還有《經文選》、《啟應輪唱詩歌集》與《聖詩集》。

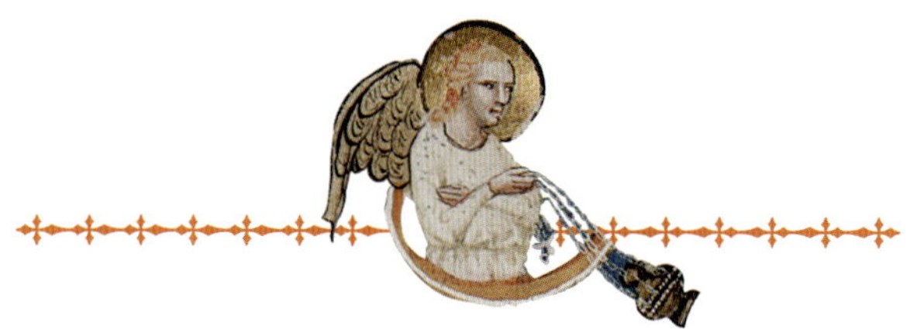

more manuscripts had decorated or historiated initials, and manuscripts essentially for study regularly contained some images, often not in colour. This trend intensified during the Gothic period (12th–14th centuries), when most manuscripts had at least decorative flourishes, and an increasing number of polychrome images. A Gothic regularly contains several areas and types of decoration: a miniature in a frame, a historiated initial beginning a passage of text, and a border with drolleries—typically executed by diverse artists working on different parts of the decoration.

During the late 13th century, scribes began to create prayer books for the laity, often known as books of hours due to their use at prescribed times of the day.[4] From the middle of the 14th century, blockbooks that contained both text and images created by woodcuts appear to have become affordable for parish priests in the Low Countries, where they were most popular. By the end of the century, printed books with illustrations, still primarily on religious subjects, rapidly became accessible to the prosperous middle class. In the 15th century, the introduction of inexpensive prints, generally woodcuts, made it possible even for peasants to have devotional images at home.

Bibles, psalters and books of hours existed in parallel and were used in daily religious practice. Although different in character and size, one shared common topic is *The Life of Christ*. At the core of the Christian ceremony and devotion are hand-painted and gilded illuminations regularly depicting principal episodes, which include: *The Annunciation*, *The Nativity* and *The Adoration of the Magi*.[5] Treasured throughout time, many such miniature illustrations are finely executed polychrome paintings

則更多使用單色的插圖。這種趨勢在哥德藝術時期(十二至十四世紀)變得更為強烈，大部分的手抄本開始至少有了裝飾花紋，而且飾有彩色插圖的手抄本也不斷增加。哥德式手抄本通常擁有幾個裝飾區塊：邊框的微繪，段落文字佔行大寫首字母的花體裝飾與變形，還有飾以詼諧智趣圖案的頁邊——這些往往由不同藝術家分別製作。

十三世紀末，抄寫師開始為平信徒製作祈禱書，由於這些書是被用於一天中特定時刻的特性，而被稱為「時禱書」。[4] 始於十四世紀中期，欠發達地區的教區群眾逐漸可以支付起圖文並茂的木刻版印書籍，故而在這些區域內，木刻版印書籍變得尤為流行。到了十四世紀末，主要以宗教為主題的插圖版印刷書籍迅速成為富有的新興中產階級的新寵。在十五世紀，以木刻版印書籍為代表的廉價印刷製品的介入，使得即便是農民群體在家中也可以擁有圖畫幫助虔修敬拜。

《聖經》、《聖詠經》與《時禱書》被共同使用於每日的宗教靈修操練中。雖然風格與尺寸迥異，但「基督生平」卻是其共有的核心內容。手繪的裝飾圖畫處於基督教慶典和敬拜的核心之中，這些圖像固定描繪了一些主要場景，包括：「聖母領報」、「耶穌降生」和「博士來朝」等。[5] 許多這類的細密畫即使經過漫長歲月依然被悉心珍藏。他們都是一些技巧精妙的彩繪圖，就符號形象系統來說，他們同更大規模的藝術作品比如主要是聖壇或者其他虔修敬拜繪畫同屬

---

[4] The earliest known example seems to have been written for an unknown laywoman living in a small village near Oxford, England, in about 1240. Nobility frequently purchased such texts, paying handsomely for decorative illustrations; among the most well-known creators of these is Jean Pucelle (c.1300–1355), whose Hours of Jeanne d'Évreux (c.1324–1328) was commissioned by King Charles IV of France (1294–1328) as a gift for his queen, Jeanne d'Évreux (1310–1371).
已知最早的實例似乎是為了女平信徒而製，她於一二四零年左右住在英國牛津附近一個小村莊。貴族經常購買此類文本，並且為其泥金裝飾插畫支付豐厚的報酬，其中最著名的裝飾家為讓．皮塞勒(約一三零零年至一三五五年)，他受法國國王查理四世(一二九四年至一三二八年)的委託，為其王后貞德(一三一零年至一三七一年)製作了《貞德時禱書》(約一三二四年至一三二八年)。

[5] See the following chapter for the original Gospel texts and the catalogue section of this book for examples of illustrated scenes of *The Life of Christ*.
詳見下文中福音書原文章節，以及本圖錄中的相關場景介紹。

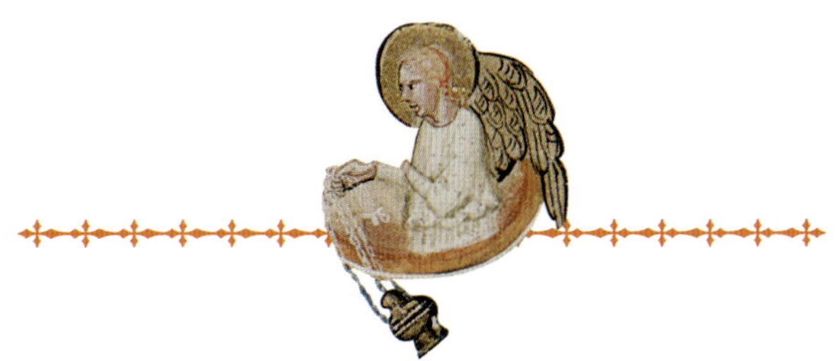

that relate in their iconography to larger, oftentimes altar or other devotional paintings, and repeat stylistically the contemporary design of Medieval, Gothic and later Renaissance (15th–16th centuries) painterly or architectural compositions. At times from the hands of the same master painters, manuscript illuminations equal in character the composition of larger scale figurative scenes, and translate some of the most valuable materials, including gold and lapis lazuli pigment, as well as celebrated painterly techniques, into a portable miniature art form that accompanied its patron in his or her everyday routine.

In the early Middle Ages, most books were produced in monasteries, whether for their own use, for presentation or for a commission. However, commercial scriptoria developed in large cities, especially Paris, as well as urban areas in Italy and the Netherlands. By the late 14th century, a significant industry producing manuscripts had developed, which included agents who would take long-distance commissions. By the end of this period, many of the painters were women, especially in Paris.

Today, illuminated manuscripts represent the most complete record of Gothic painting, preserving a testimony of styles—both leading influential examples from cultural centres and local derivatives—in places where no monumental works have otherwise survived. The earliest full manuscripts with French Gothic illustrations date to the middle of the 13th century.[6] Many such illuminated manuscripts were royal Bibles, as well as psalters, both of which included finely executed and detailed illustrations.[7]

The majority of these manuscripts are of a religious nature. However, especially from the 13th century onward, an increasing number of secular texts also were illuminated. Most illuminated manuscripts were created as codices, which had superseded scrolls. A very few illuminated manuscript fragments survive on papyrus, which does not last nearly as long as vellum or

於一個體系，不僅如此，他們還呼應了諸如中世紀藝術、哥德藝術和文藝復興(十五至十六世紀)晚期藝術的繪畫和建築創作中的造型佈局風格。有時，出自同一位繪畫大師之手的手抄本裝飾插圖與具象的大型場景繪畫，具有相似的特徵與構圖，並且將一些珍貴材料，包括黃金和青金石顏料，通過高超的繪畫技巧融入此種便攜式的微繪藝術形式，得以伴隨主顧們的每日靈修操練。

中世紀早期，大部分書籍主要由修道院製作，或為自用，或為陳設，抑或為了來自外部的委託；然而，具有商業性質的繕寫室亦逐漸在一些大城市中發展起來，特別是在巴黎、意大利與荷蘭的城區。到了十四世紀晚期，製作手抄本的重要工業已經發展完備，還出現了可接受跨地區製書委託的代理商。到這個時期的末尾，特別是在巴黎，大部分從事此項事業的畫家們都是女性。

今日，泥金插畫裝飾手抄本最完整記錄了哥德時期的繪畫藝術，亦保留了諸多藝術風格的特點——這些風格的產生地並無不朽作品傳世。最早的配有法國哥德風格插畫的完整手抄本可以追溯到十三世紀中期。[6] 許多此類的泥金裝飾手抄本都是《聖經》正典，以及《聖詠經》，兩者皆飾有精妙製作的細緻插圖。[7]

大部分此類抄本都有宗教本質。然而，特別是從十三世紀開始，飾有插圖的世俗文本也不斷湧現。許多的彩繪手抄本被製作並取代了之前的捲軸。只有極少數以莎草紙製作的彩繪手抄本碎片得以傳世，因為莎草紙無法像犢皮紙或羊皮紙那樣持久保存。中世紀手抄本中的絕大多數，無論是否配有插圖，皆是書寫於羊皮紙(主要是牛犢，綿羊或山羊的皮)上，而那些飾以插圖

6 Stokstad 2005, p. 540.

7 The Parisian Psalter of Saint Louis, dating from 1253 to 1270, features 78 full-page illuminations in tempera paint and gold leaf. 《巴黎的聖路易斯聖詠經》，始於一二五三年至一二七零年間，以七十八幅全版裝飾畫為特徵，為蛋彩畫與金葉。

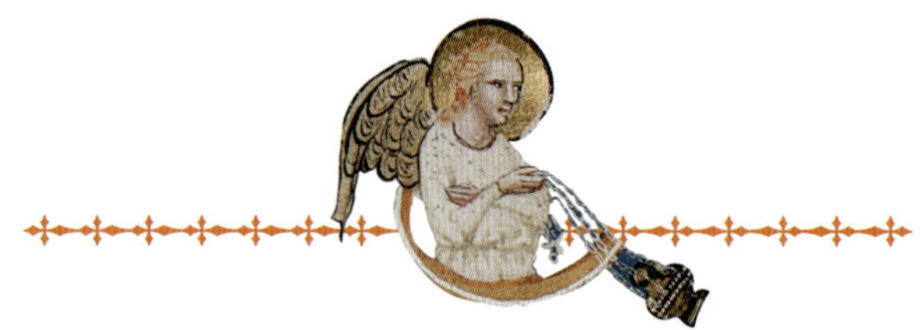

parchment. A majority of medieval manuscripts, illuminated or not, were written on parchment (commonly calf, sheep or goat skin), and most manuscripts important enough to illuminate were written on the best quality parchment, known as vellum, which was made exclusively from calf skin.

Beginning in the late Middle Ages, manuscripts began to be produced on paper.[8] Very early printed books were sometimes produced with spaces left for rubrics and miniatures, or were given illuminated initials or decorations in the margin. The introduction of printing rapidly led to the decline of illumination. Illuminated manuscripts continued to be produced in the early 16th century, but in much smaller numbers, and primarily for the very wealthy.

The illumination and decoration were normally planned at the inception of the work, although the text was generally written before the illumination work began. After the general layout of the page was planned (e.g., the historiated initial letter or borders), the page was lightly ruled with a pointed stick, and the scribe went to work with ink that he applied either with a sharpened quill feather or reed pen.[9] In the Early Medieval period, the text and illumination were often done by the same artist, usually monks. By the High Middle Ages, the roles were typically separated, except for routine initials and flourishes. By at least the 14th century, there were secular manuscript workshops, and by the beginning of the 15th century these workshops were producing most of the best work, and were being commissioned even by monasteries. When the text was completed, the illustrator set to work. Complex designs were planned out beforehand, and the design was traced or drawn onto the vellum.

的重要手抄本則會大部分書寫於質量最優良的上等羊皮紙之上，被稱為犢皮紙，這些犢皮紙只能以牛犢皮製成。

自中世紀晚期，手抄本開始以紙張製作。[8]最早期的印刷書籍往往在頁左為紅字標題或微繪裝飾留位，或者繪以圖畫的變形佔行首字母，或者裝飾頁邊紋路。印刷術的引進迅速導致插畫的沒落。泥金裝飾手抄本直至十六世紀早期依然維持製作，但是數量已大幅減少，且主要供應給富有的群體。

雖然大部分文字通常都會寫於繪圖工作之前，但是圖畫與裝飾工作卻往往是在書本製作之初便已規劃完畢。在常規的頁面設計完成之後(例如首字母變形與邊框裝飾)，會用一根尖頭木條在頁面畫出格線，之後抄寫師開始用削尖的鵝毛筆或蘆葦筆蘸墨水抄寫文字。[9]在中世紀早期，文字與圖畫通常由同一位修士藝術家完成；而到了中世紀中期，首字母變形與裝飾花紋之外的其他事項開始產生分工。最晚到十四世紀的時候，世俗的手抄本作坊已經存在，而到了十五世紀初，這些作坊已能製作出最傑出的作品，甚至還能得到修道院的書籍製作委託。當文字抄寫完畢，插畫家開始根據之前的設計規劃著手繪圖，將設計圖樣實施於犢皮紙上。

一本插畫裝飾手抄本，唯有在其插圖飾有金箔或以拋光的方式塗繪金斑的時候，才可以被認作泥金插畫手抄本。黃金的使用對於其所修飾的文本有著多重可能性的註解。如果在宗教性質的文本中，黃金的使

8 De Hamel 1992, p. 45.
9 Calkins, 1978.

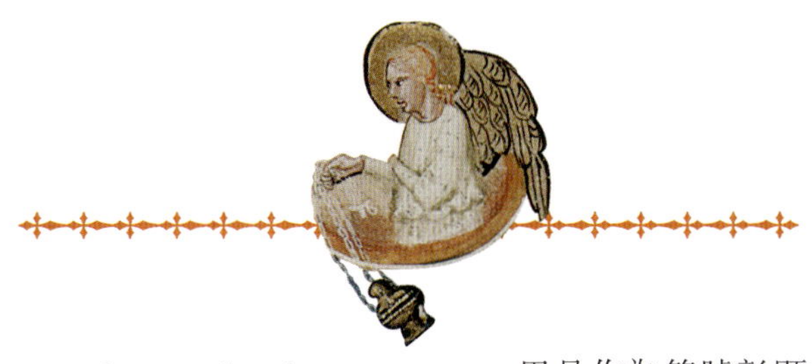

An illuminated manuscript is only considered illuminated if the illustrations contain gold leaf, or are brushed with gold specks, a process known as burnishing. The inclusion of gold on an illumination alludes to many different possibilities for the text. If the text is of a religious nature, the gold is a sign of exalting the text. In the early centuries of Christianity, Gospel manuscripts were sometimes written entirely in gold. Aside from adding lavish decoration to the text, scribes during this period considered themselves to be praising God with their use of gold. Furthermore, gold was used if a commissioning patron wished to display his wealth by paying for the costly materials, both gold and lapis lazuli pigment, and the application of gold leaf or dust to an illumination, which consisted of an extremely detailed process that only the most skilled illuminators could accomplish.[10]

用是作為符號彰顯文本的神聖。在早期的基督宗教世代中，福音書有時會全部用黃金抄寫。除了為文本添加奢華的裝飾，此時期內的抄寫師認為使用黃金來抄寫是對上帝的敬拜。此外，黃金的使用還有一種情況：即如果一個主顧想要展現他的財力，他會因此而購買貴重的材料，黃金和青金顏料以及繪圖中金箔和金粉的使用，都在此類，特別是金箔和金粉的使用，通常會被認為是唯有技藝非凡的插圖師才能夠成就的精工細作。[10]

[10] De Hamel, 1992, p. 49.
Over time, however, the price of gold decreased and its inclusion in an illuminated manuscript accounted for only a tenth of the cost of production.
然而之後隨著黃金價格的降低，泥金裝飾手抄本的製作成本也降低了九成。

THE LIFE OF CHRIST 基督生平
THE BIBLE, NEW INTERNATIONAL VERSION (NIV)
【新國際版聖經】

Numerous illuminated manuscripts depict episodes from *The Life of Christ*, as told by Gospels in the New Testament. Both Luke and Matthew describe *The Nativity*, and state that Jesus was born in Bethlehem in Judea, to a virgin mother. Of the most commonly illustrated chapters, The Gospel of Luke tells *The Annunciation to the Virgin Mary* (Luke 1:26–33), *The Nativity* (Luke 2:1–7), *The Annunciation to the Shepherds* (Luke 2:8–12), *The Circumcision* (Luke 2:21) and *The Presentation in the Temple* (Luke 2:22), whereas the Gospel of Matthew describes *The Nativity*, *The Adoration of the Magi*, and *The Flight into Egypt* (Matthew 1:18–2:23). [11]

許多泥金插畫手繪本中描繪的場景皆取材自新約聖經福音書中講述的「基督生平」。《路加福音》與《馬太福音》都描述了「耶穌降生」，並敘說耶穌生於猶太的伯利恆，受孕於一位童女。插畫裝飾中最為常見的故事章節是《路加福音》中的「聖母領報」（《路加福音》第一章二十六至三十三節）、「耶穌降生」（《路加福音》第二章一至七節）、「天使向牧羊人報喜」（《路加福音》第二章八至十二節）、「基督割禮」（《路加福音》第二章二十一節）與「獻主於聖殿」（《路加福音》第二章二十二節），《馬太福音》中敘述了「耶穌降生」、「博士來朝」與「逃往埃及」（《馬太福音》第一章十八節至第二章二十三節）。[11]

THE GOSPEL OF LUKE

***The Annunciation to The Virgin Mary* (Luke 1:26–33)**

[26] In the sixth month of Elizabeth's pregnancy, God sent the angel Gabriel to Nazareth, a town in Galilee, [27] to a virgin pledged to be married to a man named Joseph, a descendant of David. The virgin's name was Mary. [28] The angel went to her and said, "Greetings, you who are highly favoured! The Lord is with you."

[29] Mary was greatly troubled at his words and wondered what kind of greeting this might be. [30] But the angel said to her, "Do not be afraid, Mary; you have found favour with God. [31] You will conceive and give birth to a son, and you are to call him Jesus. [32] He will be great and will be called the Son of the Most High. The Lord God will give him the throne of his father David, [33] and he will reign over Jacob's descendants forever; his kingdom will never end."

《路加福音》

「聖母領報」

（《路加福音》第一章二十六至三十三節）

[26] 到了第六個月，天使加百列奉上帝的差遣往加利利的一座城去，這城名叫拿撒勒，[27] 到一個童女那裏，她已經許配大衛家的一個人，名叫若瑟；童女的名字叫馬利亞。[28] 天使進去，對她說：「蒙大恩的女子，你好，主和你同在！」

[29] 馬利亞因這話就很驚慌，又反覆思考這樣問候是甚麼意思。[30] 天使對她說：「馬利亞，不要怕！你在上帝面前已經蒙恩了。[31] 你要懷孕生子，要給他起名叫耶穌。[32] 他將要為大，稱為至高者的兒子；主上帝要把他祖先大衛的王位給他。[33] 他要作雅各家的王，直到永遠；他的國沒有窮盡。」

***The Birth of Christ* (Luke 2:1–7)**

[1] Caesar Augustus issued a decree that a census should be taken of the entire Roman world.

[2] This was the first census that took place while Quirinius was governor of Syria.

[3] And everyone went to their own town to register.

[4] So Joseph also went up from the town of Nazareth in Galilee to Judea, to Bethlehem the town of David, because he belonged to the house and line of David. [5] He went there to register with Mary, who was pledged to be married to him and was expecting a child. [6] While they were there, the time came for the baby to be born, [7] and she gave birth to her firstborn, a son. She wrapped him in cloths and placed him in a manger, because there was no guest room available for them.

「耶穌降生」（《路加福音》第二章一至七節）

[1] 在那些日子，凱撒奧古斯都降旨，叫全國人民都登記戶籍。

[2] 這第一次登記戶籍是在居里扭作敘利亞總督的時候行的。

[3] 眾人各歸各城，辦理登記。

[4] 若瑟也從加利利的拿撒勒城上猶太去，到了大衛的城名叫伯利恆，因為他是大衛家族的人，[5] 要和他所聘之妻馬利亞一同登記戶籍。那時馬利亞已經懷孕。[6] 他們在那裏的時候，馬利亞的產期到了，[7] 就生了頭胎的兒子，用布包起來，放在馬槽裏，因為客店裏沒有地方。

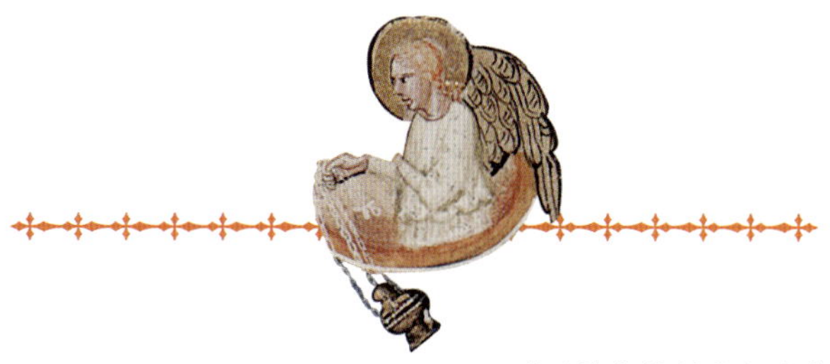

The Annunciation to the Shepherds (Luke 2:8–12)
8 And there were shepherds living out in the fields nearby,
keeping watch over their flocks at night. 9 An angel of the
Lord appeared to them, and the glory of the Lord shone
around them, and they were terrified. 10 But the angel said
to them, "Do not be afraid. I bring you good news that will
cause great joy for all the people. 11 Today in the town of
David a Saviour has been born to you; he is the Messiah, the
Lord. 12 This will be a sign to you: You will find a baby
wrapped in cloths and lying in a manger."

「天使向牧羊人報喜」
(《路加福音》第二章八至十二節)
8在伯利恆的野外有牧羊人，夜間值班看守羊
群。9有主的一個使者站在他們旁邊，主的榮光
四面照著他們，牧羊人就很懼怕。10那天使對他
們說：「不要懼怕！看哪！因為我報給你們大喜
的信息，是關乎萬民的：11因今天在大衛的城
裏，為你們生了救主，就是主基督。12你們要看
見一個嬰孩，包著布，臥在馬槽裏，那就是給
你們的記號。」

The Circumcision (Luke 2:21)
21 On the eighth day, when it was time to circumcise the
child, he was named Jesus, the name the angel had given
him before he was conceived.

「基督割禮」(《路加福音》第二章二十一節)
21滿了八天，他們就給孩子行割禮，又給他起名
叫耶穌；這是他還沒有在母腹裏成胎以前天使
所起的名。

The Presentation in the Temple (Luke 2:22)
22 When the time came for the purification rites required by
the Law of Moses, Joseph and Mary took him to Jerusalem
to present him to the Lord.

「獻主於聖殿」(《路加福音》第二章二十二節)
22按摩西律法滿了潔淨的日子，他們就帶著孩子
上耶路撒冷去，要把他獻給主。

THE GOSPEL OF MATTHEW

The Birth of Christ (Matthew 1:18–25)
18 This is how the birth of Jesus the Messiah came about:
His mother Mary was pledged to be married to Joseph, but
before they came together, she was found to be pregnant
through the Holy Spirit. 19 Because Joseph her husband was
faithful to the law, and yet did not want to expose her to
public disgrace, he had in mind to divorce her quietly.
20 But after he had considered this, an angel of the Lord
appeared to him in a dream and said, "Joseph son of David,
do not be afraid to take Mary home as your wife, because
what is conceived in her is from the Holy Spirit. 21 She will
give birth to a son, and you are to give him the name Jesus,
because he will save his people from their sins."
22 All this took place to fulfil what the Lord had said through
the prophet: 23 "The virgin will conceive and give birth to a
son, and they will call him Immanuel" (which means "God
with us").
24 When Joseph woke up, he did what the angel of the Lord
had commanded him and took Mary home as his wife.
25 But he did not consummate their marriage until she gave
birth to a son. And he gave him the name Jesus.

《馬太福音》

「耶穌降生」
(《馬太福音》第一章十八至二十五節)
18耶穌基督降生的事記在下面：他母親馬利亞已
經許配給若瑟，還沒有迎娶，馬利亞就從聖靈
懷了孕。19她丈夫若瑟是個義人，不願意當眾羞
辱她，想要暗地裏把她休了。
20正考慮這些事的時候，忽然主的使者在若瑟夢
中向他顯現，說：「大衛的子孫若瑟，不要怕，
把你的妻子馬利亞娶過來，因她所懷的孕是從
聖靈來的。21她將要生一個兒子，你要給他起名
叫耶穌，因他要將自己的百姓從罪惡裏救出
來。」
22這整件事的發生，是要應驗主藉先知所說的
話：23「必有童女懷孕生子；人要稱他的名為以
馬內利。」(以馬內利翻出來就是「上帝與我們同
在」。)
24若瑟醒來，就遵照主的使者的吩咐把妻子娶過
來；25但是沒有和她同房，直到她生了兒子，就
給他起名叫耶穌。

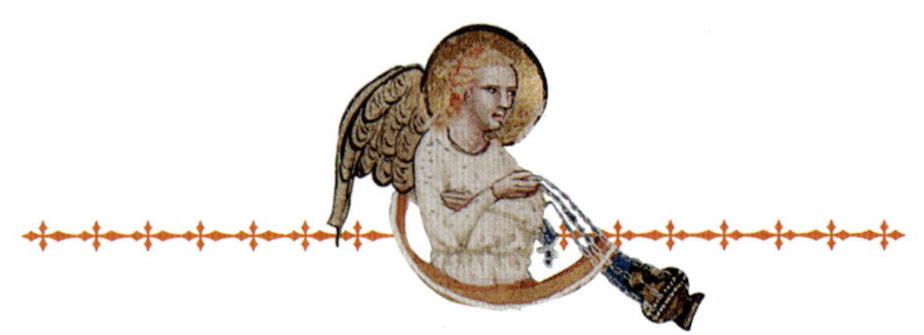

The Adoration of the Magi (Matthew 2:1–12)
1 After Jesus was born in Bethlehem in Judea, during the
time of King Herod, Magi from the east came to Jerusalem
2 and asked, "Where is the one who has been born king of
the Jews? We saw his star when it rose and have come to
worship him."
3 When King Herod heard this he was disturbed, and all
Jerusalem with him. 4 When he had called together all the
people's chief priests and teachers of the law, he asked them
where the Messiah was to be born. 5 "In Bethlehem in
Judea," they replied, "for this is what the prophet has
written: 6 'But you, Bethlehem, in the land of Judah, are by
no means least among the rulers of Judah; for out of you
will come a ruler who will shepherd my people Israel.'"
7 Then Herod called the Magi secretly and found out from
them the exact time the star had appeared. 8 He sent them
to Bethlehem and said, "Go and search carefully for the
child. As soon as you find him, report to me, so that I too
may go and worship him."
9 After they had heard the king, they went on their way, and
the star they had seen when it rose went ahead of them
until it stopped over the place where the child was. 10 When
they saw the star, they were overjoyed. 11 On coming to the
house, they saw the child with his mother Mary, and they
bowed down and worshiped him. Then they opened their
treasures and presented him with gifts of gold, frankincense
and myrrh. 12 And having been warned in a dream not to go
back to Herod, they returned to their country by another
route.

「博士來朝」(《馬太福音》第二章一至十二節)
1在希律作王的時候，耶穌生在猶太的伯利恆。
有幾個博學之士從東方來到耶路撒冷，說：
2「那生下來作猶太人之王的在哪裏？我們在東
方看見他的星，特來拜他。」
3希律王聽見了，就心裏不安；耶路撒冷全城的
人也都不安。4他就召集了祭司長和民間的文
士，問他們：「基督該生在哪裏？」5他們說：
6「在猶太的伯利恆。因為有先知記著：『猶大地
的伯利恆啊，你在猶大諸城中並不是最小的；
因為將來有一位統治者要從你那裏出來，牧養
我以色列民。』」
7於是，希律暗地裏召了博學之士來，查問那星
是甚麼時候出現的，8就派他們往伯利恆去，
說：「你們去仔細尋訪那小孩子，找到了就來報
信，我也好去拜他。」
9他們聽了王的話就去了。忽然，在東方所看到
的那顆星在前面引領他們，一直行到小孩子所
在地方的上方就停住了。10他們看見那星，就非
常歡喜；11進了房子，看見小孩子和他母親馬利
亞，就俯伏拜那小孩子，揭開寶盒，拿出黃
金、乳香、沒藥，作為禮物獻給他。12因為在夢
中得到主的指示，不要回去見希律，他們就從
別的路回自己的家鄉去了。

The Flight into Egypt (Matthew 2:13–14)
13 When they had gone, an angel of the Lord appeared to
Joseph in a dream. "Get up," he said, "take the child and his
mother and escape to Egypt. Stay there until I tell you, for
Herod is going to search for the child to kill him."
14 So he got up, took the child and his mother during the
night and left for Egypt, 15 where he stayed until the death
of Herod. And so was fulfilled what the Lord had said
through the prophet: "Out of Egypt I called my son."

「逃往埃及」(《馬太福音》第二章十三至十四節)
13他們走後，忽然主的使者在若瑟夢中向他顯
現，說：「起來！帶著小孩子和他母親逃往埃
及，住在那裏，等我的指示；因為希律要搜尋
那小孩子來殺害他。」
14若瑟就起來，連夜帶著小孩子和他母親往埃及
去，15住在那裏，直到希律死了。這是要應驗
主藉先知所說的話：「我從埃及召我的兒子
出來。」

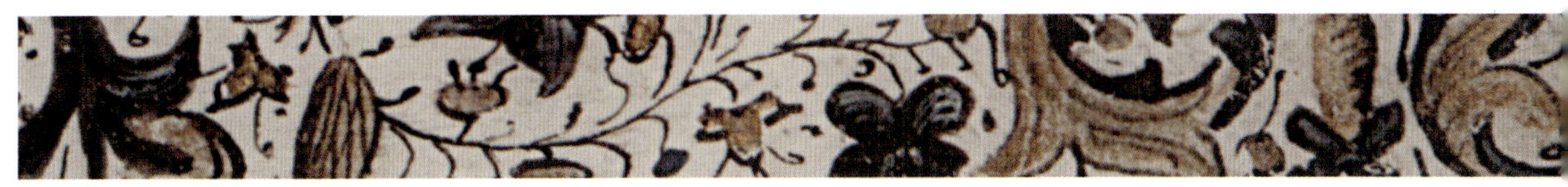

ILLUSTRIOUS ILLUMINATIONS: CHRISTIAN MANUSCRIPTS

輝煌的啟示：基督宗教手稿

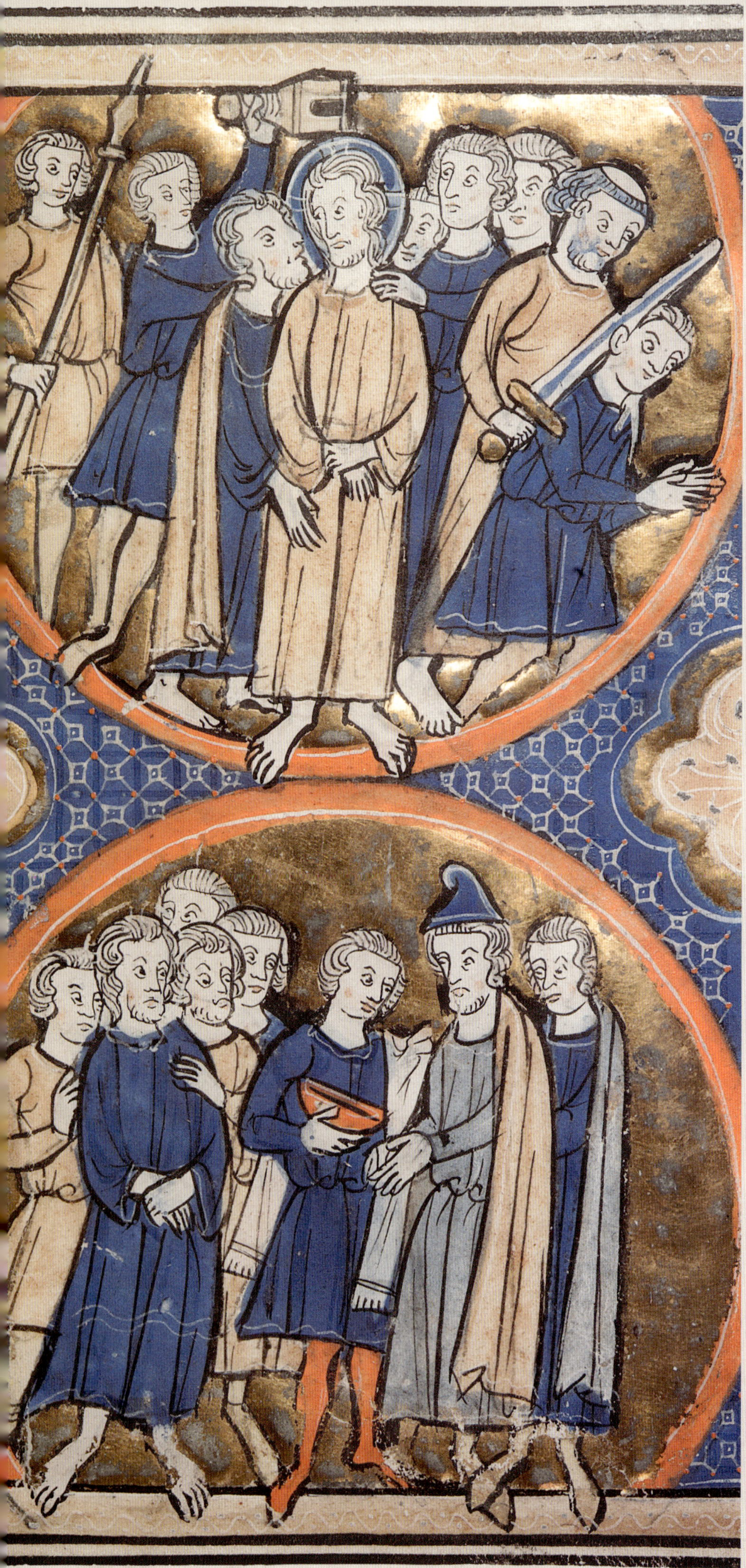

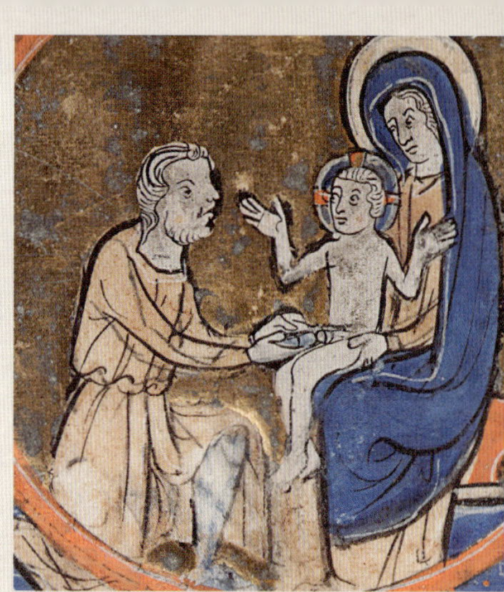

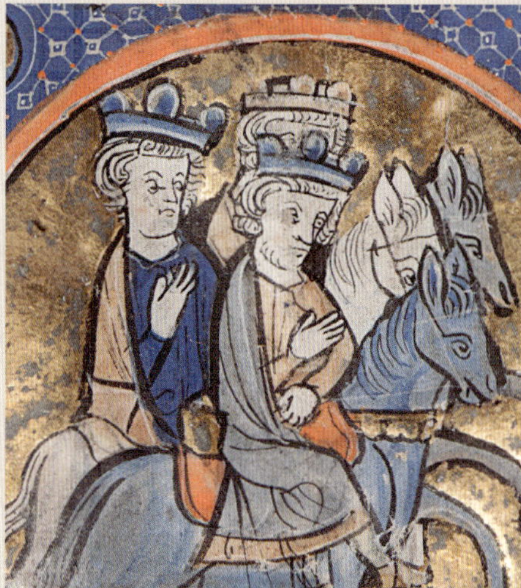

1a (detail 局部)

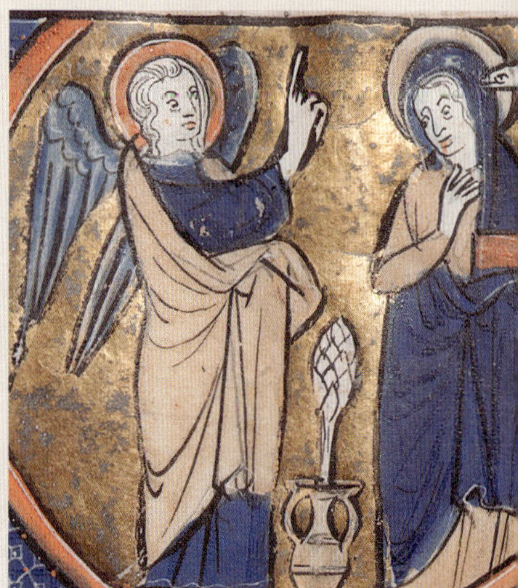

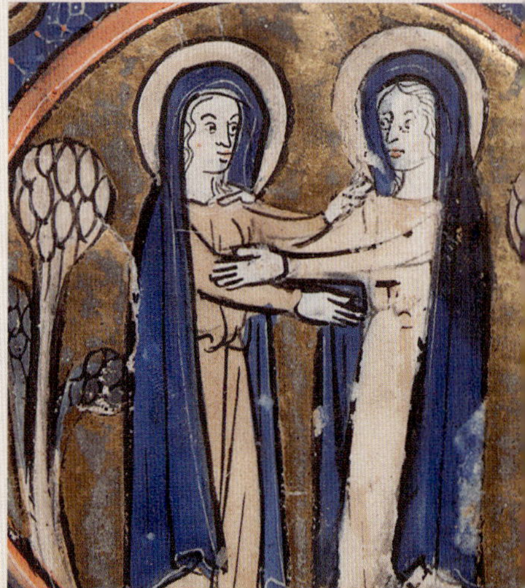

1c (detail 局部)

1b (detail 局部)

The Phillips Miniatures
菲利普斯微繪

Cat. 1a–c

Catalogue numbers 1a–c represent three of the surviving ten so-called Phillips Miniatures that are well preserved and lightly detailed, illuminating the opening of the cycles of the Infancy and the Passion. The sequence of miniatures originally faced each other in pairs and must have prefixed a luxury psalter. Sections of a similar cycle in almost the same format and dimensions are held in the Bodleian Library (MS. Douce 50). The style is quite similar to that of illuminations from the so-called Guines workshop, and particularly the miniature on f.93 of a pontifical now in the British Library (MS. lat. 1246). Other books, partly or wholly from the same workshop, include British Library Add. MS. 30045, a psalter which belonged to the Counts of Guines (datable to after 1228); a psalter of Franciscan use, datable between 1235 and 1255 (Bodleian Library MS. Douce 48); Fitzwilliam Museum MS.300, the Hours of Isabella of France, sister of St. Louis, datable before 1270 (Fitzwilliam Museum MS. 300); and a psalter that later belonged to Henry VIII (British Library, Yates Thompson MS. 18).

Literature: Branner 1977, fig. 133; Stork 1992; and Zeitleis 2004, cat. no. 134, pp. 394–398.

圖錄編號1a–c是現存的十幅所稱「菲利普斯微繪」中保存最完好、藝術最精細的三幅傑出代表，描繪了「嬰孩基督」系列故事與「耶穌受難」系列故事的開始。這些微繪最初依順序成雙相對，而且一定置於一本奢華的《聖詠經》之前。博德利圖書館的藏書中可見到類似系列故事中的章節，並以幾乎相同的版式與尺寸表現（編號：MS. Douce 50）。這些作品與所謂的吉訥工作坊的插畫具有類似的藝術風格，這突出表現在一本現存於大英圖書館的《主教儀典書》f.93的微繪（編號：MS. lat. 1246）。其他書籍中部分或全部的插畫皆製作於同一工作坊，包括《吉訥伯爵聖詠經》（現存於大英圖書館，編號：Add. MS. 30045）（年代推定至一二二八年之後）、方濟各會使用的《聖詠經》（現存於博德利圖書館，編號：MS. Douce 48）（年代推定至一二三五年至一二五五年間）、聖路易之妹伊莎貝拉的《法蘭西伊莎貝拉時禱書》（現存於菲茨威廉博物館，編號：MS. 300）（年代推定至一二七零年之前）以及之後歸亨利八世所有的《聖詠經》（現存於大英圖書館，編號：Yates Thompson MS. 18）。

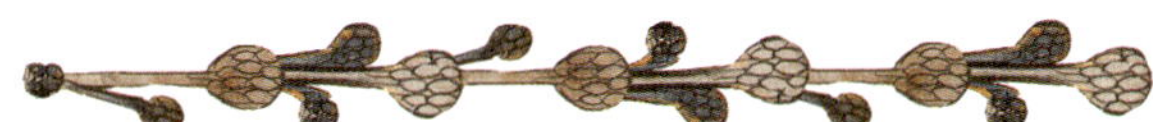
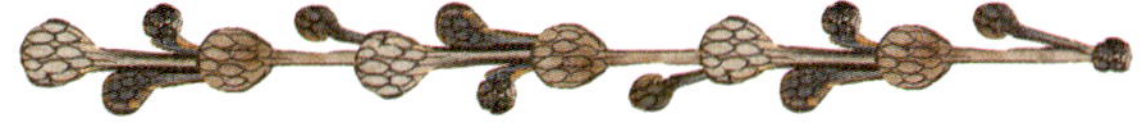

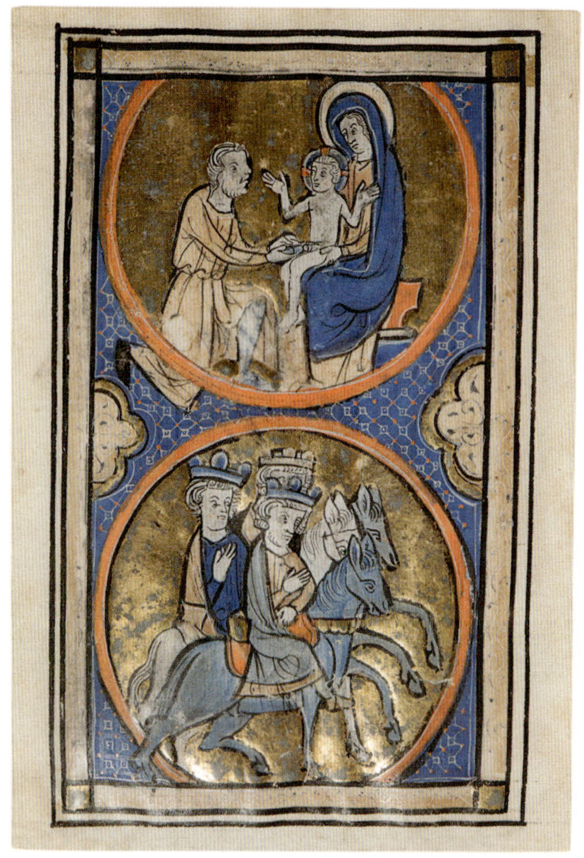

(actual size 原大)

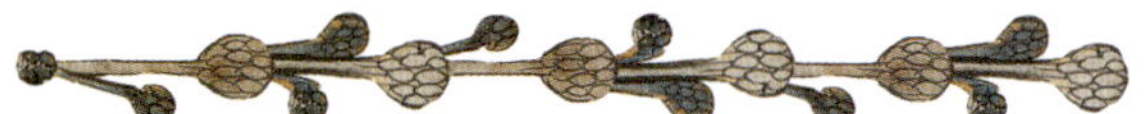
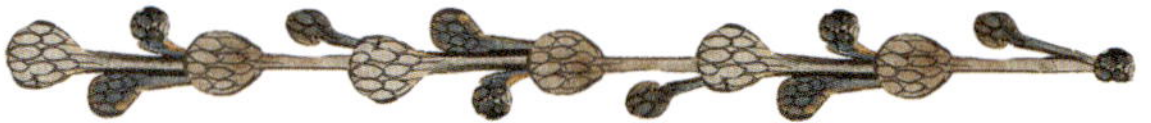

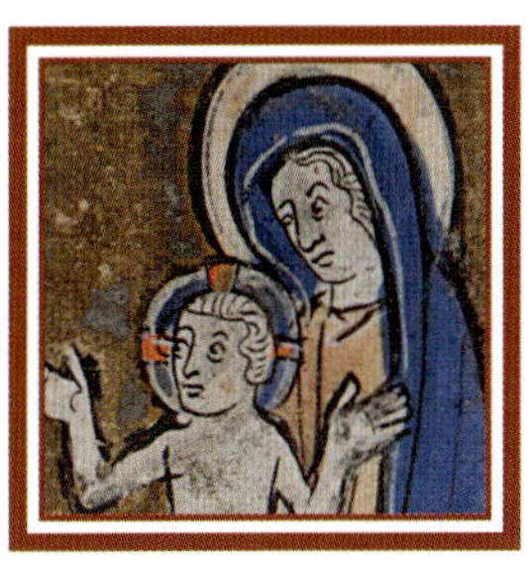

Cat. 1a | Reference 參考編號: BM 1003

Psalter Leaf with Roundel Scenes Depicting *The Circumcision* and *The Three Kings*

《聖詠經》書頁，圓形圖版中描繪「基督割禮」與「三博士來朝」

Anonymous, attributed to the Guines workshop
Paris, France, c.1250–1270
Tempera, gold and ink on vellum
H. 105 mm W. 65 mm

This psalter leaf presents two nearly complete roundels, each 52 mm in diameter, which appear on a blue background placed one above the other. The leaf is flattened along the top of the upper roundel and along the bottom of the lower roundel on the verso page. The upper roundel depicts a representation of *The Circumcision*. The Virgin is seated with Christ in her lap and Zacharias is kneeling in front of them to perform the circumcision. The lower roundel displays a representation of the Three Kings on horseback, again on a gold background. Each page is located within double borders of blue or pale pink, with white tracers and burnished gold corners. The miniatures are in full colour (predominantly blues, pale browns, whites and oranges, with heightening in black and white) on heavily raised burnished gold ground (gesso without bole, a characteristic feature of Parisian illumination). Each page of the Phillips Miniatures is within double borders of blue or pale pink with white tracery, burnished gold corners (105 mm x 65 mm) and cusped compartments. The outer interstices between the roundels and surrounds are infilled with very fine designs of geometric patterns in colour with a delicate tracery that resembles tapestry designs. On the middle right and left of the leaf are two half-quatrefoils.

匿名，被認作吉訥工作坊作品
製作於巴黎，法國，約一二五零年至一二七零年
蛋彩、泥金與墨水，犢皮紙
高105公釐，寬65公釐

此片《聖詠經》書頁以藍色為背景，內含兩個接近正圓形（直徑52公釐）的圖版，並上下分置，其中上圖版的上緣及下圖版的下緣皆沿書頁邊框切平。上圖「基督割禮」場景中，聖母呈坐姿，基督坐其腿上，撒迦利亞則跪在面前施行割禮；下圖「三博士來朝」場景中三博士（或帝王）騎於馬背，背景同為金色。每張菲利普斯微繪書頁皆採用藍色或淡粉色的雙邊框，並配有白色窗格花飾，四角則為拋光泥金。圓形圖版中的微繪為全彩色（主要有藍色、淡褐色、白色與橙色，這些顏色更因黑白印刷而得到加強），背景則是強力拋光的泥金顏料（不添加紅玄武土的石膏底料，巴黎式彩飾的典型特徵）。圓形圖版與環繞物之間的外間隙由精細的彩色幾何圖樣填充，並配有類似緙織壁毯式樣的精美窗格花飾。書頁的正中左右兩邊分別有一個四瓣葉紋飾。

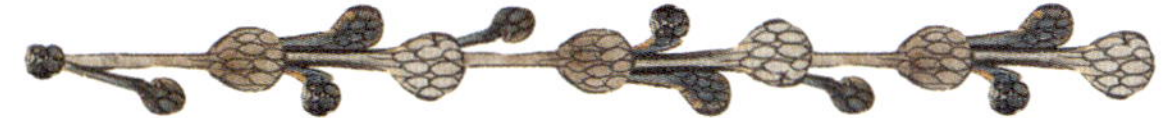 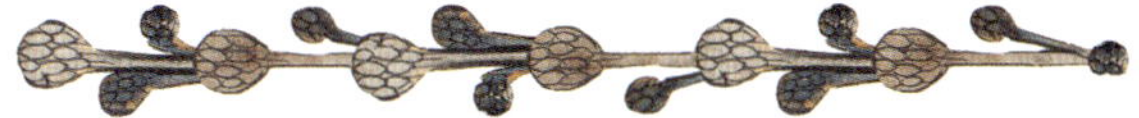

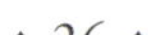

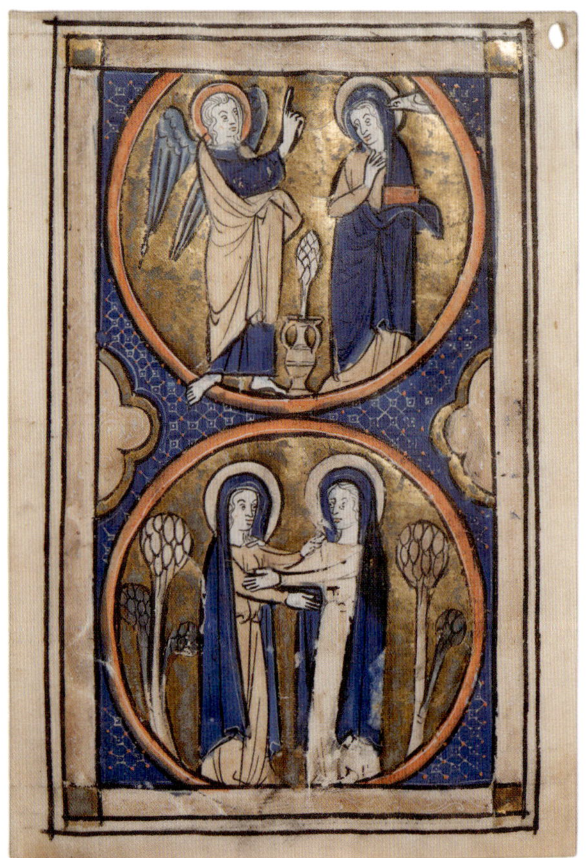

(actual size 原大)

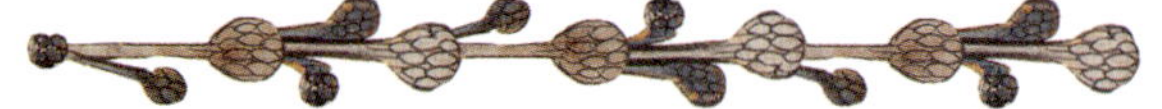
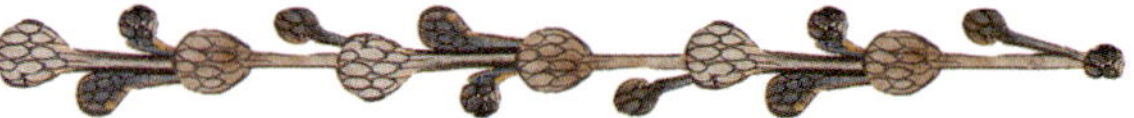

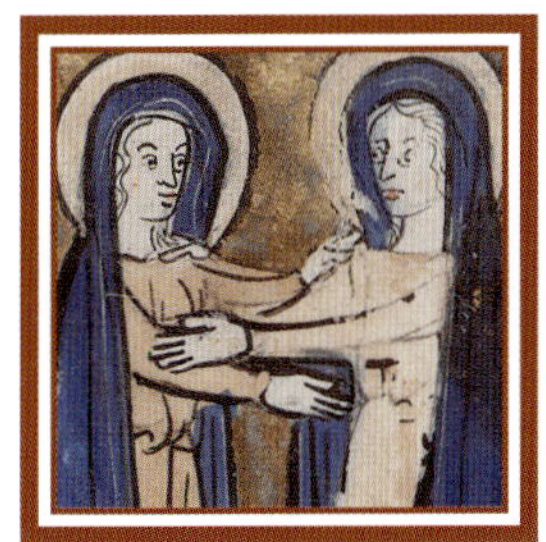

Cat. 1b | Reference 參考編號: BM 1052a; SF 3912

Psalter Leaf with Roundel Scenes Depicting *The Annunciation* and *The Visitation*
《聖詠經》書頁，圓形圖版中描繪「聖母領報」與「聖母訪親」

Anonymous, attributed to the Guines workshop
Paris, France, c.1250–1270
Tempera, gold and ink on vellum
H. 105 mm W. 65 mm

Description as in cat. no. 1a (BM 1003), on a blue background with two roundels placed vertically on the page. The top roundel contains a representation of the *The Annunciation* and the bottom roundel depicts a representation of *The Visitation*. In *The Annunciation*, Gabriel and the Virgin are both standing with Gabriel pointing upwards. The Virgin is holding a book, with the Holy Dove at her ear and a lily in a vase between them. *The Visitation* shows the Virgin and St. Elizabeth clasping each other's arms, with trees placed on either side. There is minor worming in the margins and the lower compartment is slightly rubbed.

匿名，被認作吉訥工作坊作品
製作於巴黎，法國，約一二五零年至一二七零年
蛋彩、泥金與墨水，犢皮紙
高105公釐，寬65公釐

與圖錄編號1a（BM 1003）的描述相同，此片書頁中的兩個圓形圖版亦垂直分置於藍色背景之上。上圖「聖母領報」場景中，天使加百列與聖母皆呈站姿，天使加百列手指上方，聖母則手持一本書，且有代表聖靈的白鴿在耳側，兩人之間的花瓶中插有一支百合花；下圖「聖母訪親」場景中的聖母與聖以利沙伯抱緊對方的手臂，樹木分置兩人身側。頁邊有較小的龜裂紋，下部區間略遭磨損。

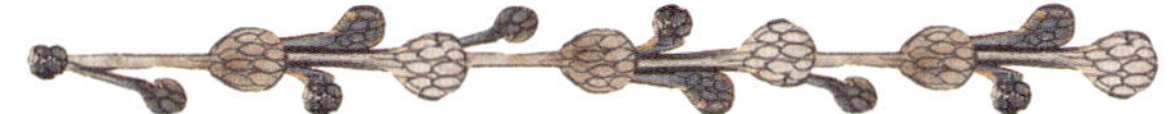
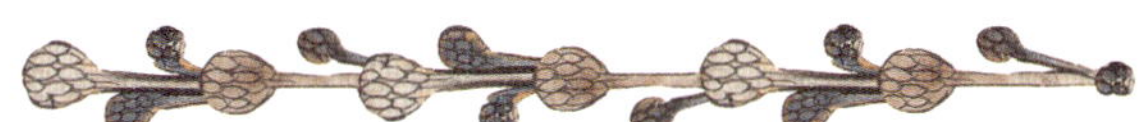

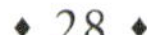

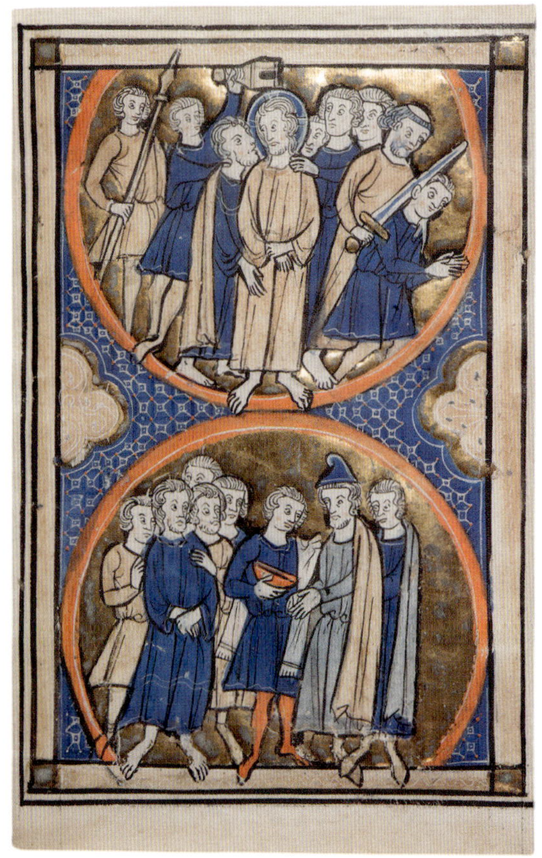

(actual size 原大)

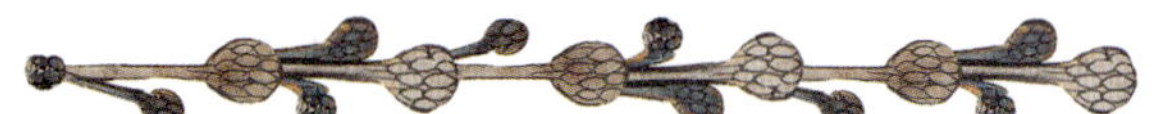
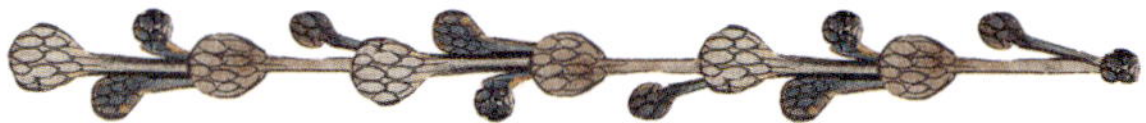

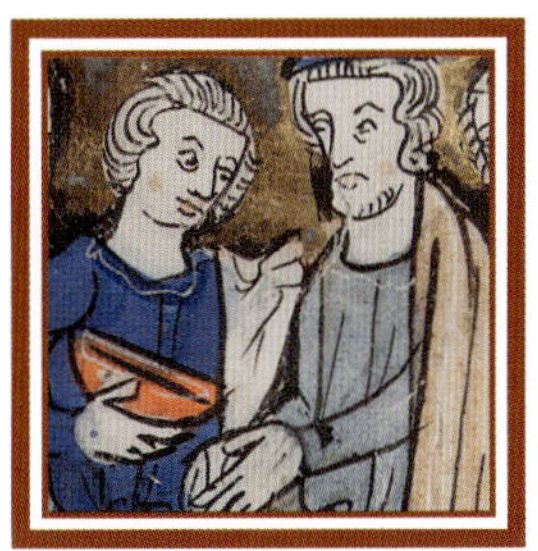

Cat. 1c | Reference 參考編號: BM 1052b

Psalter Leaf with Roundel Scenes Depicting *The Betrayal of Christ* and *The Washing of Hands*
《聖詠經》書頁，圓形場景描繪「基督被賣」與「彼拉多洗手」

Anonymous, attributed to the Guines workshop
Paris, France, c.1250–1270
Tempera, gold and ink on vellum
H. 105 mm W. 65 mm

Description as in cat. no. 1a (BM 1003), on a blue background with two roundels placed vertically on the page. The top roundel contains a representation of *The Betrayal* and the bottom roundel contains *The Washing of Hands*, which is placed on the verso page. *The Betrayal* shows Judas kissing Jesus among a crowd of people, one of whom is holding a lance, another a lantern, while on the right Saint Peter is cutting off the ear of Malchus. *The Washing of Hands* depicts Christ being led before Pilate, who washes and dries his hands from a bowl that is held by an attendant.

匿名，被認作吉訥工作坊作品
製作於巴黎，法國，約一二五零年至一二七零年
蛋彩、泥金與墨水，犢皮紙
高105公釐，寬65公釐

與圖錄編號1a（BM 1003）的描述相同，此片書頁中的兩個圓形圖版亦垂直分置於藍色背景之上。上圖「基督被賣」場景中，猶大在人群間獻吻耶穌，人群中一人手執騎槍，另一人手執燈籠，右邊的聖彼得正砍下馬勒古的耳朵；下圖「彼拉多洗手」場景中，基督被帶到彼拉多前，彼拉多在一個侍從所持的碗中洗手並擦乾。

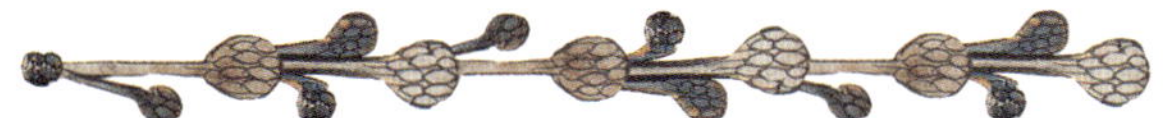 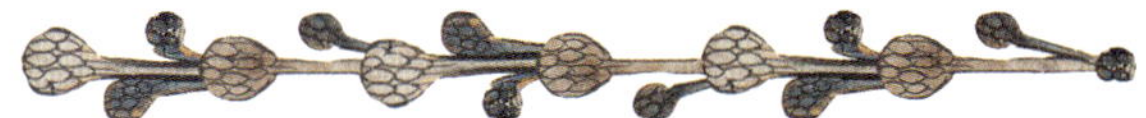

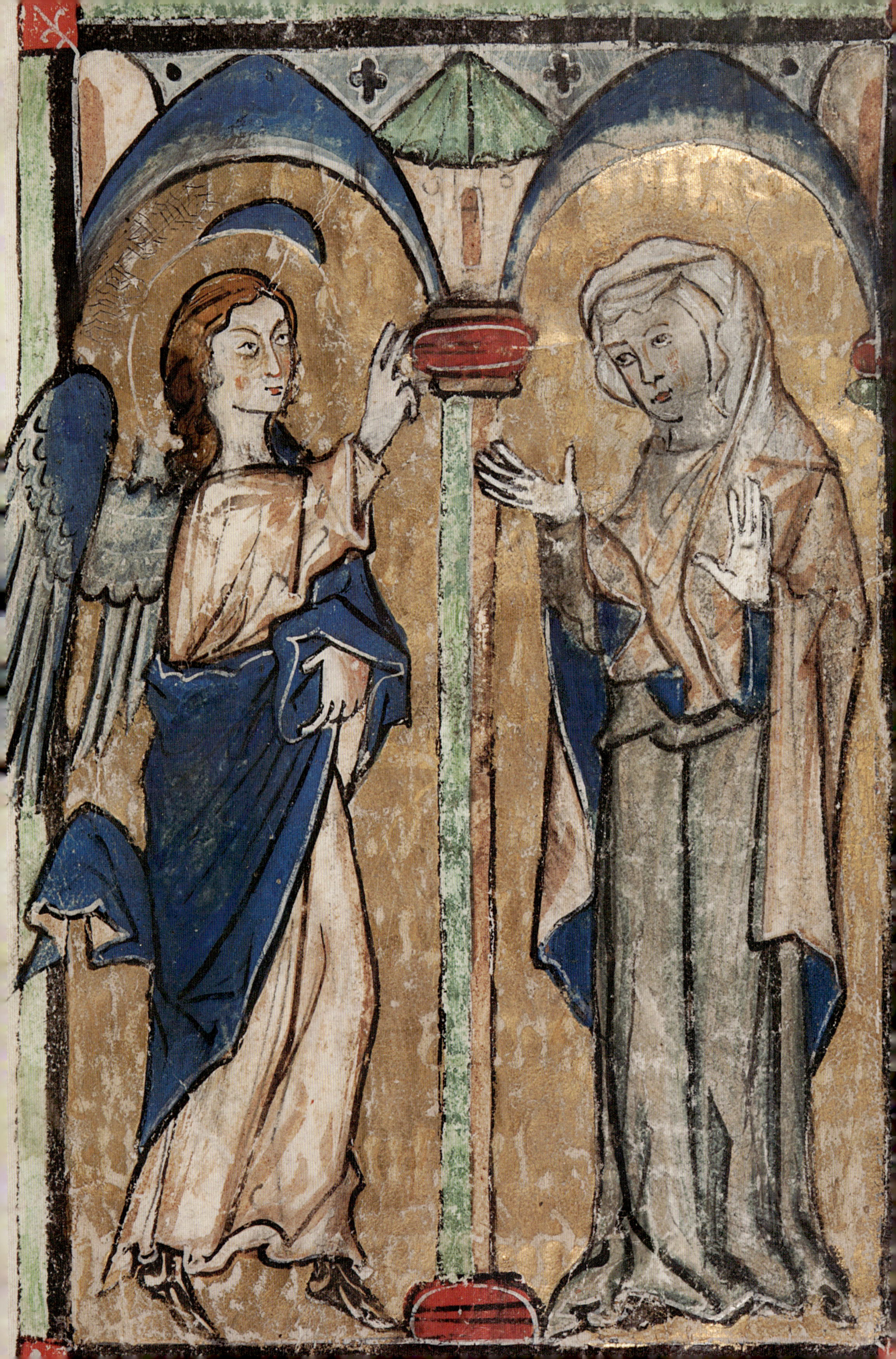

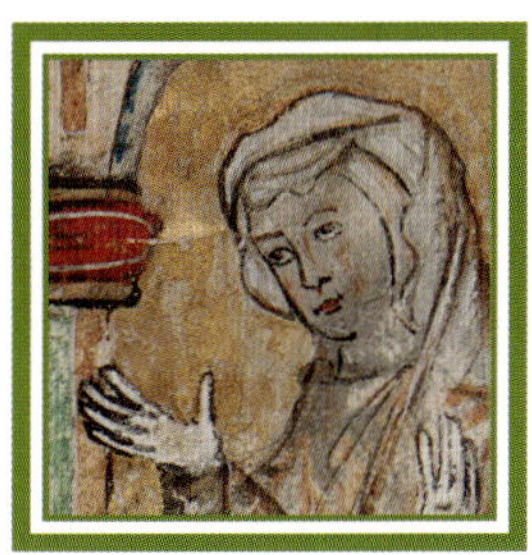

Cat. 2 | Reference 參考編號: BM 1938

Prayer Book or Psalter Leaf with Full-page Miniature Depicting *The Annunciation*
《祈禱書》或《聖詠經》中全版微繪書頁，描繪「聖母領報」

Anonymous
Lake Constance or possibly Upper Rhine, Germany, c.1260
Ink, wash, paint and gold on vellum
H. 180 mm W. 135 mm

This miniature (156 mm x 105 mm) represents *The Annunciation* on the recto, whereas the verso is ruled for 15 lines (156 mm x 105 mm) and contains a complete prayer written in red and blue ink that is introduced by a blue initial D with red penwork. The text is written in *Textualis Formata*. *The Annunciation* depicts the Archangel Gabriel entering the scene from the left, greeting the Virgin Mary with his raised right arm. Mary, standing on the right, is surprised by his appearance, as indicated by her raised hands and palms. Both figures are framed, as well as separated from each other, in architectural compartments; thus, indicating that the angel has entered a room. The illuminator has stressed Gabriel's dynamic movement by allowing his right wing and gown to overlap the painted frame of the image—a motif that is relatively common in 13th-century southern German book illumination. The letters for "angel" are incised into the gold ground in a half-circle in the upper left of Gabriel's halo. Apart from this, the illuminator trusted that the readers of the book would recognize and understand the depicted scene, as he refrained from employing script rolls for the figures, which are found in numerous other parallel depictions from the same time. Christological illuminations, or even cycles in German psalter illustrations, are so varied that no regional cycles have yet to be established. Certain German psalters made

匿名
製作於博登湖或上萊茵，德國，約一二六零年
墨水、淡水彩、彩漆與泥金，犢皮紙
高180公釐，寬135公釐

此幅書頁正面的微繪(156 x 105公釐)描繪了「聖母領報」，然而書頁背面則由十五條線佔據(156 x 105公釐)，以及以紅藍墨水寫就的完整禱文(由藍色大寫首字母「D」作為開頭，紅色筆繪裝飾)，文字為哥德體。「聖母領報」描繪的是，天使長加百列由左側進入該場景，舉起右手向聖母致意；站在場景右側的聖母則吃驚於加百列的出現，她舉起手與手掌表示驚訝；同時，兩個人物被分別框於建築物區隔之中，這表明天使已經進入房間。插畫師通過將天使的右翼與長袍同繪製的畫框重合，來強調加百列的動感——此種圖樣相對多見於十三世紀德國南部的書籍插畫中。在加百列頭頂光環的左上方，單詞「Angel」(天使)的字母以半圓形狀被刻入泥金料底。除此之外，插畫師避免將經卷加入畫中人物場景中——這種經卷形象大量見於同時代的同類作品中——作者相信讀者能夠認出並理解這些場景。有關基督的插畫或甚至是德國《聖詠經》中的系列故事插畫，往往複雜多樣，以至於地區性的故事系列不能被建立。許多熱衷於某一類特定主題的專業畫室，當他們製作某些德國《聖詠經》的插圖時，多樂於從「基督生平」(見 Oliver 2004,

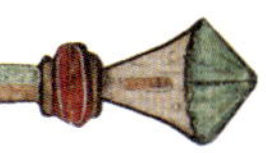
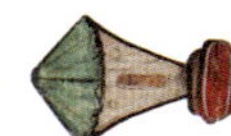

by professional ateliers adhere to a definable thematic group, their illustrative cycle drawn from *The Life of Christ* (see Oliver 2004, p. 263). However, stylistic characteristics such as the outline of the garments' folds and drapery with strong contours—the prevailing modest colours especially of green hues, and the delicate faces with their sweet expression—imply an Upper Rhenish / Lake Constance origin of the miniature and the book it was taken from. The painter displays remarkable artistic skill and inventiveness as he allows the angel's left wing, which is largely covered, to show only a slight bit above the angel's halo, like a blue echo of the golden gloriole. In this way, the latter is visible in front of the golden background. In parallel illustrations of the *The Annunciation* in 13th-century German book illustration, the angel's left wing is generally either omitted or shown completely stretched above Gabriel's head.

This miniature was most likely taken from a psalter manuscript where it could have served as the first illumination. 13th-century psalters from the Upper Rhine region generally presented illumination cycles that preceded either the entire text in a separate section of the book, or else figured at standard divisions of the text; i.e., with Psalms 51 and 101 and/or 2, 26, 38, 80, 109. When, as with this leaf, the illumination was Christological, the introductory text had no direct connection to the text of the psalms. In some of these cycles, prayers had been written on the verso of the illumination, which might correlate with another illustration on the following leaf. The prayer we find on the verso of the miniature could thus have referred to the subsequent Crucifixion. The surface of the miniature is slightly rubbed, with the colours partly flaked off, particularly on the archangel's dress. There is also rubbing on the burnished gold ground, especially where the letters from the verso show through.

p. 263）中取材。然而，一些風格特徵，比如有著鮮明輪廓的服飾褶皺及布料——特別是以綠色系為偏好的溫和色調的流行，以及帶有甜美表情的精緻面容，皆體現出上萊茵 / 博登湖作為此插畫及該書之源起的事實特徵。天使的大部分左翼應被掩蓋，但畫家卻有意在光環上方顯露出左翼的一小部分，好似金色光環的藍色重影，恰能在金色的背景下襯托出金色的光環，這展現了畫家卓越的藝術技巧與創造才能；在十三世紀德國書籍同樣描繪「聖母領報」的插畫中，天使的左翼通常被略去，抑或完全舒展於頭頂。

此微繪極有可能是一本《聖詠經》手卷中的第一幅插畫。十三世紀上萊茵地區的《聖詠經》通常會以插畫展示系列故事，不是放置於單獨文字框之前，就是在文字頁中標準的獨立區域展現；即《詩篇》五十一篇與一百零一篇，與 / 或二篇，二十六篇，三十八篇，八十篇，一百零九篇。如同此頁一般，其插畫也是基督論的題材，而介紹文字卻與詩篇內容無直接連繫。在許多這些故事系列中，禱文被寫在插圖的背頁，而與下頁的插畫相關聯，因此，此幅微繪背頁的禱文與隨後的「耶穌被釘十字架」場景相關聯。微繪表面遭輕微磨損，顏色部分脱落（注意天使長的服裝），拋光泥金料底也有磨損（尤其是背頁透印的地方）。

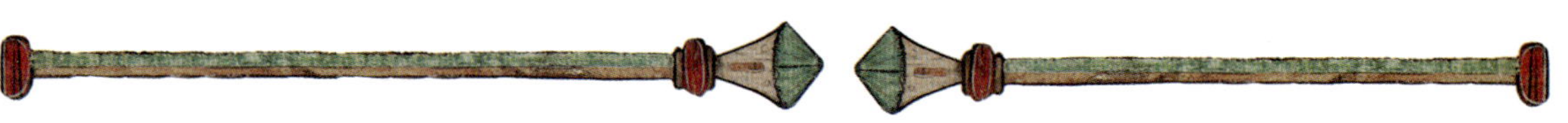

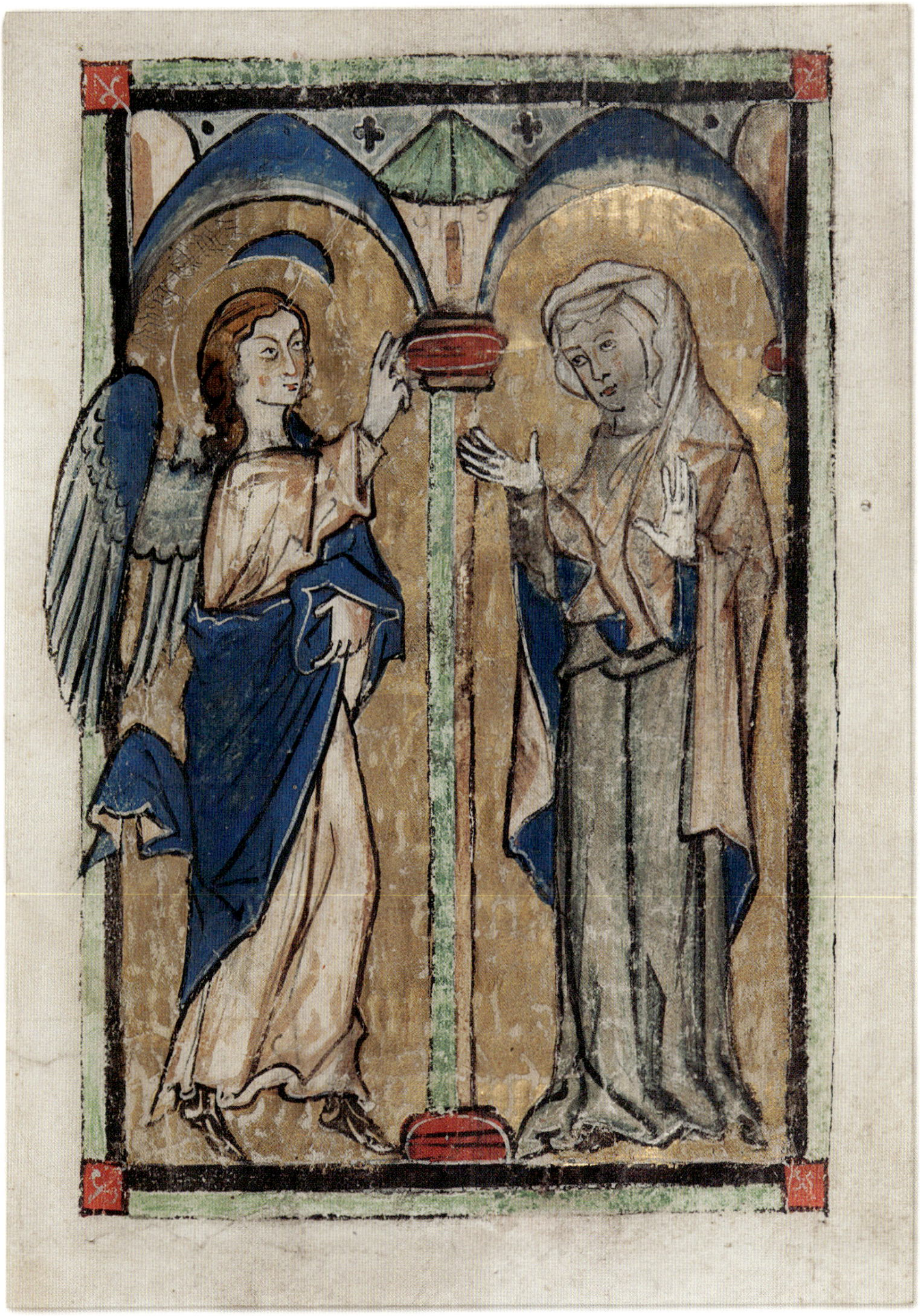

(actual size 原大)

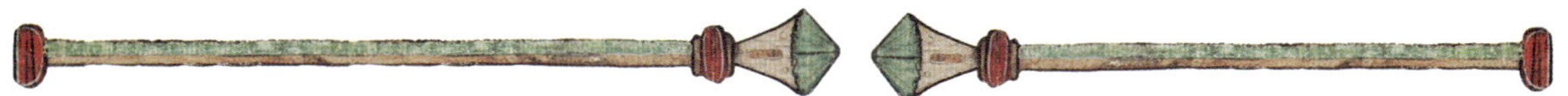

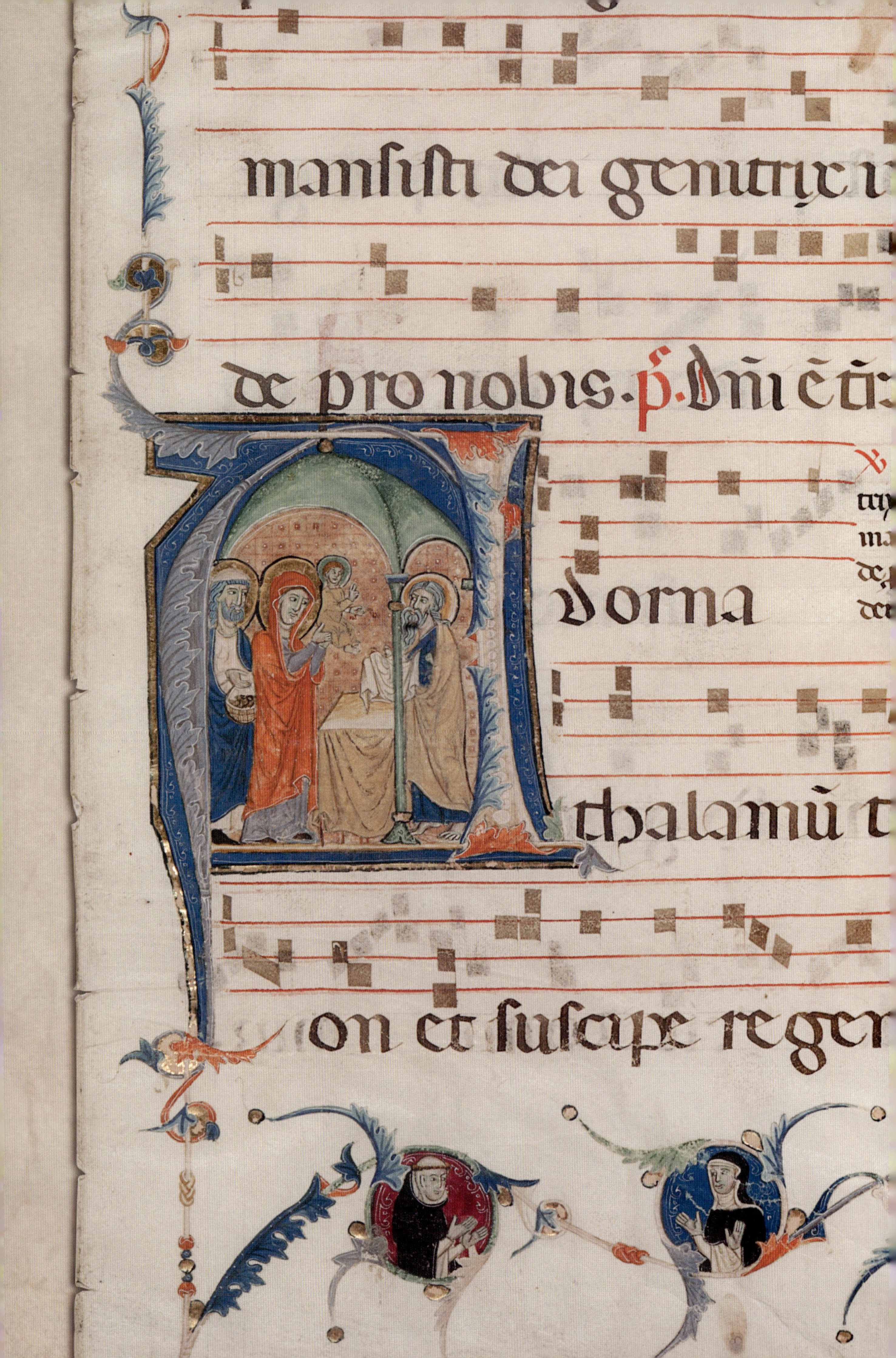
mansisti dei genitrix
de pro nobis.
dorna
thalamu
on et suscipe regem

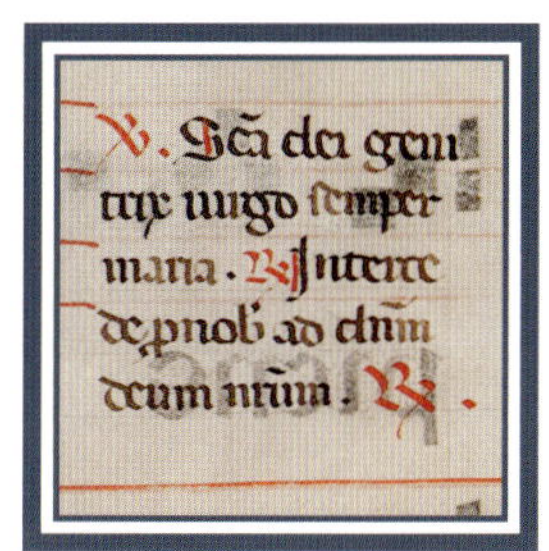

Cat. 3 | Reference 參考編號: BM 1417; SF 9515

Leaf from an Antiphonary Depicting *The Presentation in the Temple* and a Historiated Initial "A"
《啟應輪唱詩歌集》書頁，描畫「獻主於聖殿」，佔行大寫首字母「A」經中世紀傳統出版風格修飾與變形

Jacobellus of Salerno (active around 1270)
Bologna, Italy, c.1270
Tempera, gold and ink on vellum
H. 528 mm W. 350 mm

薩雷諾的雅各（活躍於一二七零年前後）
製作於博洛尼亞，意大利，約一二七零年
蛋彩、泥金與墨水，犢皮紙
高528公釐，寬350公釐

Text: *Adorna thalamu[m] tuu[m] Syon* . . . (Sion, adorn your dwelling . . .) is the first Matins response for the Feast of the Purification of the Virgin (February 2).

On a recto page from a choir book, Jacobellus's *The Presentation in the Temple* is the traditional illustration for the Feast of the Purification of the Virgin celebrated on 2 February. The feast commemorates the purification of the Virgin and the presentation of Christ in the Temple, which took place forty days after Christ's birth, in accordance with Jewish law. Stylistic elements and motifs employed by Jacobellus can be found in the parent manuscripts and sister leaves. The canopy over the figures and the diapered background in the Breslauer initial are similar to those in a Nativity found in the Stockholm Antiphonary (cf. Nordenfalk 1979, no. 18, fig. 104). The roundels in the bottom border with busts of Dominican monks and nuns are also found in the Stockholm Antiphonary (Nordenfalk 1979, figs. 104 and 107), the Chicago Antiphonary (cf. Nordenfalk 1979, fig. 222), the Getty Gradual (Euw–Plotzek 1979, pp. 171–172, and illus. p. 263) and a leaf in a German private collection (see Mickenberg 1985).

文字：「*Adorna thalamu[m] tuu[m] Syon* . . . 」（錫安，裝飾你的居所……）是第一次晨禱，響應聖母取潔日（二月二日）。

雅各的「獻主於聖殿」位於一本聖詩集的右頁，乃是二月二日聖母取潔日的傳統插畫。此節紀念聖母的淨潔，以及獻主於聖殿，根據猶太人的律法，此項禮儀需在基督降生後第四十日進行。雅各此處所使用的風格及圖樣元素均可發現於該圖所在的書籍及其姊妹書頁之中。人物上方的華蓋，以及對布雷斯勞爾菱形花紋背景的使用，皆與斯德哥爾摩《啟應輪唱詩歌集》（cf. Nordenfalk 1979, no. 18, fig. 104）中的「耶穌降生」場景類似。底部邊緣兩個圓圖版為道明會修士與修女的半身像，也同樣見於斯德哥爾摩《啟應輪唱詩歌集》（Nordenfalk 1979, figs. 104 and 107），芝加哥《啟應輪唱詩歌集》（cf. Nordenfalk 1979, fig. 222），蓋提《階台經》（Euw–Plotzek 1979, pp. 171–172, and illus. p. 263），以及一張德國私人收藏書頁（Mickenberg 1985）。

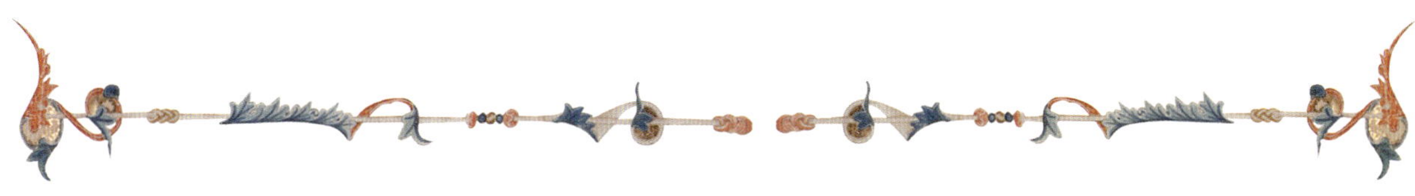

The many roundels of Dominican monks and nuns that occur throughout the original manuscripts, as well as textual elements in the signed Gradual, indicate that the choir books were made for a Dominican institution. Because of the many nuns, Euw and Plotzek (p. 264) have suggested that it was modeled after the Convent of San Guglielmo in Bologna. The choir books, however, could have been made for any number of Dominican institutions established during the century following St. Dominic's founding of his order in 1216.

This leaf once belonged to a set of choir books consisting of at least four volumes: a Gradual and a three-volume Antiphonary, of which two volumes survive. The third exists only in a few leaves. The set was written, illuminated and notated by Jacobellus, known as Muriolus of Salerno. His unusually specific colophon in Latin is found on folio 159v of the Getty Gradual, one of the parent set: "I, Jacobellus, known as 'muriolus', of Salerno, wrote, illuminated and notated this book, which was the first work by my hand" (Euw–Plotzek 1979, vol. I, p. 262). Since Jacobellus does not preface his name with "frater" (as expected from a monastic scribe in this period), he might have been a lay scribe who, as his name indicates, came from the southern Italian city of Salerno. His manner of painting differs from the Bolognese "First Style".

Literature: Voelkle and Wieck 1992, no. 57.

原始手抄本中隨處可見的道明會修士與修女圓像，與署名的《階台經》中的文本元素一樣，皆表明此類聖詩集是為道明會而製。由於出現許多修女，故而艾烏和普羅澤科 (Euw–Plotzek) (p. 264) 認為這是在模仿博洛尼亞的聖古列爾莫女修道院；然而，這些聖詩集可能是一二一六年聖道明建立了他的修會之後由道明會製作而成。

此書頁曾經屬於一套四卷本以上的《聖詩集》——一卷《階台經》與三卷《啟應輪唱詩歌集》——其中兩卷較完整存世，而第三卷只殘留幾張書頁而已。全套書的文字抄寫、插圖繪製與註解工作皆由雅各完成，他常被稱作薩雷諾的穆瑞奧勒斯。蓋提《階台經》159v 中發現拉丁文的版權信息：「我，雅各，被稱作薩雷諾的穆瑞奧勒斯，抄寫、插圖並註解此書，這亦是我的第一部手工作品」(Euw–Plotzek 1979, vol. I, p. 262)。由於雅各並未在他的名字前署稱「會士」(同時期的修道院抄寫員通常會如此署名)，因此他可能是一位世俗抄寫員；而正像他的名字表明的那樣，他來自意大利南部城市薩雷諾。他的繪畫習慣與博洛尼亞式的「第一樣式」不同。

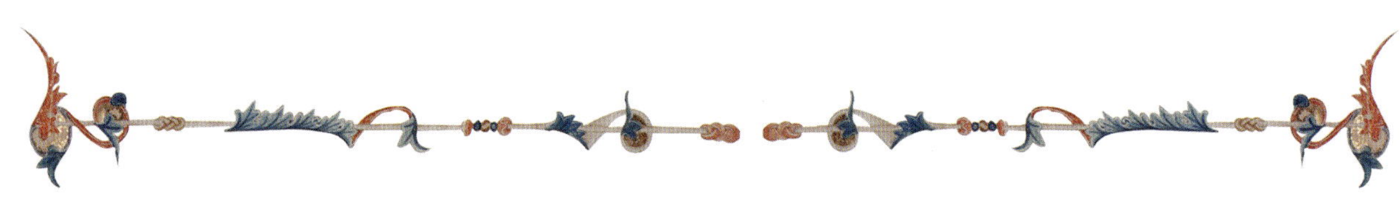

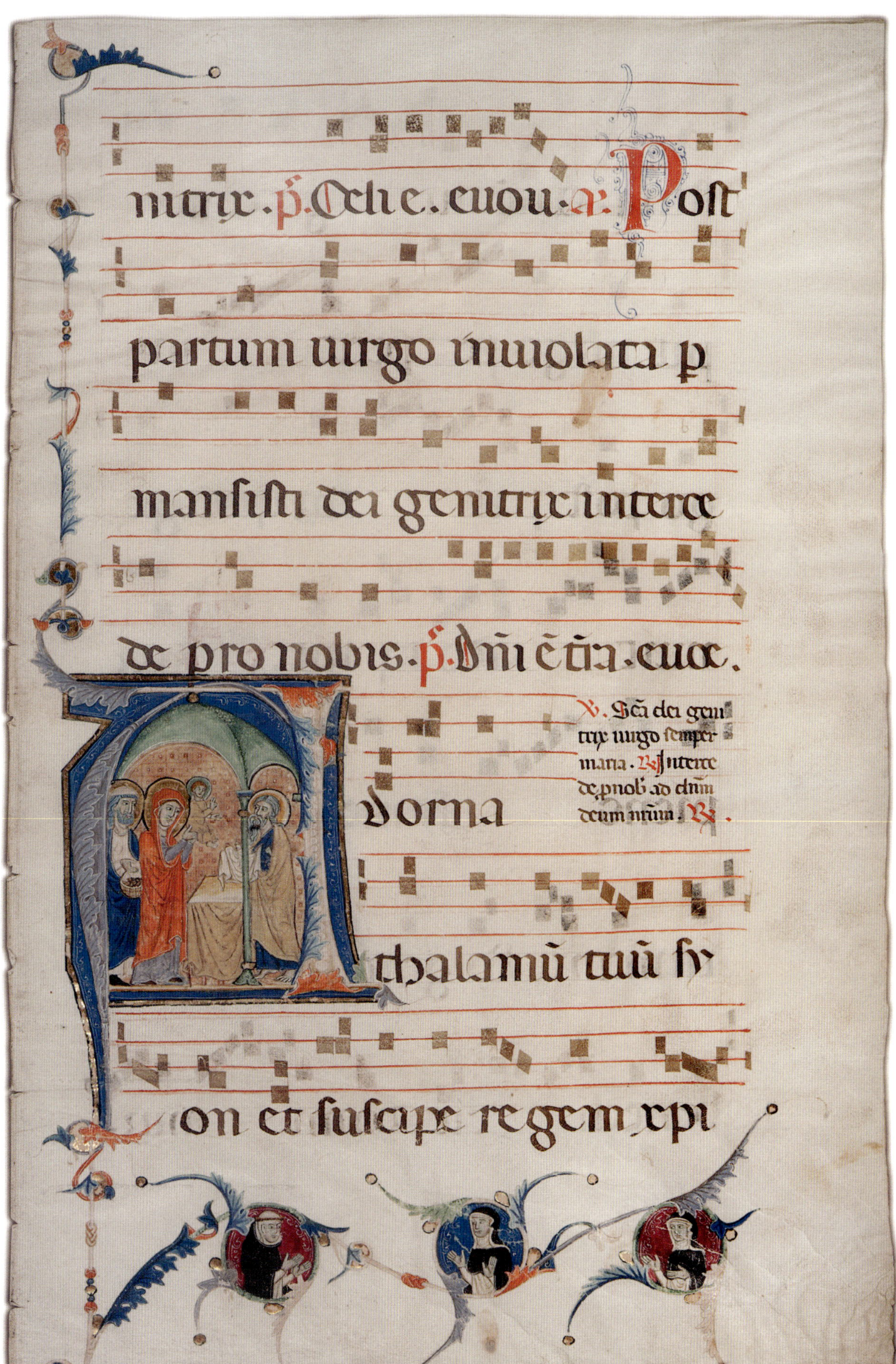
partum uirgo inuiolata p
mansisti dei genitrix interce
de pro nobis
Adorna
thalamū tuū sy
on et suscipe regem xpi

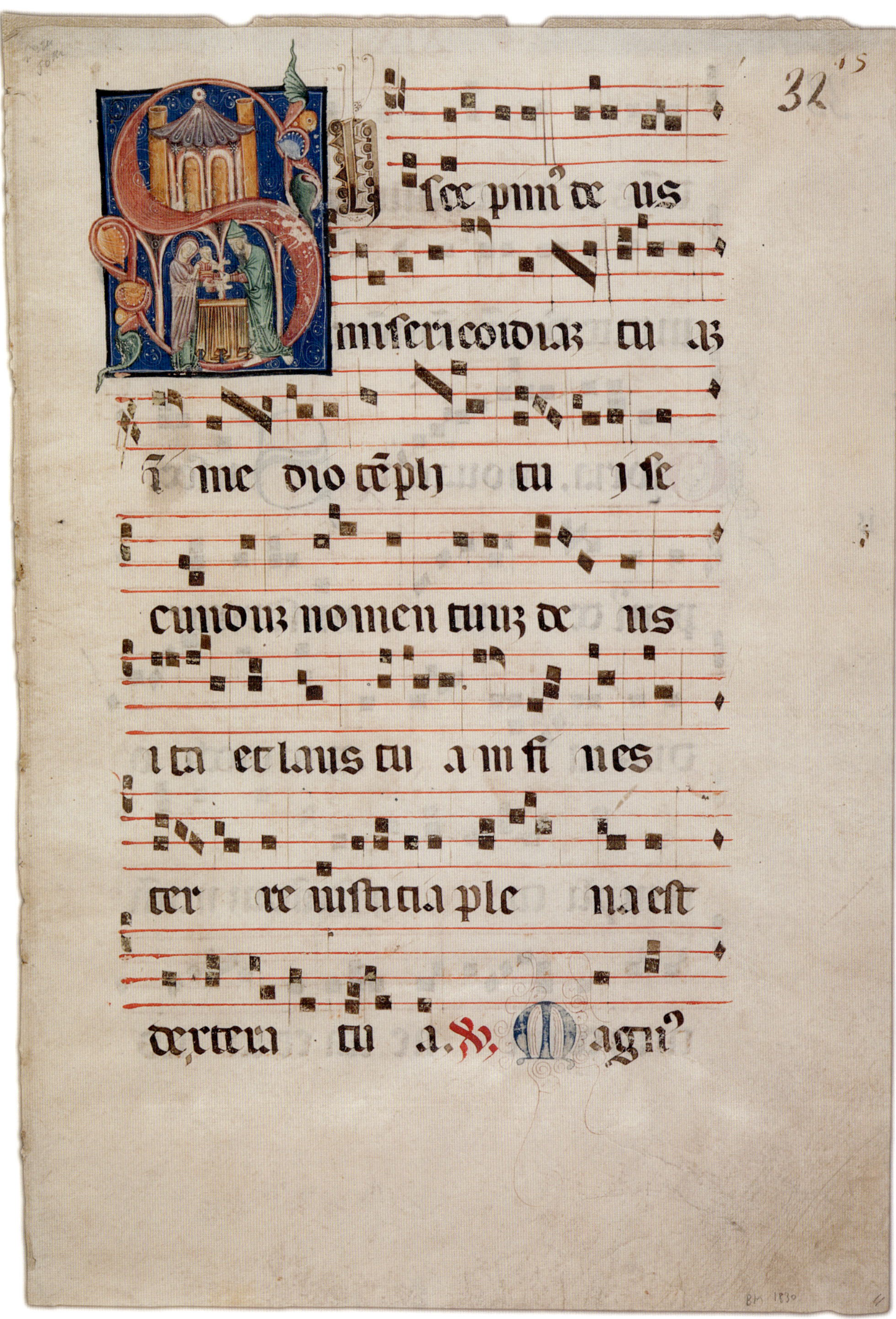
cundum nomen tuum de us
ita et laus tua in fi nes
ter re iustitia ple na est
32

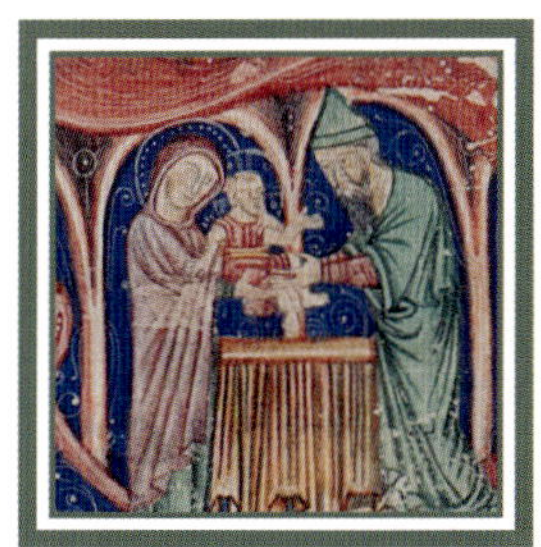

Cat. 4 | Reference 參考編號: BM 1830; SF 54

Leaf from a Gradual Depicting *The Presentation in the Temple* and a Historiated Initial "S"
《階台經》書頁，描繪「獻主於聖殿」，佔行大寫首字母「S」經中世紀傳統出版風格修飾與變形

Anonymous
Umbria or southern Italy, c.1270–1280
Tempera and gold on parchment
H. 48.2 cm W. 33.2 cm

Text on recto: *Suscepim[us] deus/ misericordia[m] tua[m]/ i[n] medio te[m]pli tui se/cundu[m] nomen tuu[m] deus/ ita et laus tua in fines/ terre iustitia plena est/ dextera tua. [rubr.] V. Magn[us].*

Text on verso: *d[omi]n[u]s et laudabilis nimis in ci/vitate d[e]i n [ost]ri i[n]mo[n]te s[an]c[t]o eius./ Gloria.euouae. [rubr.] R. Susce/pim[us] deus misericor/dia[m] tua[m] in medio/ templi tui sec[n]du[m] nom[en]/ tuu[m] domine ita et laus*

This illumination depicts *The Presentation in the Temple*, a scene often repeated and here skillfully placed within the bulbous curves of the initial "S". The "presentation" itself is shown in the lower part of the letter as it depicts Christ held over the baptismal font and under the towering arches of the temple. The upper curve is taken up by the temple, suggesting a large and impressive structure.

Literature: De Ricci 1937, p. 1708, B.6; Palladino 2003, no. 3c, Ms. 54.

匿名
製作於溫布利亞或意大利南部
約一二七零年至一二八零年
蛋彩與泥金，羊皮紙
高48.2公分，寬33.2公分

書頁正面文字：「*Suscepim[us] deus/ misericordia[m] tua[m]/ i[n] medio te[m]pli tui se/cundu[m] nomen tuu[m] deus/ ita et laus tua in fines/ terre iustitia plena est/ dextera tua. [rubr.] V. Magn[us].*」

書頁反面文字：「*d[omi]n[u]s et laudabilis nimis in ci/vitate d[e]i n [ost]ri i[n]mo[n]te s[an]c[t]o eius./ Gloria.euouae. [rubr.] R. Susce/pim[us] deus misericor/dia[m] tua[m] in medio/ templi tui sec[n]du[m] nom[en]/ tuu[m] domine ita et laus*」

書頁插圖描繪了一個經常重複出現的場景——「獻主於聖殿」，並被巧妙放置於球莖狀曲線變形的佔行大寫首字母「S」中。「獻主」的過程在「S」的下半部分出現，其中基督被抱於洗禮池之上，也位於聖殿高大拱門的下方；「S」上半部分的曲線則由聖殿充滿，營造了一種巨大且令人印象深刻的結構。

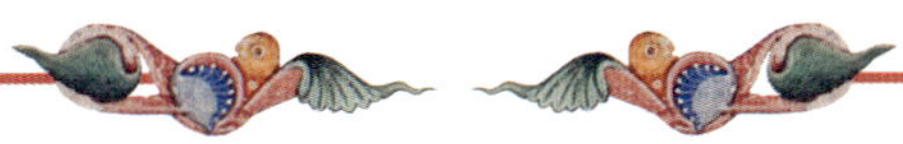

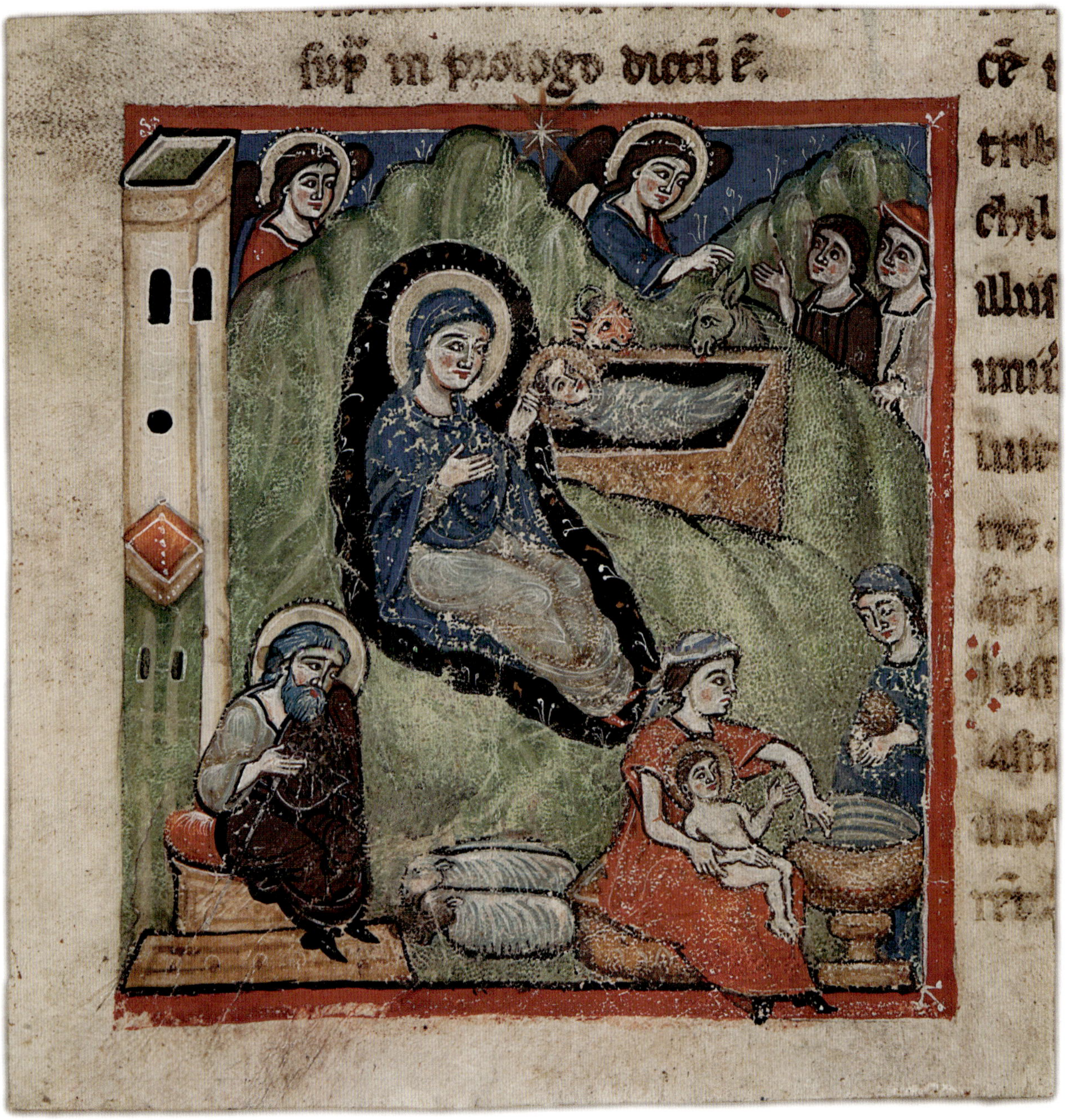

(actual size 原大)

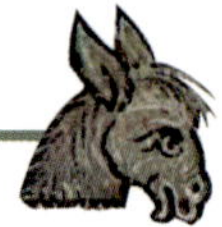
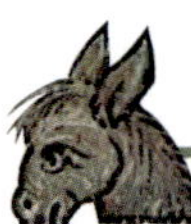

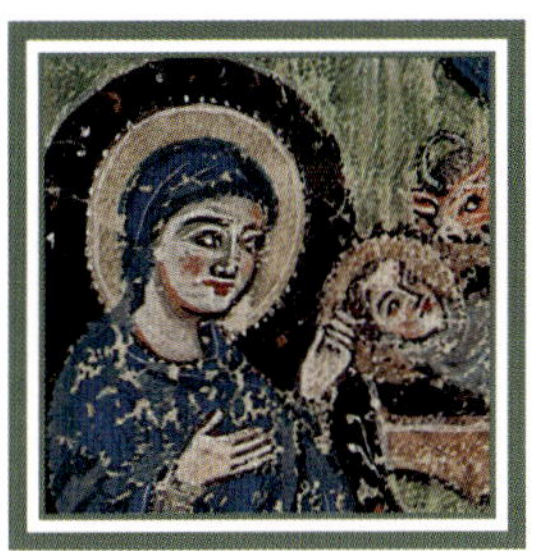

Cat. 5 | Reference 參考編號: BM 1276

Manuscript Cutting from an Early Illustrated Version of Jacopo da Voragine's *Golden Legend* with a Miniature Depicting *The Nativity*
雅各・德・佛拉金的早期插畫版《黃金傳説》中截取的微繪，描繪「耶穌降生」

Master of Monza (active c.1270–1290)
Monza, Italy, c.1275–1285
Tempera and ink on vellum
H. 137 mm W. 135 mm

來自蒙扎的大師
(活躍於約一二七零年至一二九零年)
製作於蒙扎，意大利，約一二七五年至一二八五年
蛋彩與墨水，犢皮紙
高137公釐，寬135公釐

This animated illumination depicts the birth of Christ from a manuscript of Jacobus de Voragine's *Golden Legend*, which contains the lives of the saints. As in the Byzantine tradition, the Virgin Mary appears in the centre, nestled in a cave, with the Christ Child situated in front of her. Below and to the left, Joseph is shown sitting with two sheep by his feet, whereas on the right two women are washing the Child. Above the scene are two angels with the Star, which is guiding two shepherds (upper right corner).

While the Master of Monza remains anonymous to date, this leaf is described as having been completed by the same illuminator who was responsible for an important choir book made for the Cathedral of Monza between 1280 and 1285 (now in Cracow, Bibl. Jagiellonska, Rps. akc. 20/ 1951). The artist's stylistic features are easily analyzed in the more extensive Cracow Antiphonary: towers with turrets framing the scenes, white highlighting and dots of snowflakes on the garments, and finely modeled Byzantine faces. The secure localization of the choir book provides the first compelling evidence for the locus of activity of this talented artist.

Literature: Forrer 1902, vol. 1, pls. VI–VIII; Boskovits 1997, no. 5, pp. 34–45.

此幅裁自雅各・德・佛拉金《黃金傳説》的生動插畫描繪了「耶穌降生」場景，亦包含了聖人們的生活。聖母根據拜占庭傳統在畫中心出現，安坐於洞穴中，聖嬰在其身前；約瑟呈坐姿於畫作的左下部，腳前另有兩隻羊，右側的兩位女性在為聖嬰洗浴；上部場景為兩個天使以及晨星，正在指引兩名牧羊人(右上角)。

迄今為止，我們依然不知這位來自蒙扎的大師的具體名姓，但普遍認為他亦於一二八零年至一二八五年間負責為蒙扎大教堂製作了一本重要的《聖詩集》(現存於克拉科夫，亞捷隆大學圖書館，編號：Rps. akc. 20/ 1951)。藝術家的風格特點在克拉科夫《啟應輪唱詩歌集》中更為突出：有角樓的高塔構成了場景的框架，服裝上的高光點與許多雪花圓點，以及拜占庭式的精緻面容。《聖詩集》確鑿的起源第一次展現了這位天賦異稟的藝術家的活動軌跡。

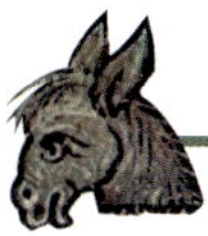

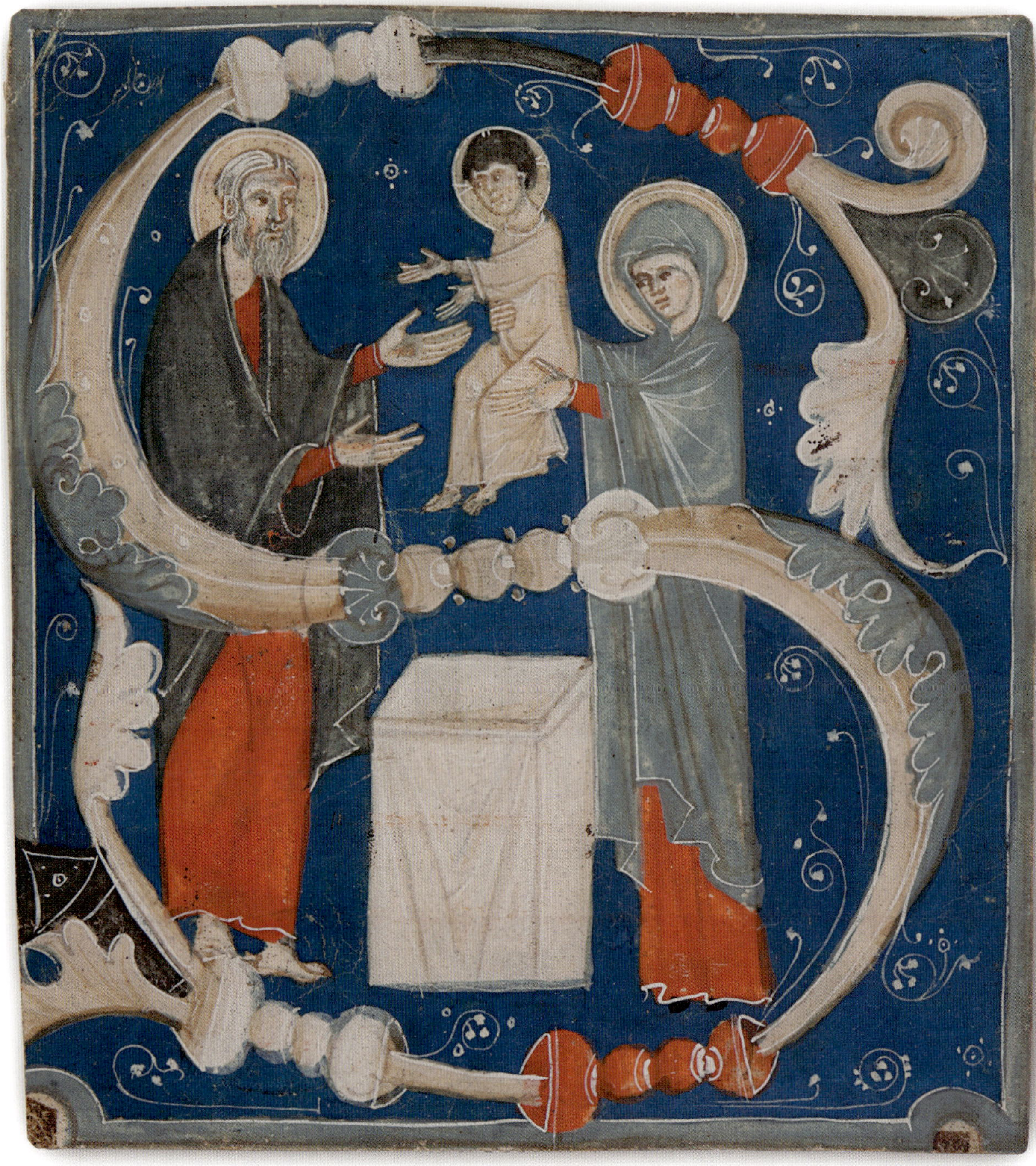

(actual size 原大)

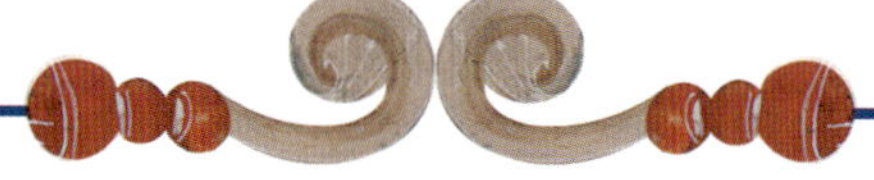

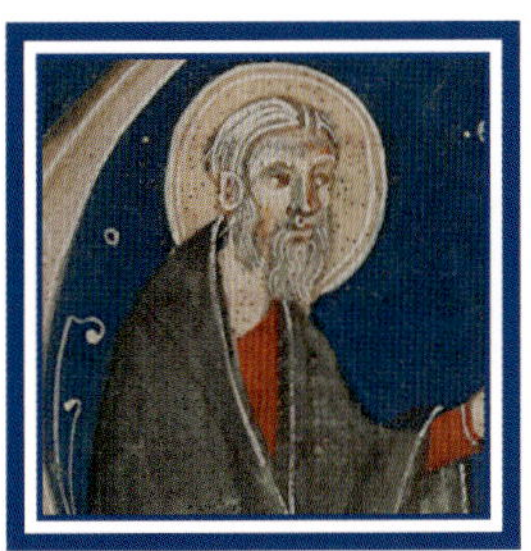

Cat. 6 | Reference 參考編號: BM 2470; SF 21

Choir Book Leaf with a Miniature Depicting *The Presentation in the Temple*
《聖詩集》書頁中的微繪，描繪「獻主於聖殿」

Italian Master
Italy, second half of the 13th century
Tempera and ink on parchment
H. 175 mm W. 165 mm

This polychrome painting illustrates *The Presentation in the Temple* which is developed within the letter "S" on a dark blue background in light-blue framing. Behind the letter is the scene of Christ in the Temple. The altar is represented in the lower register of the letter, while the moment in which the Child is being presented to the priest is represented in the upper register. Figures and initials are rendered in light colours and covered in a delicate white net of ornamental lines and ridges, providing a "glassy" quality to the image. This high-quality image resembles other works of art created in Bologna in the second half of the 13th century.
The verso depicts neumes (square notes) and Latin text in brown, as well as a red four-line note system.

意大利大師
製作於意大利，十三世紀下半葉
蛋彩與墨水，羊皮紙
高175公釐，寬165公釐

此幅多彩繪畫描繪的「獻主於聖殿」場景在字母「S」圖層之下，並被字母框住，另具深藍色背景，及淡藍色邊框。「S」下半部分中有一個聖壇，將聖嬰遞給祭司的動作則被表現於上半部分。人物與字母以淡色渲染，並被精緻的白色網狀裝飾線條和脊線覆蓋，這為圖畫融入了一種「玻璃」質感。此幅高水平的繪畫類似十三世紀下半葉製作於博洛尼亞的藝術品。而在背頁則包括褐色的紐姆符號（方形標記）與拉丁文字，以及紅色四線標記系統。

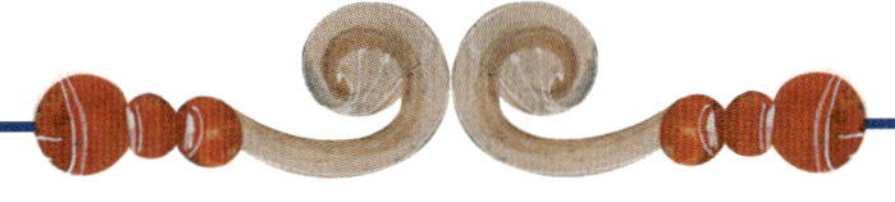

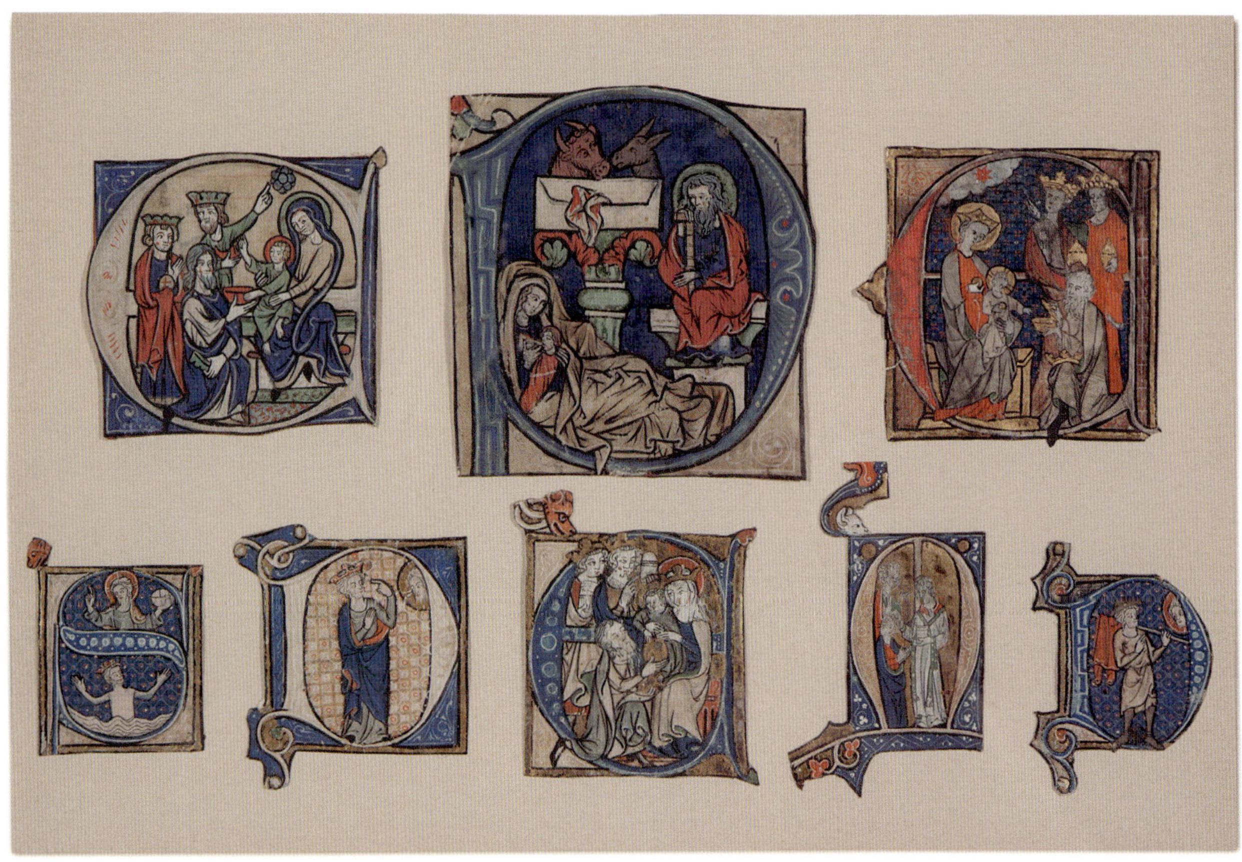

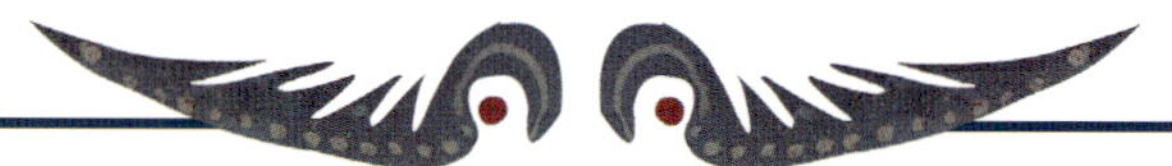

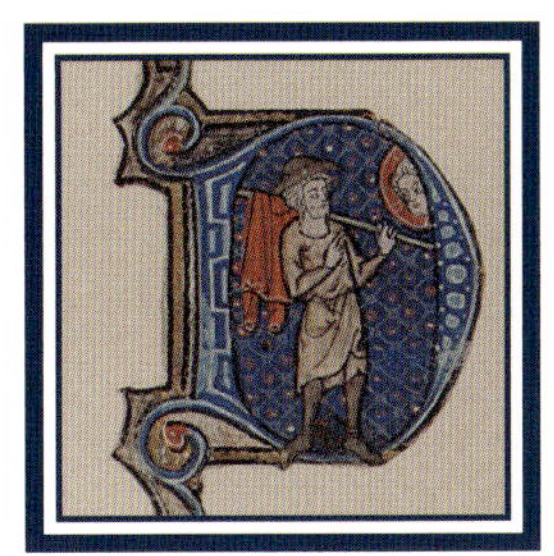

Cat. 7a–h | Reference 參考編號: BM 1207b, c, f; SF 4165

Manuscript Cuttings from German Bibles Depicting *The Nativity* and *The Adoration of the Magi*, and Historiated Initials (set of eight)
德譯版《聖經》中截取的手繪插畫，描繪「耶穌降生」與「博士來朝」，佔行大寫首字母經中世紀傳統出版風格修飾與變形（共八幅）

Anonymous
Germany, 13th century
Tempera, gold and ink on vellum
Images range from H. 73 mm W. 71 mm
to H. 40 mm W. 31 mm

These cuttings present illuminated and historiated initials that originally introduced the page and chapter. The letters are drawn in varied sizes and each illustrate a biblical scene (clockwise): *The Adoration of the Magi*, *The Nativity*, *The Adoration of the Magi*, *The Annunciation to Joseph*, *The Benediction*, *The Adoration of the Magi*, *The Annunciation to Joseph*, *Christ Pantocrator* (top) and *Knight at Sea* (bottom). Although isolated from their former context—the larger pages and book they were painted for—all eight depictions beautifully display the fine quality and style of 13th-century German illuminations. Notwithstanding the lack of depth and perspective, these illustrations demonstrate how the artist filled the volume of each initial and how the juxtaposition of figures creates an illusion of space and complexity.

匿名
製作於德國，十三世紀
蛋彩、泥金與墨水，犢皮紙
由高73公釐，寬71公釐
至高40公釐，寬31公釐

這些裁取的插畫展現了一系列經過修飾與變形的佔行大寫首字母，皆被用以領啟頁面與章節。這些字母尺寸不同，每一個都表現了「聖經」場景，由左上起沿順時針方向依次為：「博士來朝」、「耶穌降生」、「博士來朝」、「若瑟領報」、「祝福」、「博士來朝」、「若瑟領報」與「『基督普世君王』(上)『海上騎士』」(下)。雖然與之前的文字脱離，但所有八幅微繪確實完美展現了十三世紀德國插畫的風格與藝術品質。儘管缺乏景深和透視，這些插畫卻詳細展示了如何填滿每一個變形字母的空間，以及人物的鋪陳如何帶出空間感與複雜感。

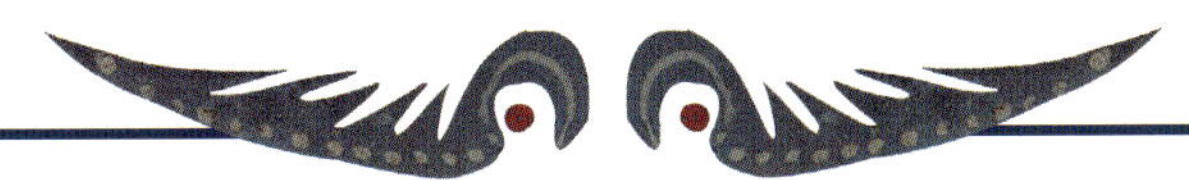

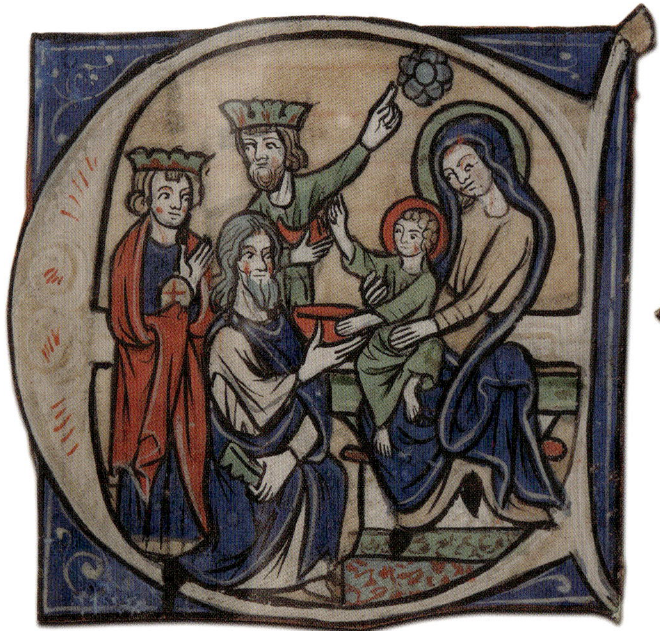

The Adoration of the Magi
「博士來朝」

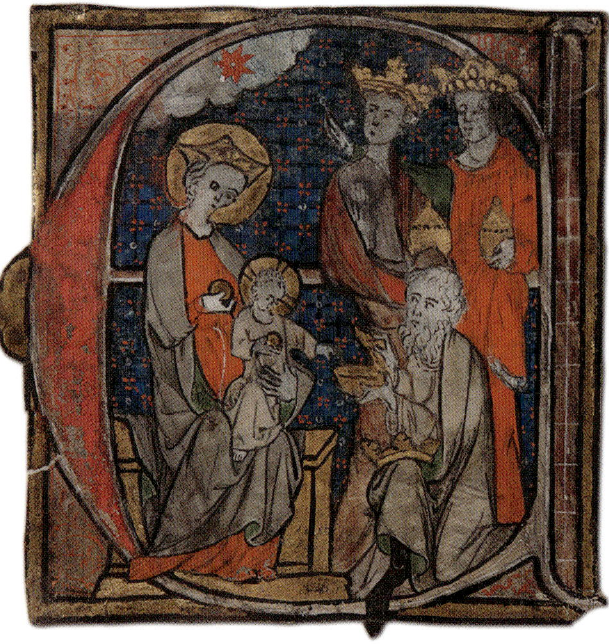

The Adoration of the Magi
「博士來朝」

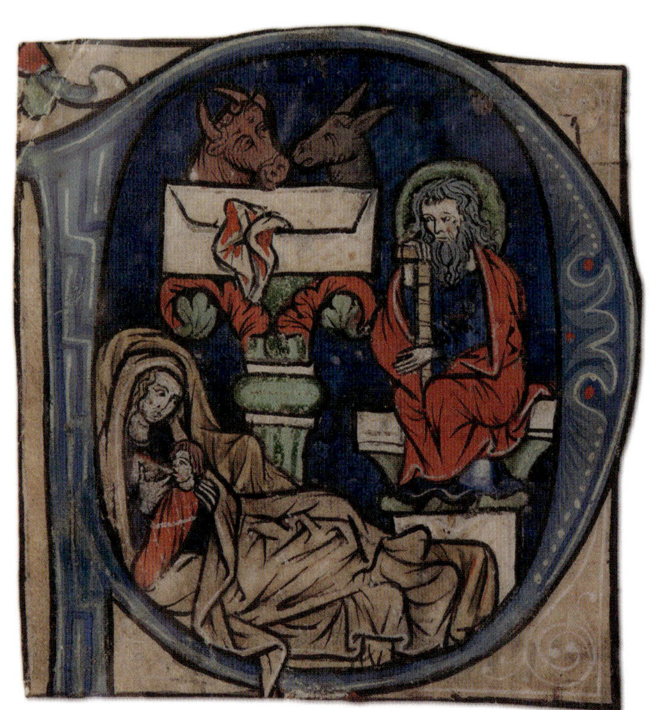

The Nativity
「耶穌降生」

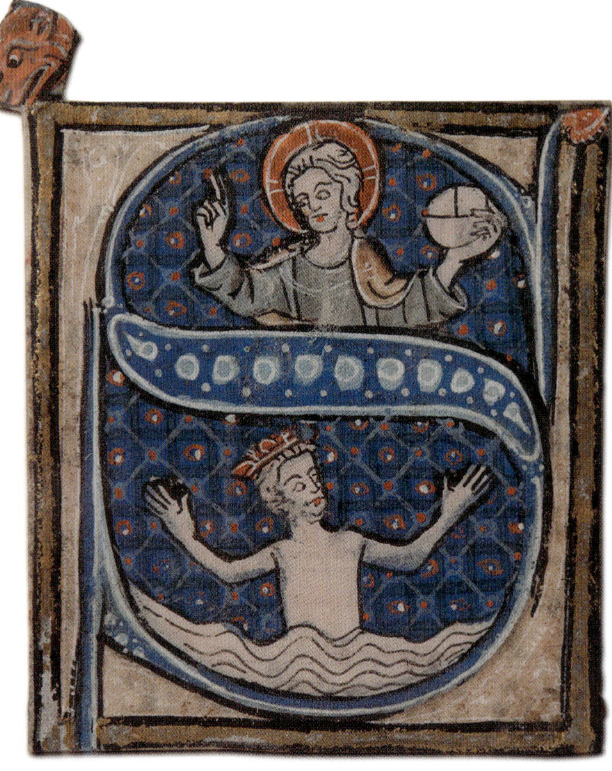

Christ Pantocrator (top) and *Knight at Sea* (bottom)
「『基督普世君王』(上)『海上騎士』」(下)

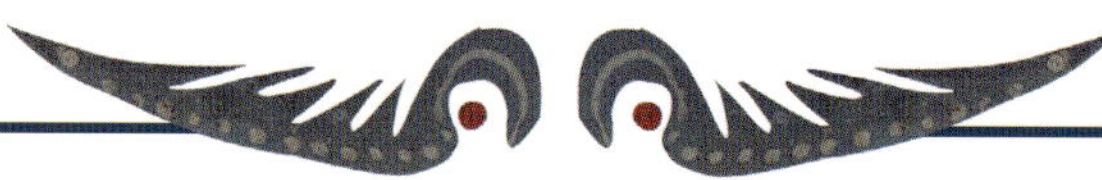

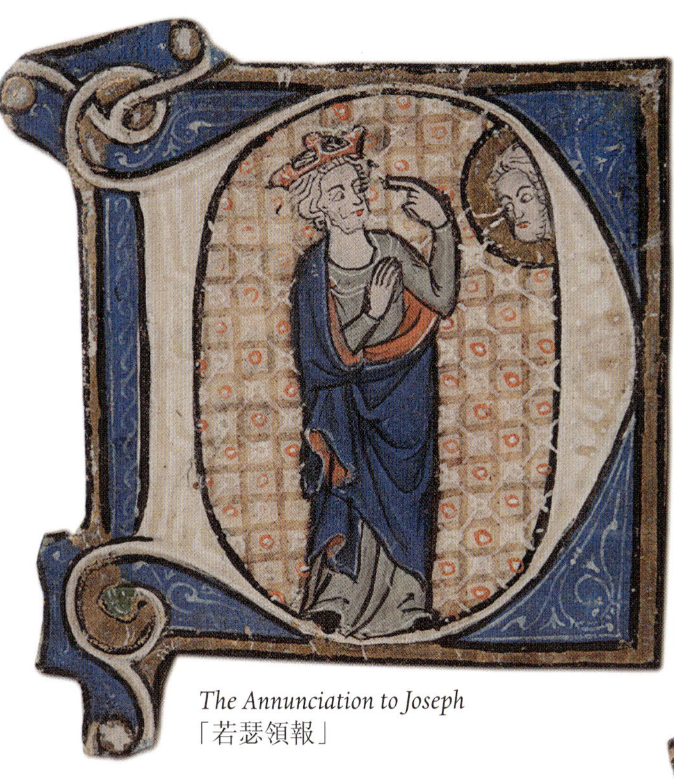

The Annunciation to Joseph
「若瑟領報」

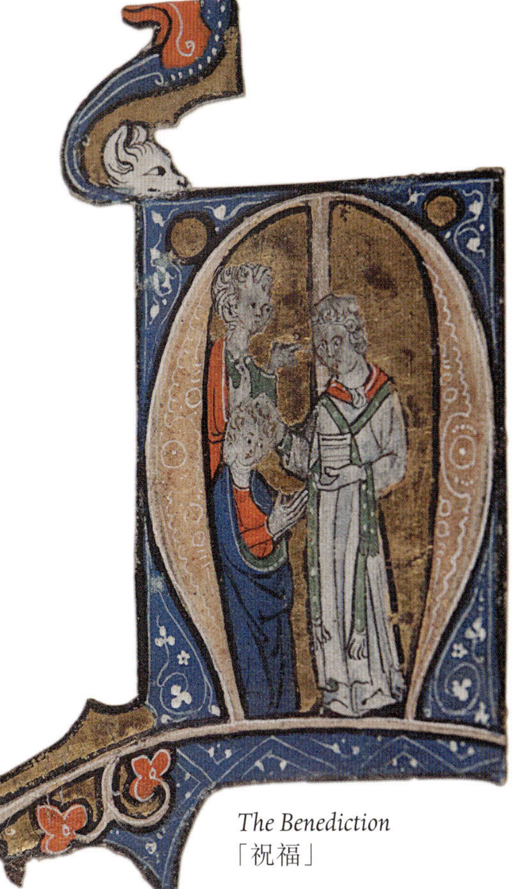

The Benediction
「祝福」

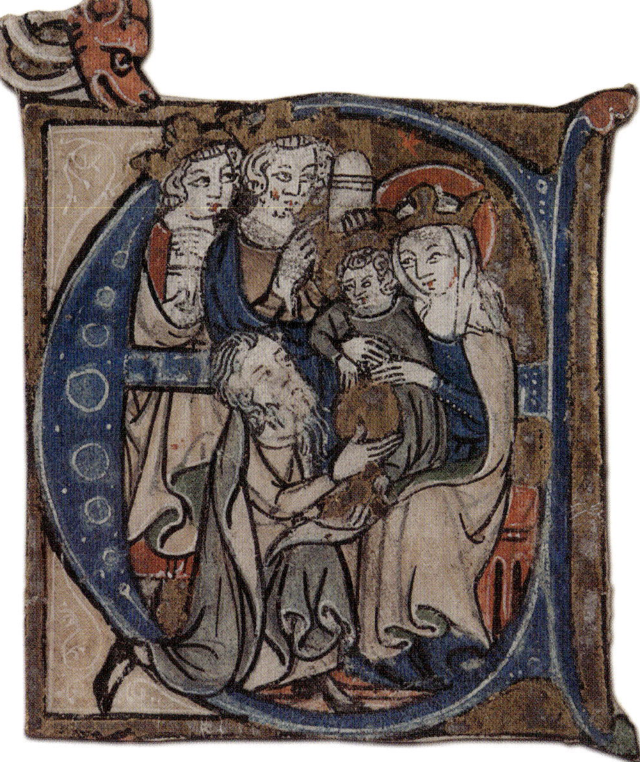

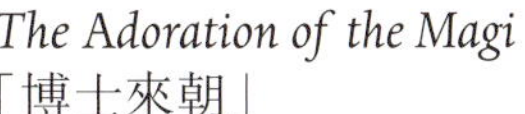

The Adoration of the Magi
「博士來朝」

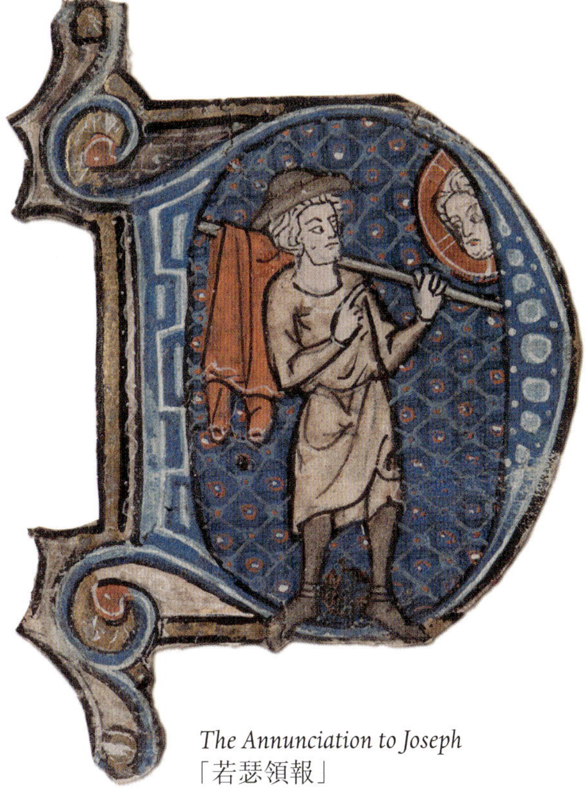

The Annunciation to Joseph
「若瑟領報」

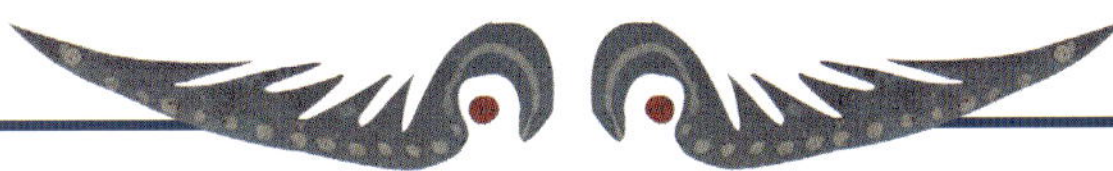

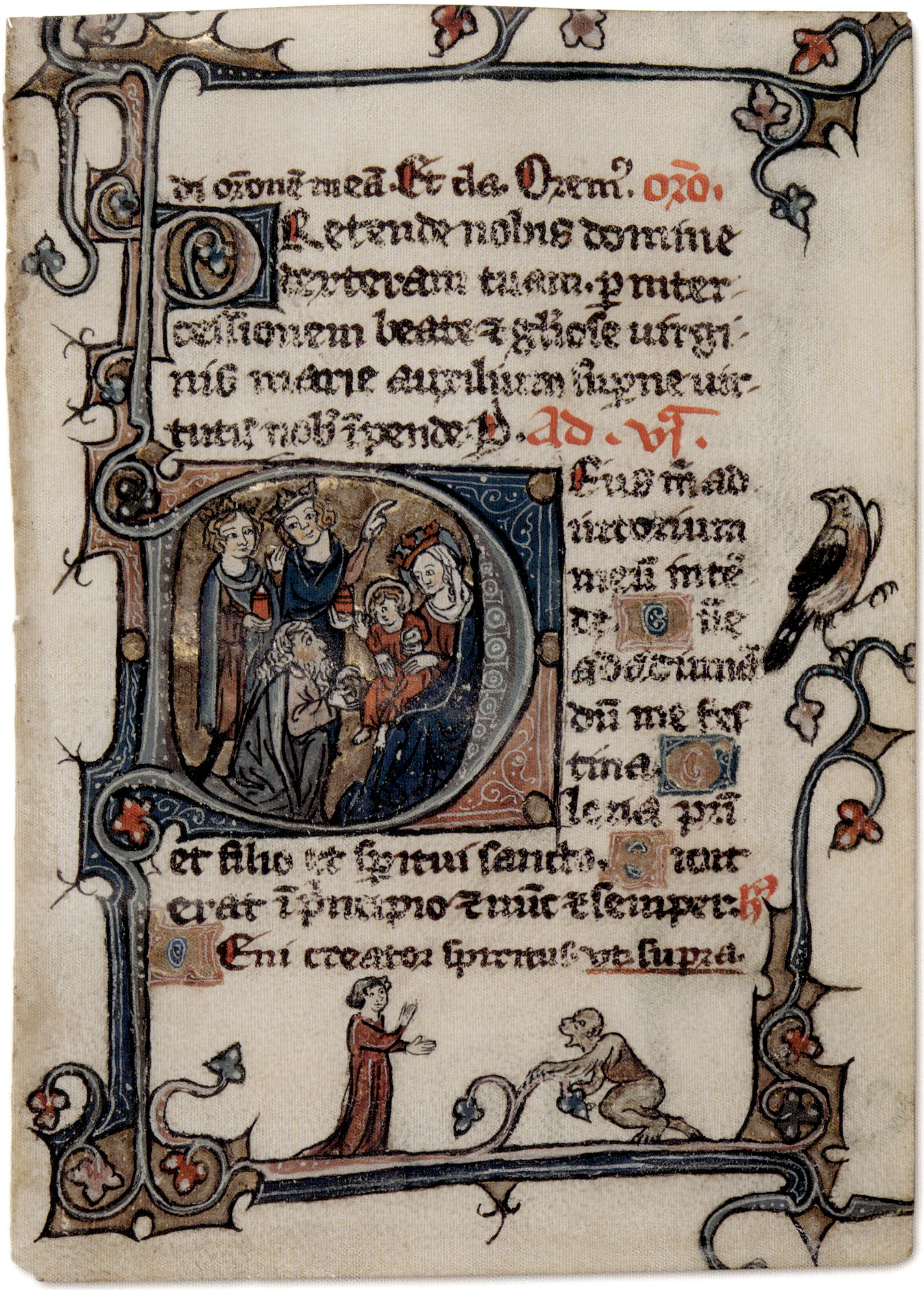

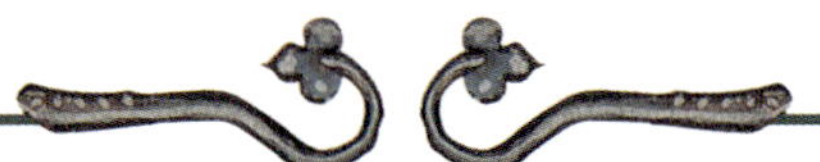

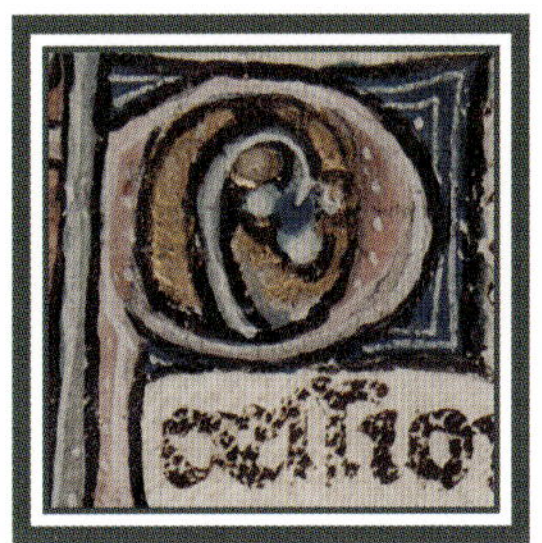

Cat. 8 | Reference 參考編號: BM 1181; SF 59

Psalter Leaf Depicting *The Adoration of the Magi* and a Historiated Initial "D"
《聖詠經》書頁，描繪「博士來朝」，佔行大寫首字母「D」經中世紀傳統出版風格修飾與變形

Anonymous
France, late 13th century
Tempera, gold and ink on vellum
H. 127 mm W. 95 mm

The manuscript depicts *The Adoration of the Magi* in which the Virgin and Child are shown seated on the right, and the Kings on the left. One of the Kings is kneeling and the others standing. The scene's background is gilded and the halos are yellow (Christ) and blue (Virgin). This initial also contains elaborate extenders with a foliate decorative motif, a bird on the right margin, and a monkey and standing female figure at the lower margin. It is drawn in light blue on a red and blue background.

匿名
製作於法國，十三世紀晚期
蛋彩、泥金與墨水，犢皮紙
高 127 公釐，寬 95 公釐

書頁內的「博士來朝」場景中，聖母與聖嬰坐於右側，三位博士居左側，其一正行跪拜，另兩位則站立。微繪圖版以紅色與藍色為底，其上塗繪淡藍色，再經泥金裝飾場景之背景，圖中的基督光環為金色，聖母光環為藍色。此佔行大寫首字母也有精心設計的延伸部分，包括葉狀裝飾圖樣，右頁邊的鳥，以及下頁邊的猴與站立的女子形象。

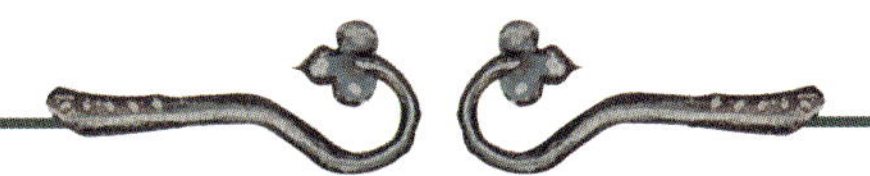

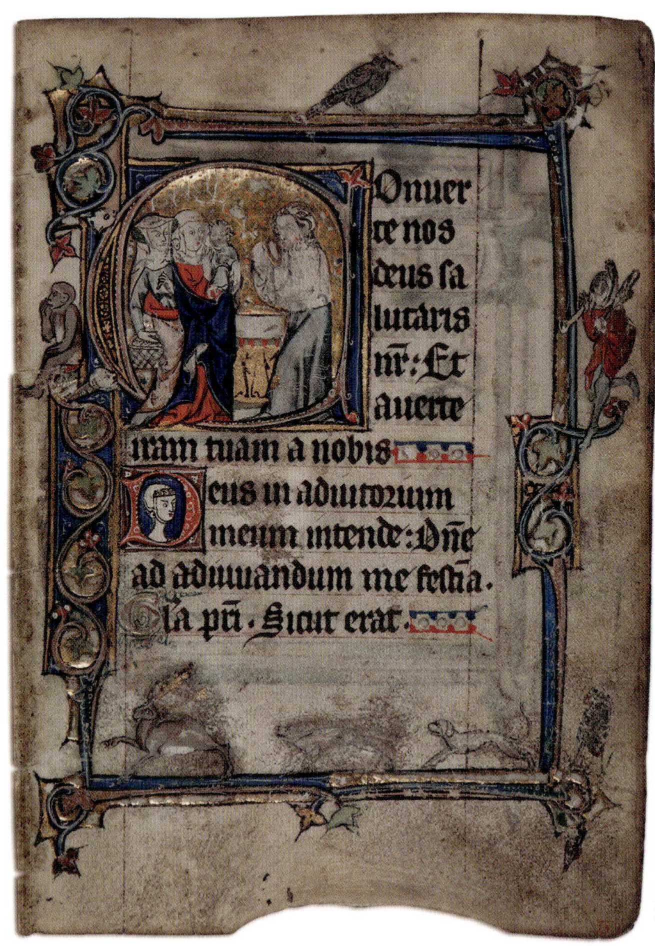
Onuer
te nos
deus sa
lutaris
nr̄: Et
auerte
iram tuam a nobis
Deus in adiutorium
meum intende: Dn̄e
ad adiuuandum me festia.
Gl'a pr̄i. Sicut erat.

9a (actual size 原大)

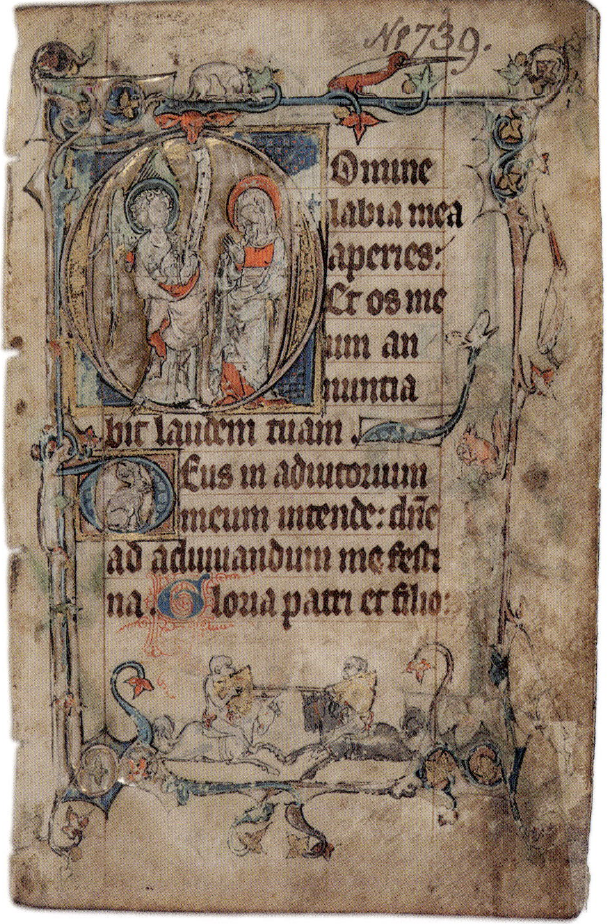
N° 739.
Omine
labia mea
aperies:
Et os me
um an
nuntia
bit laudem tuam
Eus in adiutorium
meum intende: dn̄e
ad adiuuandum me fest
na. Gloria patri et filio:

9b (actual size 原大)

The Calendar of the Ghistelles Hours
希斯特爾斯時禱書禮儀年曆

Cat. 9a–c

The Calendar of the Ghistelles Hours is an illuminated manuscript on vellum that consists of 14 leaves (final blank), which was possibly made for John III of Ghistelles (d.1315), Lord of Ghistelles and Ingelmuster, whose coat of arms appear on other pages of the book. The incomplete set of pages is lacking a first leaf with the beginning of January (the present first page is the second half of January, rubbed and stained to such an extent that the book must have been imperfect for many centuries, and without a binding). It also contains the entire Calendar, together with a full-page table for identifying Easter in each year from 1300 to 1316, along with a list of the days of fairs in Bruges, St. Trond, Lille and "Mesine" (perhaps Mesen, between Lille and Ypres). It is written in Latin and French in dark brown, red and blue ink in a small gothic liturgical hand. Each month begins on a verso with a large illuminated initial and three-quarter illuminated branching ivy leaf border. Included along the upper margins: a hound chasing a hare, a hare chasing a stag, several birds, grotesques, a unicorn, a hare confronting a bird and a boy with a trumpet and monkey. In the lower margins are eleven miniatures of the occupations of the months—the Easter table begins with a historiated initial of a man's head—fol.13v blank, fol.14, a flyleaf which doubtless faced the opening of Matins, worn and rubbed, corners creased and thumbed, fragile, and loosely stitched with two paper flyleaves still attached.

《希斯特爾斯時禱書禮儀年曆》是一本使用犢皮紙的泥金裝飾手抄本，共十四頁(最後為空白頁)，這可能是為希斯特爾斯與英厄爾蒙斯特之王——希斯特爾斯的約翰三世(一三一五年)而製，因為他的盾徽出現於書的其他書頁中。現存全套書頁缺少以一月份為起始的首頁(現首頁為一月份後半期，被摩擦與染色到了一個嚴重的程度，可見原首頁早已散佚許多世紀，而且長期無裝訂)。也包括了全部禮儀年曆，以及一個全版面的表格，上面標示著從一三零零年至一三一六年每年的復活節日期，連同一個羅列著於布魯日、聖特雷登、里爾與「Mesine」(可能是梅森，位於里爾與伊珀爾之間)舉辦市集的日子。文字為深褐色的拉丁文與法文，紅色與藍色墨水的小型哥德禮拜儀式手寫體。每個月份開始於背頁的大型裝飾首字母，以及三邊常春藤纏枝式樣的邊框。上頁邊還有：一條追逐野兔的獵犬，一隻追逐鹿的野兔，幾隻鳥，一些滴水簷怪獸，一隻獨角獸，一隻與鳥面對面的野兔，一位吹號的男孩，以及許多猴子。下頁邊有十一幅關於對應月份之「日常活動」的微繪——復活節表格以變形為人首形狀的大寫首字母開始—— fol.13v blank，fol.14，一張無疑放置在晨禱文對面的飛頁，蟲蛀和磨損嚴重，被大拇指反復按壓過的頁腳也已捲邊，脆弱的它鬆散地同另外兩張至今附著其上的飛頁裝訂在一起。

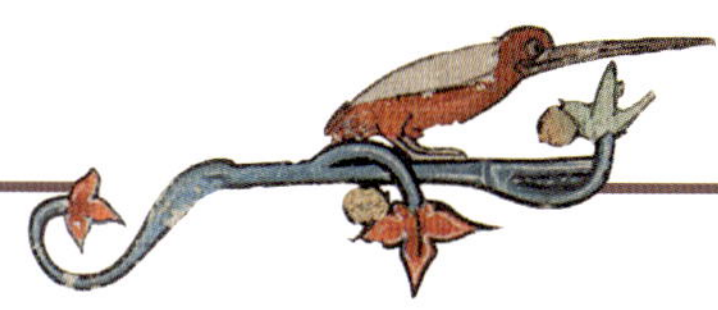

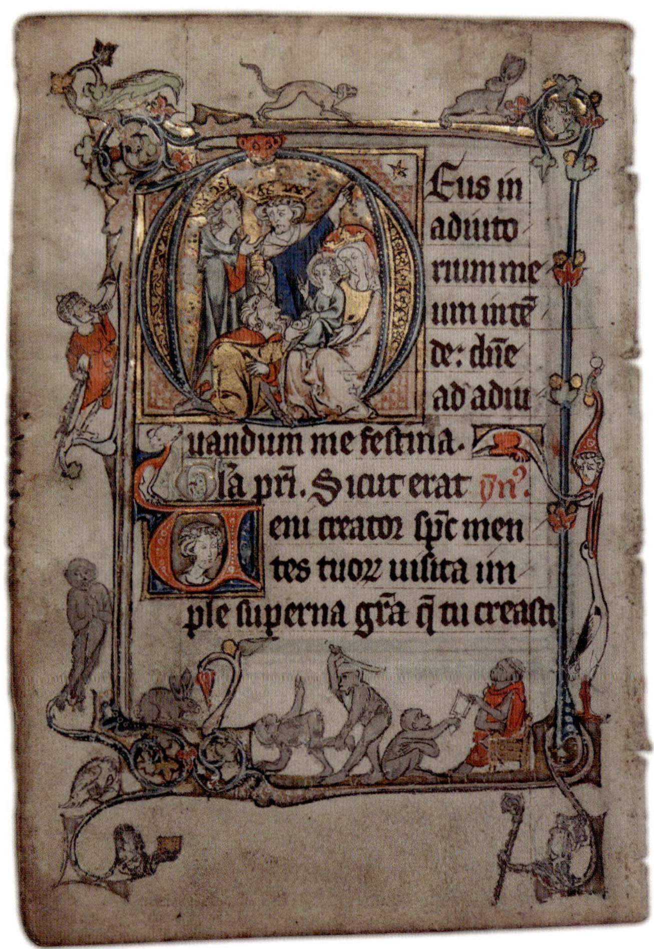

9c (actual size 原大)

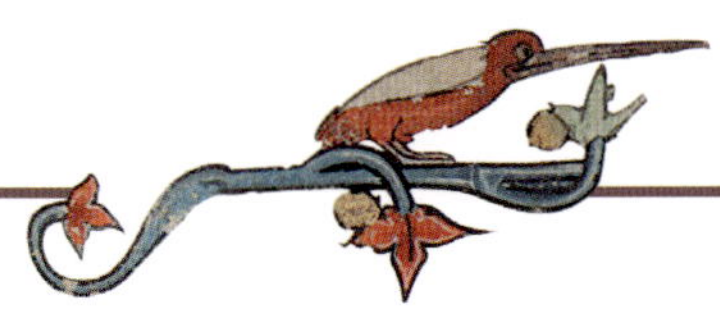

The opulent Calendar has a wonderful series of secular occupations of the months: 1) February: a girl with a tall candle (Candlemas is on 2 February); 2) March: a hooded peasant chopping down a tree; 3) April: a man holding two vertical rods, and two apes—one seated in a basket showing the blisters on his foot to the other (perhaps aping humans who take their first unaccustomed Spring walk in April); 4) May: a nobleman riding his horse with a hawk on his arm and a hound behind; 5) June: a peasant carrying a full sack on his back, watched by a hare (presumably a miller with a sack of flour); 6) July: a peasant mowing with a scythe, as a unicorn bounds away; 7) August: a peasant cutting tall corn with a sickle and a scatological ape defecating into a bowl; 8) September: two boys playing a game with a ball and club, supervised by their master; 9) October: a peasant reaching into a bush to pick bunches of grapes which he puts in a basket; 10) November: a swineherd knocking acorns out of a tree to feed his two pigs; and 11) December: a butcher astride a pig as he slits its throat for Christmas.

Literature: Manion–Fines–De Hamel 1989, pp. 91–92; Randal 1966, figs. 126 and 588.

這奢華的禮儀年曆中有一個精彩描繪的對應每個月份的日常活動系列：1）二月：一個女孩與一個高高的蠟燭（聖燭節為二月二日）；2）三月：一位正在砍樹的戴有頭巾的農夫；3）四月：一個手拿垂直竿的男人，以及兩隻猿，其一正坐於籃中向另一隻展示磨出水泡的腳（可能在模仿人類四月進行的踏青）；4）五月：一位騎馬的貴族，臂上站著一隻鷹，後隨一隻獵犬；5）六月：一位身背滿裝貨物的麻布袋的農夫，旁邊一隻野兔正在凝視著他（農夫大概是背著滿滿一袋麵粉的磨坊工）；6）七月：一位農民正用釤刀割草，一隻獨角獸跳走；7）八月：一位農民正用鐮刀收割穀物，一隻滿身污穢的猿正向碗中排便；8）九月：兩個男孩在他們老師的監督下用球與棍玩遊戲；9）十月：一位農夫正伸手進灌木叢中摘取成串的葡萄並放於籃中；10）十一月：一位豬倌正在從樹上搖下橡子，用來餵食他的兩頭豬；11）十二月：一位屠戶為了聖誕節正跨在一頭豬上將之割喉。

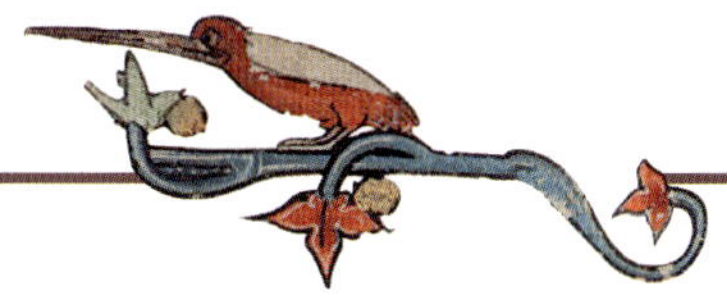

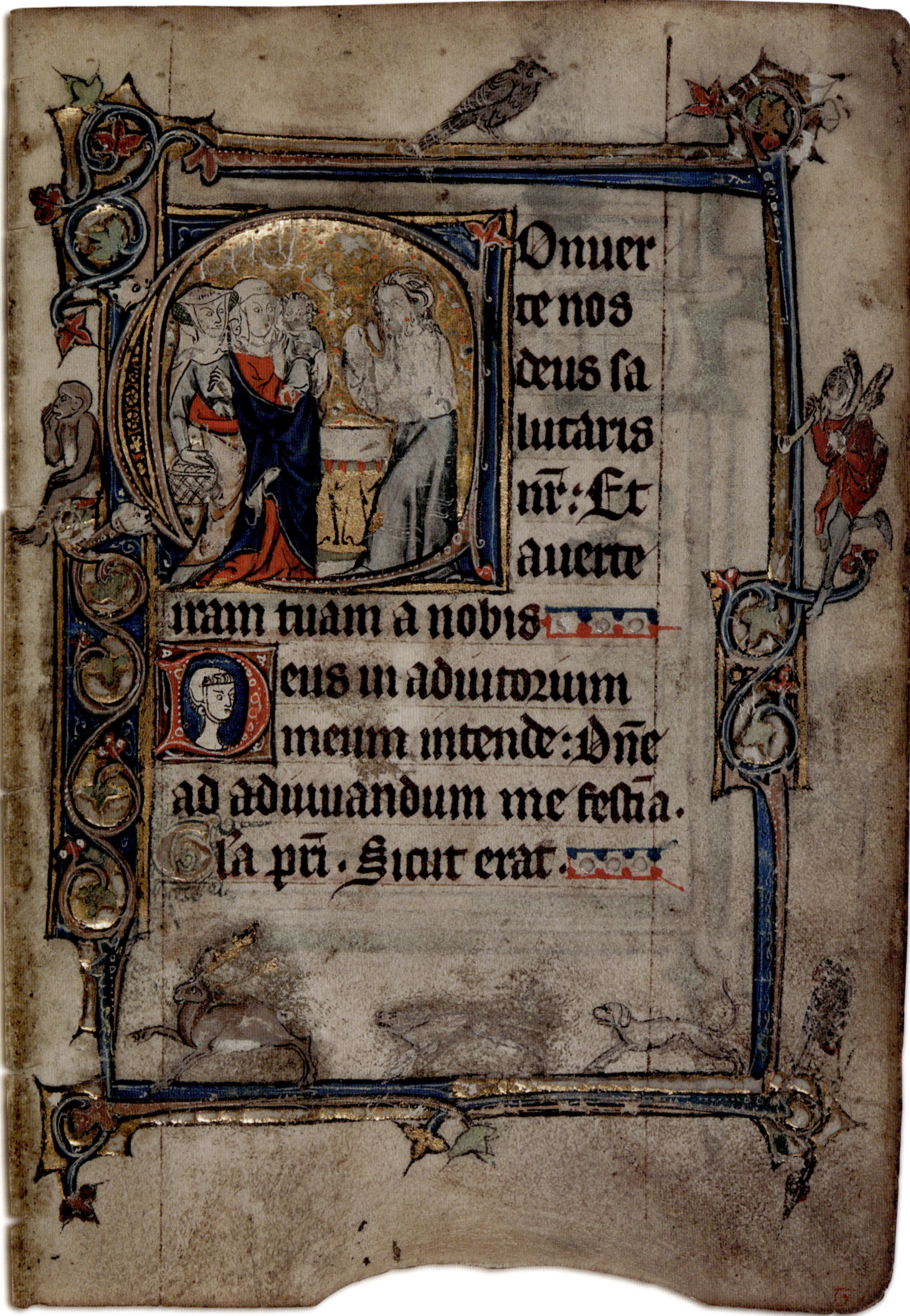
Conuer
te nos
deus sa
lutaris
nr̄: Et
auerte
iram tuam a nobis
Deus in adiutorium
meum intende: Dn̄e
ad adiuuandum me festīa.
Gl'a pr̄i. Sicut erat.

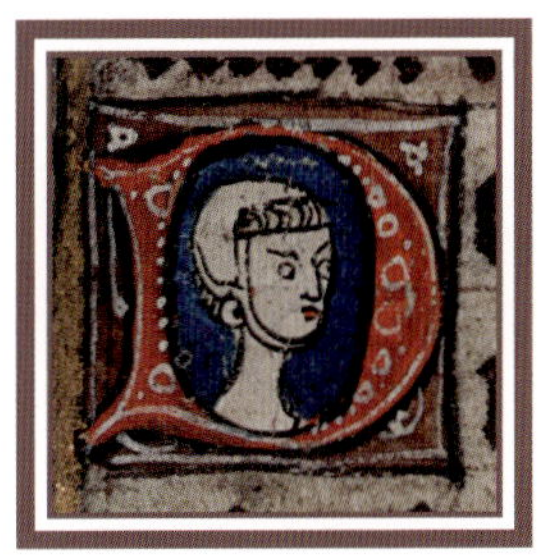

Cat. 9a | Reference 參考編號: BM 1162; SF 51

Psalter Leaf from the Ghistelles Hours Depicting *The Presentation in the Temple* and a Historiated Initial "C"
《希斯特爾斯時禱書》中的聖詩頁，描繪「獻主於聖殿」，佔行大寫首字母「C」經中世紀傳統出版風格修飾與變形

Anonymous
Possibly St-Omer, possibly Bruges, Flanders, c.1300
Tempera, gold and ink on vellum
H. 121 mm W. 85 mm

匿名
疑似製作於聖奧梅爾或布魯日，法蘭德斯
約一三零零年
蛋彩、泥金與墨水，犢皮紙
高121公釐，寬85公釐

This leaf displays *The Presentation in the Temple* on a gilded background inside the circular space of the initial "C". The initial extends to form a border around the text in blue and gilded lines, with ivy leaf decorations, a monkey, two dogs chasing a deer, a monk, a flute player and a bird. It is written in Latin in single columns with 11 lines in black ink.

Sister leaf of BM 1441.

書頁內的「獻主於聖殿」場景框於大寫首字母「C」的圓形空間之內，以泥金料底為背景，字母延伸至文字周圍的藍色與金絲邊框，並配有常春藤葉飾、一隻猴子、正在獵鹿的兩條狗、一位僧人、一位吹笛者、一隻鳥等裝飾。文字為黑色墨水的拉丁文，共單列十一行。

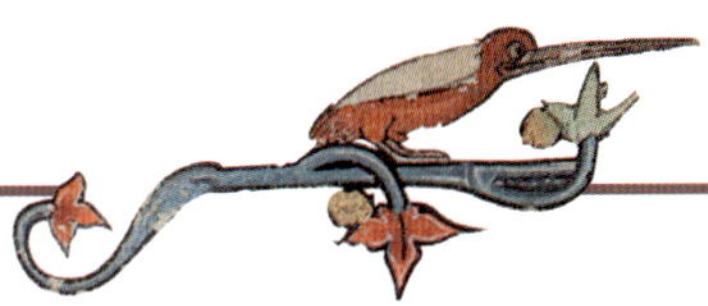

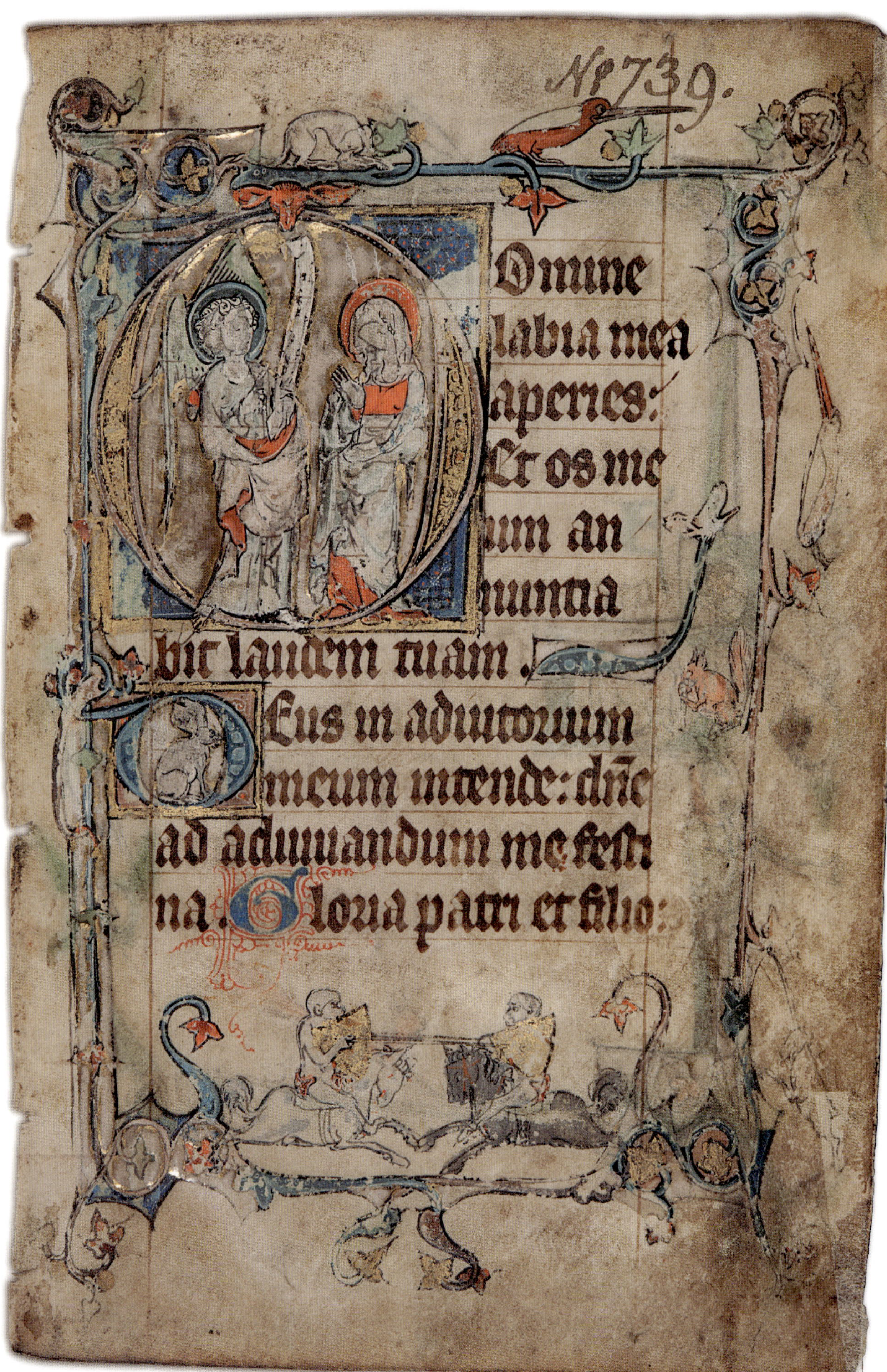
No 739.
Domine
labia mea
aperies:
Et os me
um an
nuntia
bit laudem tuam.
Deus in adiutorium
meum intende: dñe
ad adiuuandum me festi
na. Gloria patri et filio:

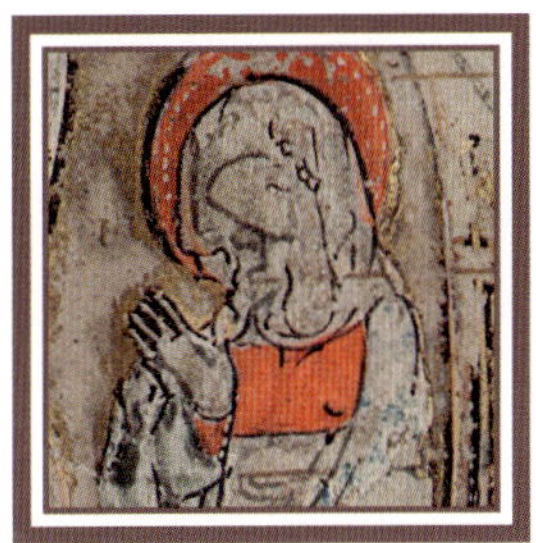

Cat. 9b | Reference 參考編號: BM 1441

Psalter Leaf from the Ghistelles Hours Depicting *The Annunciation* and a Historiated Initial "D"
《希斯特爾斯時禱書》中的聖詩頁，描繪「聖母領報」，佔行大寫首字母「D」經中世紀傳統出版風格修飾與變形

Anonymous
Possibly St-Omer, possibly Bruges, Flanders , c.1300
Tempera, gold and ink on vellum
H. 120 mm W. 79 mm

匿名
疑似製作於聖奧梅爾或布魯日，法蘭德斯，
約一三零零年
蛋彩、泥金與墨水，犢皮紙
高120公釐，寬79公釐

This leaf depicts *The Annunciation* inside the initial "D". It was the opening page of the Office of the Virgin, an important leaf from the Ghistelles Hours. Both recto and verso contain 11 lines written in brown ink in a gothic bookhand between two verticals and 12 horizontals ruled in brown. The rubric is in red with a line-ending in blue and an animal-head terminal; 3 one-line initials, two in blue with red flourishing, one in burnished gold with blue penwork decoration; 2 two-line initials, one on the recto with a blue stave on a dark pink ground with gold border, the infill inhabited by a hare, the other on the verso in pink on a patterned blue ground. The infill includes a female head with a large historiated initial with a dark pink and gold stave on a diaper-patterned blue ground. Orange dots are placed along branching full-page borders of pink, blue and burnished gold with vine-leaf finials that incorporate birds and animals, and that support two jousting monkeys on horseback. The verso incorporates a similar three-quarter branching border with an orange fox and horn-playing figure.

書頁內的「聖母領報」場景框於大寫首字母「D」中，是《聖母日課經》的開始頁，也是《希斯特爾斯時禱書》中的重要書頁。正頁與背頁皆包括十一行褐色墨水寫就的哥德體文字，位於褐色的兩條垂直線與十二條水平線分隔的區域之間。首題字為紅色，行尾結束符號為藍色獸首圖案；三個佔一行大寫首字母，其中的兩個為藍色與燦爛的紅色，另一個為拋光金色配以藍色筆繪裝飾。兩個佔兩行大寫首字母，正頁的一個為粉色底之上的藍色線譜，金色邊框，其中以野兔形象修飾；另一個位於背頁，為粉色，花飾藍底。填充物包括一個女性頭像，框於一個深粉色的大寫首字母中，為菱形花飾藍底之上的金色線譜。橙色點被置於全頁粉色、藍色與亮金色纏枝邊框內，邊框的葡萄藤葉終枝式樣的裝飾與鳥獸裝飾融合在一起，並且也為兩隻馬背上正在比賽的猴子提供支撐。背頁包含了一個類似的三邊纏枝邊框，飾以一隻橙色的狐狸與玩號角的形象。

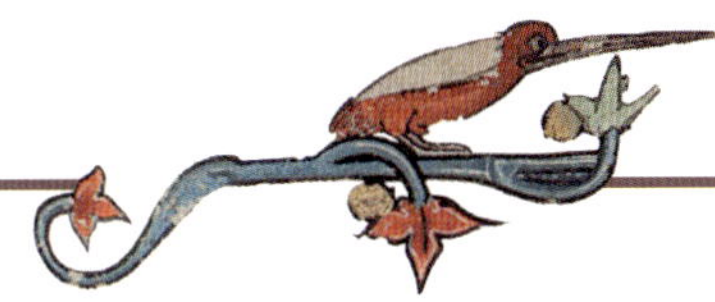

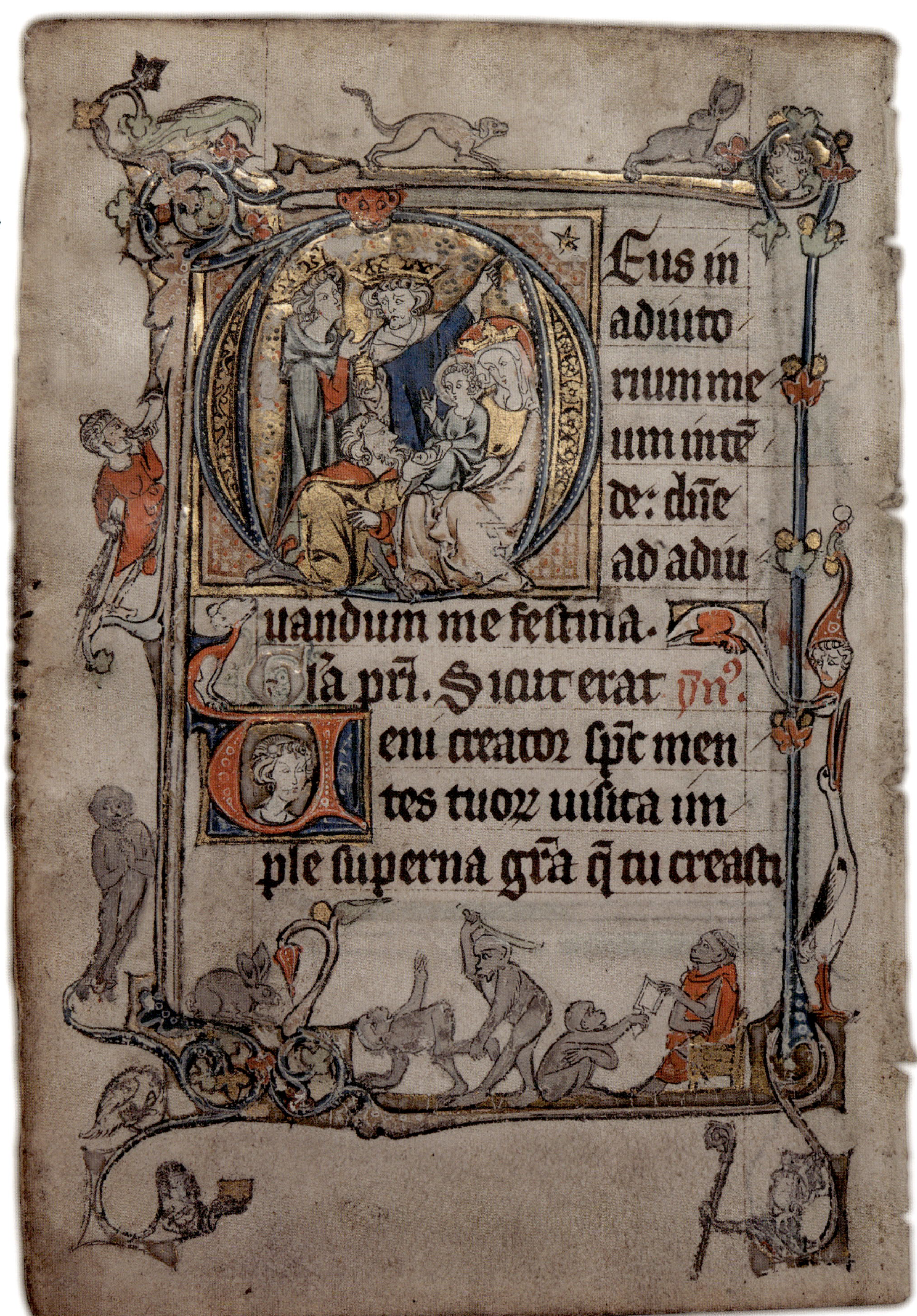

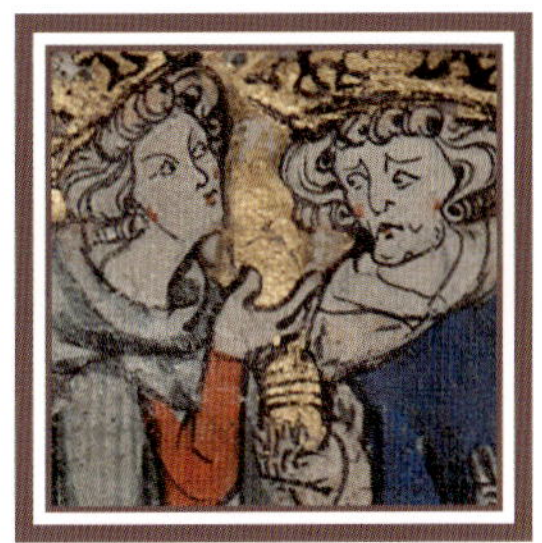

Cat. 9c | Reference 參考編號: BM 2392a; SF 16034

Psalter Leaf from the Ghistelles Hours Depicting *The Adoration of the Magi* and a Historiated Initial "D", as well as *Baboons at School*

《希斯特爾斯時禱書》中的聖詩頁，描繪「博士來朝」，佔行大寫首字母「D」經中世紀傳統出版風格修飾與變形，並飾以「求學的狒狒」場景

Anonymous
Possibly St-Omer, possibly Bruges, Flanders, c.1300
Tempera, gold and ink on vellum
H. 120 mm W. 90 mm

匿名
疑似製作於聖奧梅爾或布魯日，法蘭德斯
約一三零零年
蛋彩、泥金與墨水，犢皮紙
高120公釐，寬90公釐

The *Baboons at School* and *Baboon Hunting* scenes from the Ghistelles Hours are illuminated manuscripts on two single leaves, each 120 mm x 90 mm, with 11 lines of text and illuminated initials and borders that form the end of Terce and opening of Sext in the Hours of the Virgin. The verso of this leaf contains a 6-line historiated initial "D" illustrating *The Adoration of the Magi* (40 mm x 40 mm). In the scene the Child is seated on the Virgin's lap blessing them, one King is kneeling, and the others are looking up at the star of Bethlehem. The full border includes two birds in the foliage and the half-length figures of a woman with a book and a bishop with a crozier. Also depicted in the border are a hunter blowing a horn, a hound chasing a hare—looking around anxiously—another hare hiding, a long-necked bird pecking at a grotesque, and a school of baboons—one dressed in red and seated in the master's chair teaching a small baboon from a horn book. Another baboon is spanking a naughty pupil, which is watched approvingly by a baboon standing in prayer. This leaf has a counterpart that forms the end of the Terce and opening of Sext in the Hours of the Cross. Its border shows a baboon riding a galloping horse and blowing a golden horn as two hounds chase a stag with golden antlers.

《希斯特爾斯時禱書》中的「求學的狒狒」與「狩獵的狒狒」場景被描繪於兩張單獨的書頁中，每張為120公釐 x 90公釐，內有十一行文字，以及經過修飾的大寫首字母與邊框，構成了《聖母時禱書》中第三時的結束與第六時的開始。背頁包括框於佔六行大寫首字母「D」內的「博士來朝」場景（40公釐 x 40公釐），其中聖嬰正坐於聖母腿上祝福博士們，一位博士在跪拜，另兩位則抬頭望向伯利恆之星。全部邊框包括有兩隻葉中的鳥，拿書女性的半身像，持杖的主教，一位吹號角的獵人，一條追逐一隻焦急四望的野兔的獵犬，一隻躲藏的兔子，正在啄一個滴水簷怪獸的長頸鳥，以及一群狒狒。狒狒之一穿紅衣並坐於主人椅上，正在用角帖書教育一隻小狒狒；另有一隻狒狒在打一個頑皮的學生，一旁站著祈禱的狒狒看到此景並深感讚許。在《十字架時禱書》中有一個極類似的書頁構成了第三時的結束與第六時的開始，其邊框展示了一隻騎在烈馬上吹響金色的號角的狒狒，兩隻獵犬追逐金角鹿。

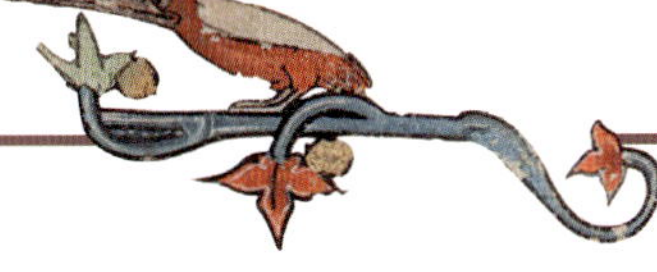

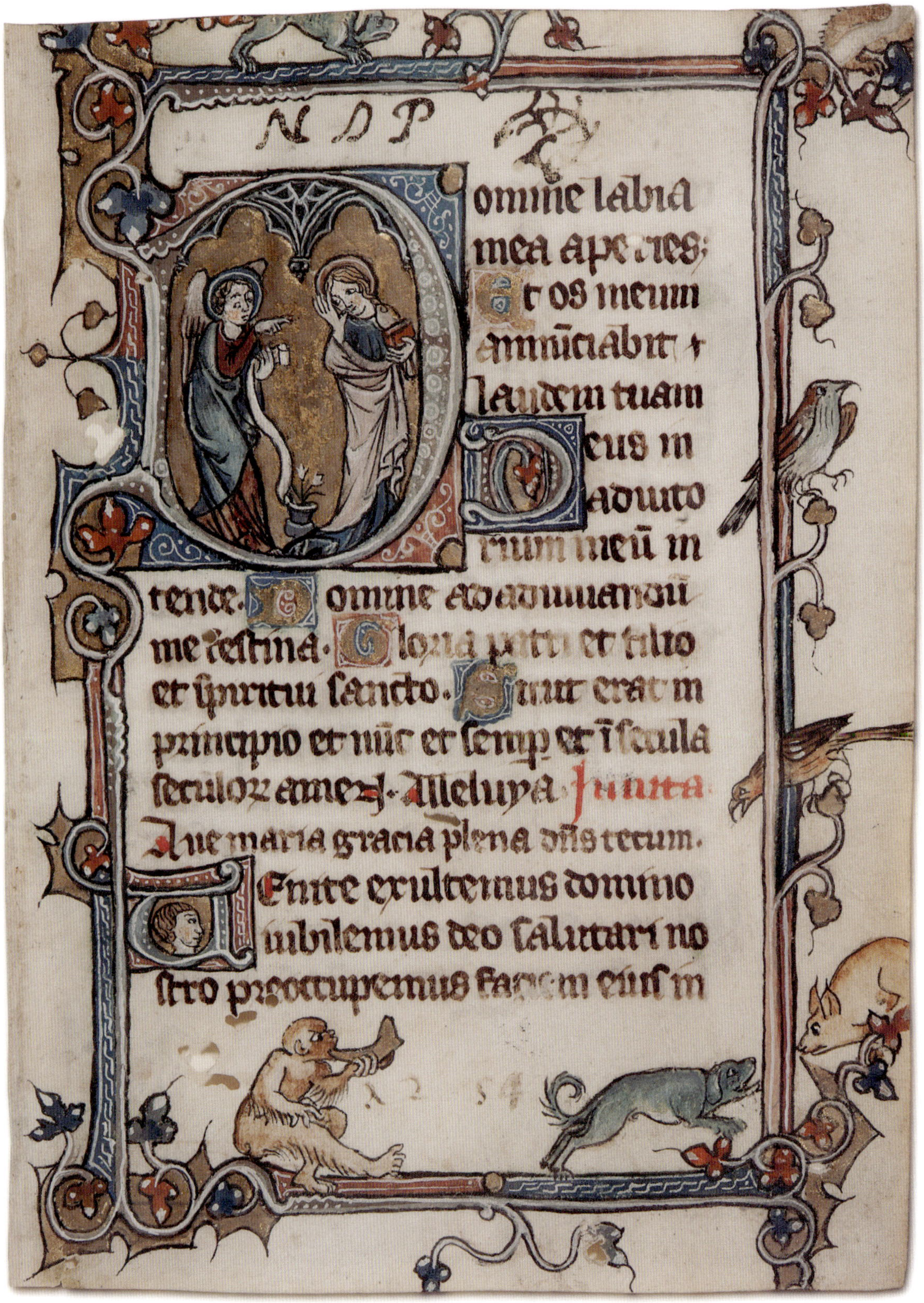

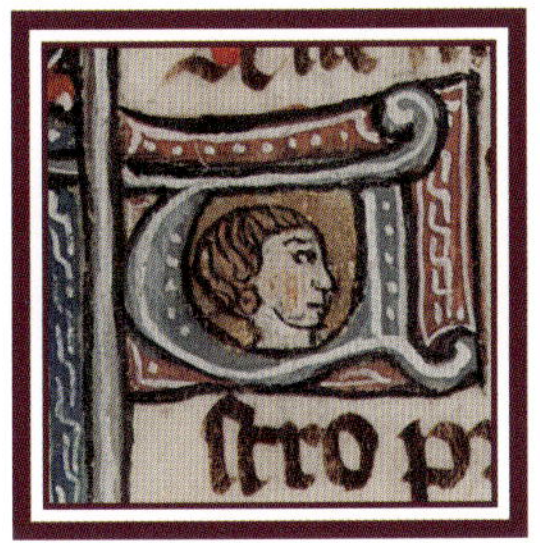

Cat. 10 | Reference 參考編號: BM 1109/BM 91 (formerly 原W47)

Psalter Leaf Depicting *The Annunciation* and a Historiated Initial "D"
《聖詠時禱書》書頁，描繪「聖母領報」，佔行大寫首字母「D」經中世紀傳統出版風格修飾與變形

Anonymous
Northern France, c.1300
Tempera, gold and ink on vellum
H. 128 mm W. 95 mm
Inscription and Marking: Inscribed in ink at the upper margin "N.D.P." with a stamp in the lower margin "1254"

This psalter leaf depicts *The Annunciation*. Two figures, including the Angel Gabriel on the left and the Vigin Mary on the right, occupy the entire space of the letter "D". The style of this scene is often repeated, while the execution varies. Both women stand before a matte gold background—a stylistic characteristic commonly found in the Gothic era—rather than in a more pictorial architectural surrounding or a landscape as in later depictions. Despite the more stylized composition, the figures are depicted in natural poses and in communication with one another.

匿名
製作於法國北部，約一三零零年
蛋彩、泥金與墨水，犢皮紙
高128公釐，寬95公釐
題字與標記：上緣以墨水題寫「N.D.P.」，下緣印有「1254」

書頁內「聖母領報」場景中共有兩個人物，一齊佔據了字母「D」中的全部空間，其中左側為天使加百列，而右側為聖母。該圖的藝術風格是重複的，但風格展現的手法卻各有不同。兩位女人的背景是哥德時期典型的純啞光黃金背景，而非後期流行的圖畫式建築物或風景背景之中。雖然構圖越發風格化，人物造型卻依然寫實，且人物與人物之間仍互有交流。

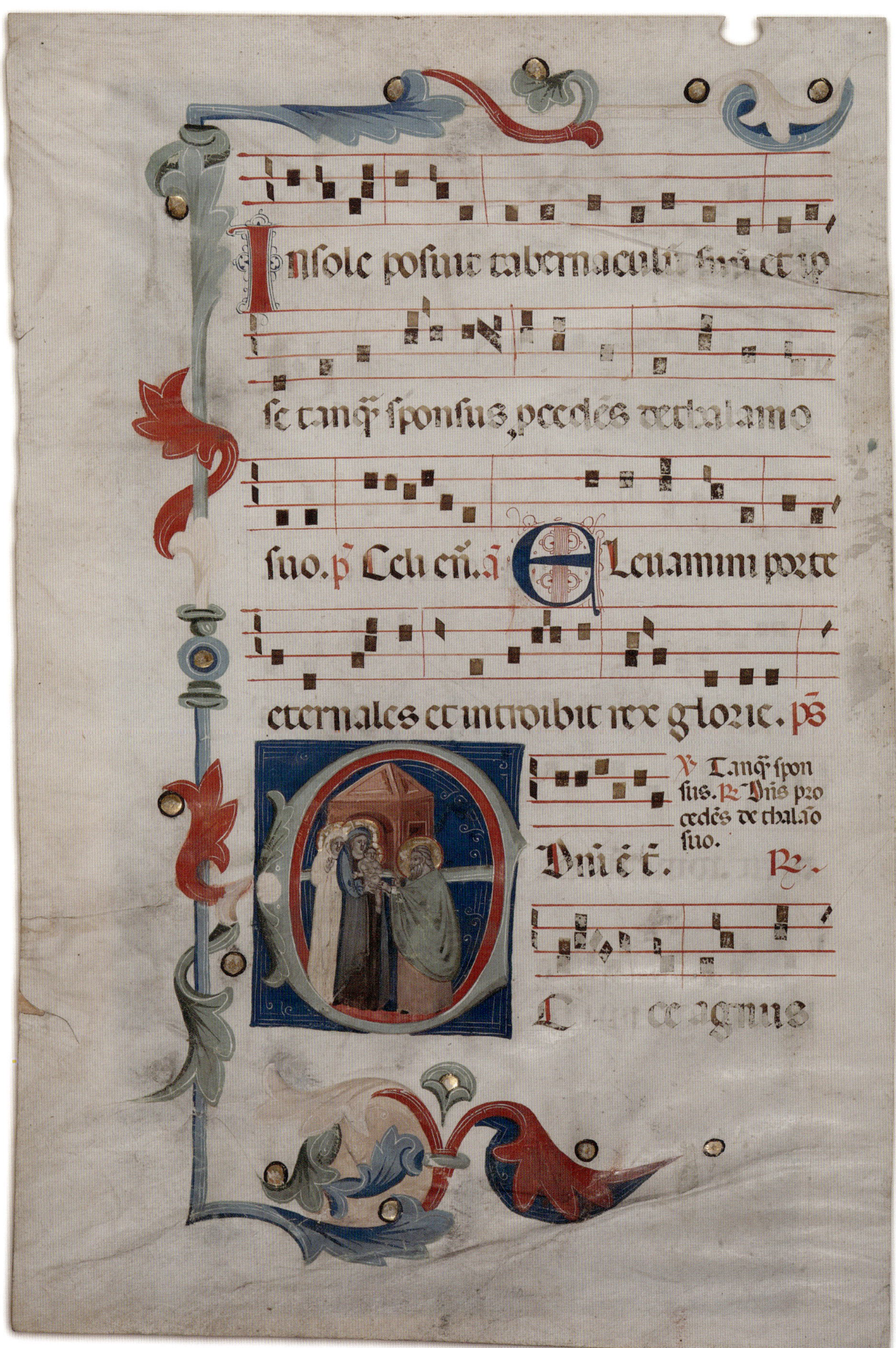
In sole posuit tabernaculū suū et ip
se tanq̄ sponsus, pcedēs de thalamo
suo. ps Celi eñ. a Eleuamini porte
eternales et introibit rex glorie. ps
ecce agnus

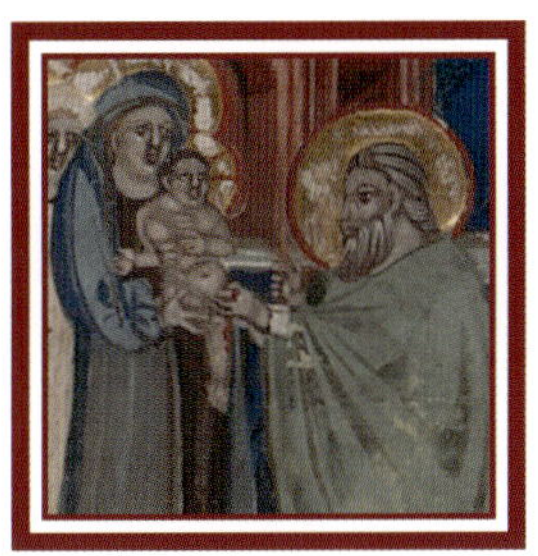

Cat. 11

Leaf from an Antiphonary Depicting *The Presentation in the Temple* and a Historiated Initial "E"
《啟應輪唱詩歌集》書頁，描繪「獻主於聖殿」，佔行大寫首字母「E」經中世紀傳統出版風格修飾與變形

Second Master of San Domenico
(Master of B18, active 1320–1340)
Bologna, Italy, c.1320
Tempera, gold and ink on vellum
H. 520 mm W. 375 mm

This leaf has been identified as originally having been part of a series of now dispersed antiphonaries made for a Bolognese Dominican convent, of which a number of leaves have been preserved in important European and American collections, including the Free Library in Philadelphia. This leaf illustrates *The Presentation in the Temple* set within a historiated initial "E" and surrounded by an elegant scrolled border of acanthus leaves in blue and red. The present leaf was decorated at the time of the better-known Master of Seneca (First master of San Domenico), by the so-called Second Master of San Domenico, who was active as an illuminator in Bologna in about 1320 to 1340. Thought to be first pupil than collaborator of Seneca, his execution of this illumination shows the influences of Byzantine art as well as of the monumental forms of his contemporary Giotto (Giotto di Bondone, 1266/1267–1337).

Literature: Freuler 2004, pp. 1–10; Freuler 2013, pp. 254–271; Zeileis 2004, pp. 28–83; Gibbs 1994.

聖道明第二院長
（活躍於一三二零年至一三四零年）
製作於博洛尼亞，意大利，約一三二零年
蛋彩、泥金與墨水，犢皮紙
高520公釐，寬375公釐

此書頁已被推定出自一套為博洛尼亞的道明會女修道院製作的《啟應輪唱詩歌集》系列，此書現已分散，其中不少書頁被保存於重要的歐洲與美國收藏中，包括費城自由圖書館。此書頁微繪為「獻主於聖殿」場景，其中的佔行大寫首字母「E」經中世紀傳統出版風格修飾與變形，精美的彎曲邊框以藍色與紅色的葉形裝飾。此書頁裝飾於以「塞內卡院長」（聖道明第一院長）的稱號而被人所知的時代，製作者為所謂的聖道明第二院長，他作為插畫家活躍於一三二零年至一三四零年間的博洛尼亞。聖道明第二院長被認為是塞內卡的第一代學徒，而非是塞內卡的合作者，製作插畫的手法深受拜占庭藝術，以及同時代的喬托（喬托．迪．邦多納，一二六六／一二六七年至一三三七年）劃時代的造型藝術風格的影響。

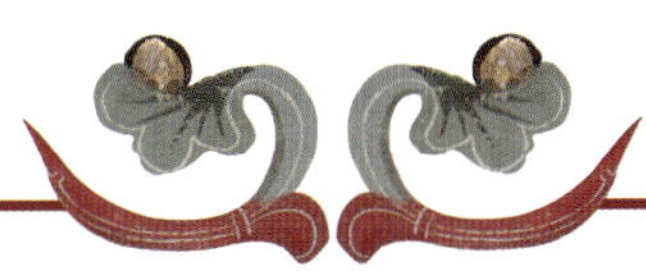

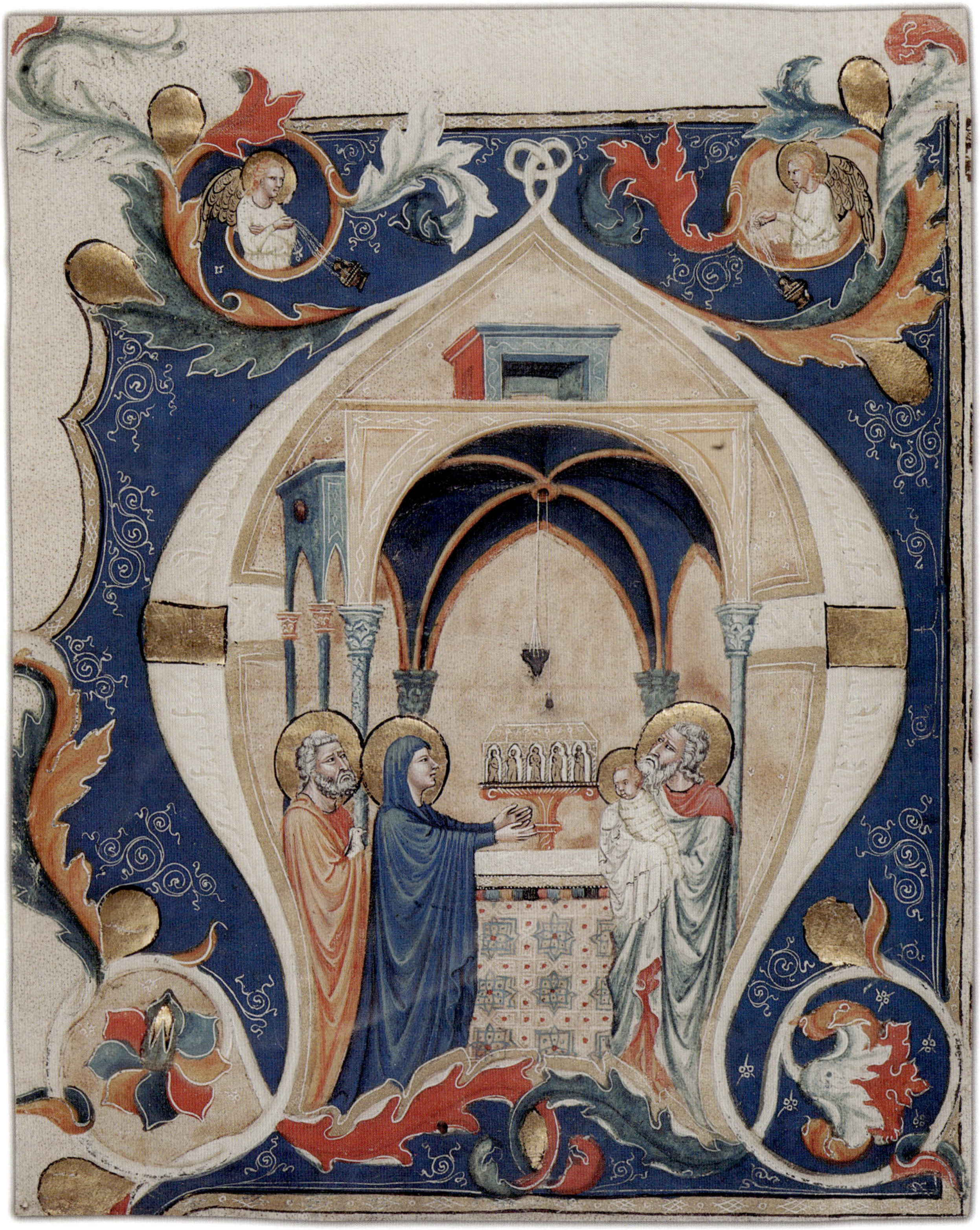

(actual size 原大)

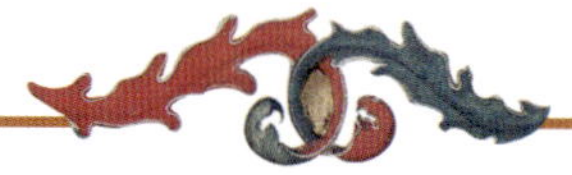

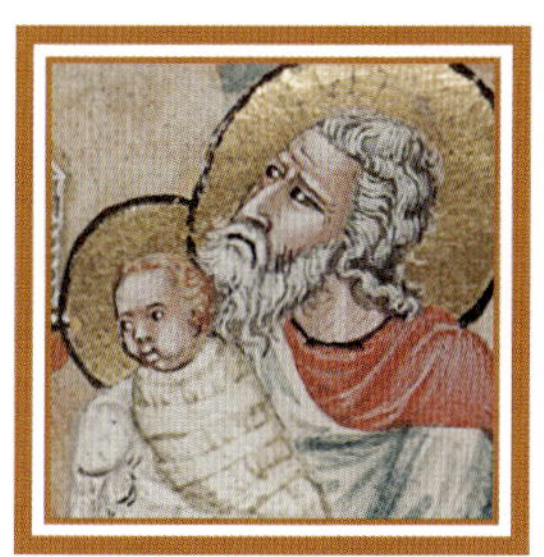

Cat. 12 | Reference 參考編號: BM 1426; SF 9518

Leaf from an Antiphonary Depicting *The Presentation in the Temple* and a Historiated Initial "A"
《啟應輪唱詩歌集》書頁，描繪「獻主於聖殿」，估行大寫首字母「A」經中世紀傳統出版風格修飾與變形

Workshop of Marino da Perugia
Perugia, Italy, c.1320–1330
Tempera and gold on vellum
H. 204 mm W. 167 mm

馬里諾 · 達 · 佩魯賈工作坊
製作於佩魯賈，意大利
約一三二零年至一三三零年
蛋彩與泥金，犢皮紙
高 204 公釐，寬 167 公釐

This leaf depicts *The Presentation in the Temple* showing Zacharias holding the Christ Child on the right, while the Virgin Mary and Joseph are standing on the left. Joseph is holding a dove. They are all placed beneath a baldachin structure, below which is an altar with what appears to be a reliquary casket with carved saints. The scene is framed by a blue background and surrounded by foliate decorative motifs with four roundels (one at each corner). The top roundels contain two angels holding censers and the bottom roundels contain flowers.

此幅「獻主於聖殿」場景中，描繪撒迦利亞在右側托抱聖嬰，而聖母與若瑟站於左側，其中若瑟還手握一隻白鴿。他們皆身處華蓋結構之下，華蓋上還附有一個聖壇，好似雕刻有聖人像的聖物箱奩。場景為藍色背景，並被葉狀裝飾圖樣及四個圓形圖版（四角各一）包圍，其中上部的兩個圖版均為持有香爐的天使，底部的兩個圖版則均是花朵。

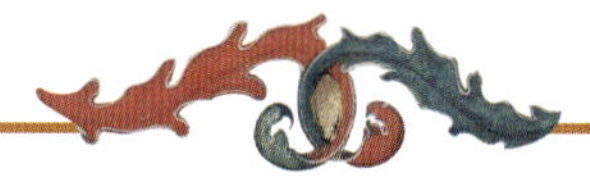

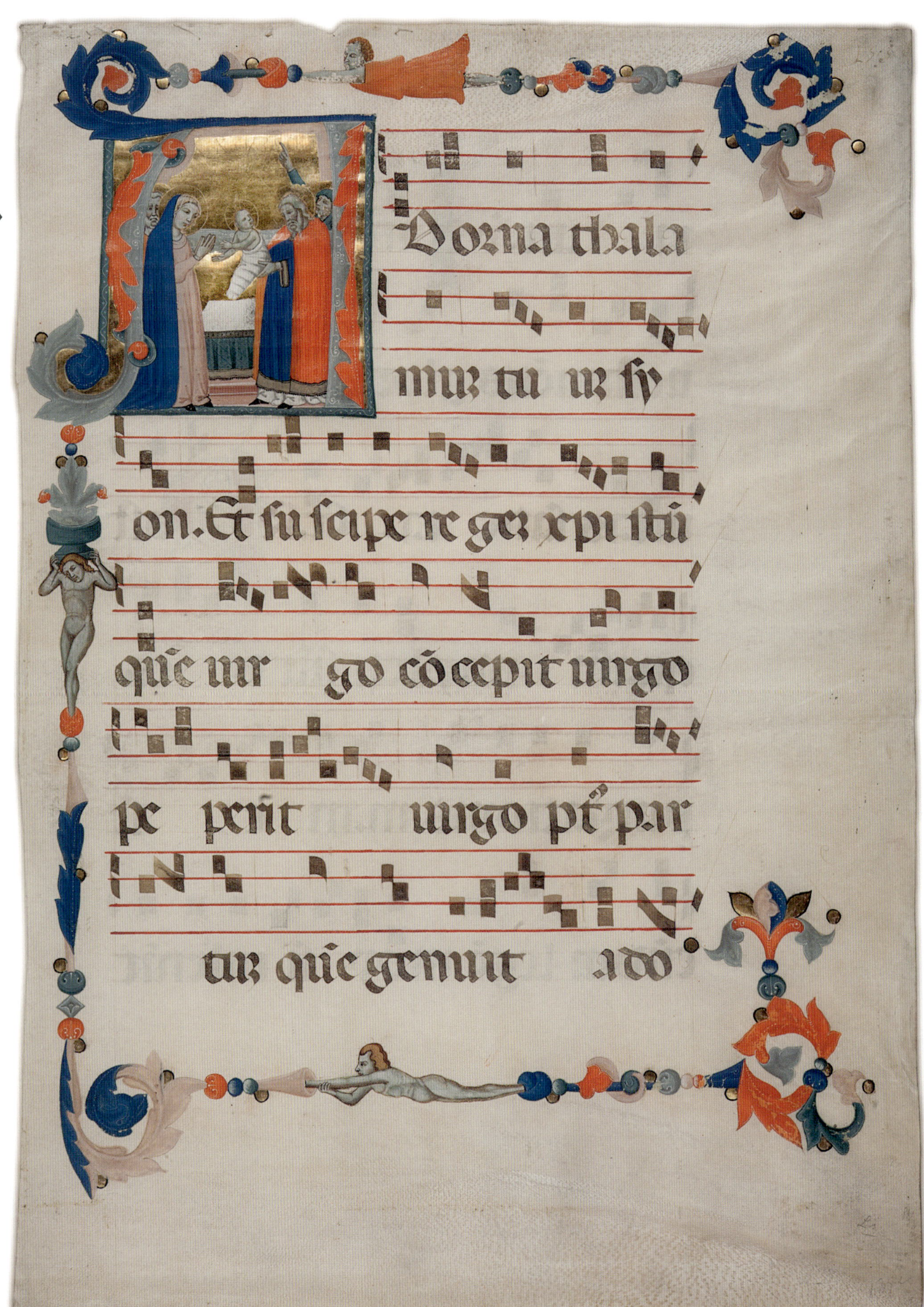
Dorna thala
mum tu um sy
on. Et su scipe re gem xpi stum
quem vir go cõ cepit virgo
pe perit virgo post par
tum quem genuit ado

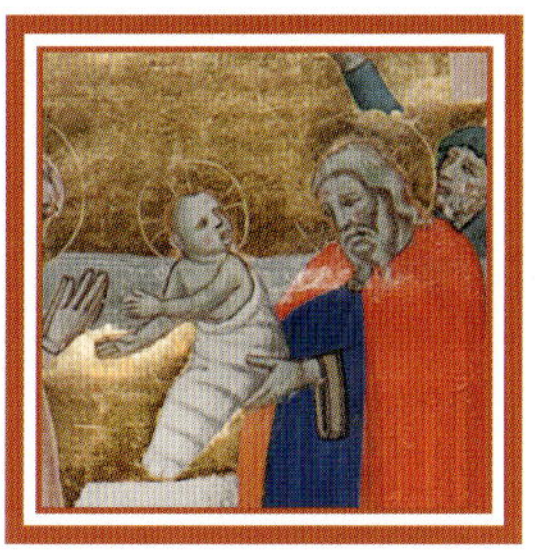

Cat. 13 | Reference 參考編號: BM 1011; SF 2859

Leaf from an Antiphonary Depicting *The Presentation in the Temple* and a Historiated Initial "A"

《啟應輪唱詩歌集》書頁，描繪「獻主於聖殿」，佔行大寫首字母「A」經中世紀傳統出版風格修飾與變形

Anonymous
Circle of Pacino da Bonaguida
Florence or Pisa, Italy, c.1320–1340
Tempera, gold and ink on vellum
H. 564 mm W. 406 mm

匿名
深受帕仙奴．達．邦納奎達風格影響的群體
製作於佛羅倫斯或比薩，意大利
約一三二零年至一三四零年
蛋彩、泥金與墨水，犢皮紙
高564公釐，寬406公釐

This leaf illustrates *The Presentation in the Temple* in which Simeon is holding the Christ Child over a draped altar as the Virgin stands in prayer and a young man points to the sky. The depiction itself is close to the style of Pacino da Bonaguida (active about 1303–1347), a leading panel painter and miniaturist of Florence in the period of Giotto (cf. Kanter 1994, pp. 44–55). It is finely painted in colour and shows highly burnished gold ground within a large initial "A" (134 mm x 120 mm). The extraordinary three-quarter illuminated border is more typical of Pisa than Florence, and can be compared to the choir books of the Ospedale degli Innocenti. The border consists of elaborate interconnected lush flowers and leaves, including two naked men and a curly-headed child in a red smock; 6 lines of text in a large rounded gothic hand; music on a 4-line red stave. The verso includes large red and blue initials with contrasting penwork.

此書頁內的「獻主於聖殿」場景中，右側的西緬將聖嬰抱於用布遮蓋的聖壇之上，聖母正在祈禱，另有一位年輕人手指天空。插畫本身接近帕仙奴．達．邦納奎達（活躍於約一三零三年至一三四七年）的風格，他乃是喬托時代佛羅倫斯首屈一指的板繪畫家與微繪畫家（cf. Kanter 1994, pp. 44–55）。微繪被框於大寫首字母「A」之中（134公釐 x 120公釐），有高度拋光的泥金料底，並細膩上色。精緻的三邊修飾框更靠近典型的比薩式，而非佛羅倫斯式，這可與佛羅倫斯孤兒院中的《聖詩集》相對比；圖中的邊框修飾包括延展的繁茂纏枝花葉紋飾，兩個裸體男性以及一個身著紅色罩衫的捲髮孩童。六行文字為飽滿的哥德體，樂符標記於紅色四線譜上。背頁包括許多紅色與藍色的大寫首字母，為對比強烈的筆繪裝飾。

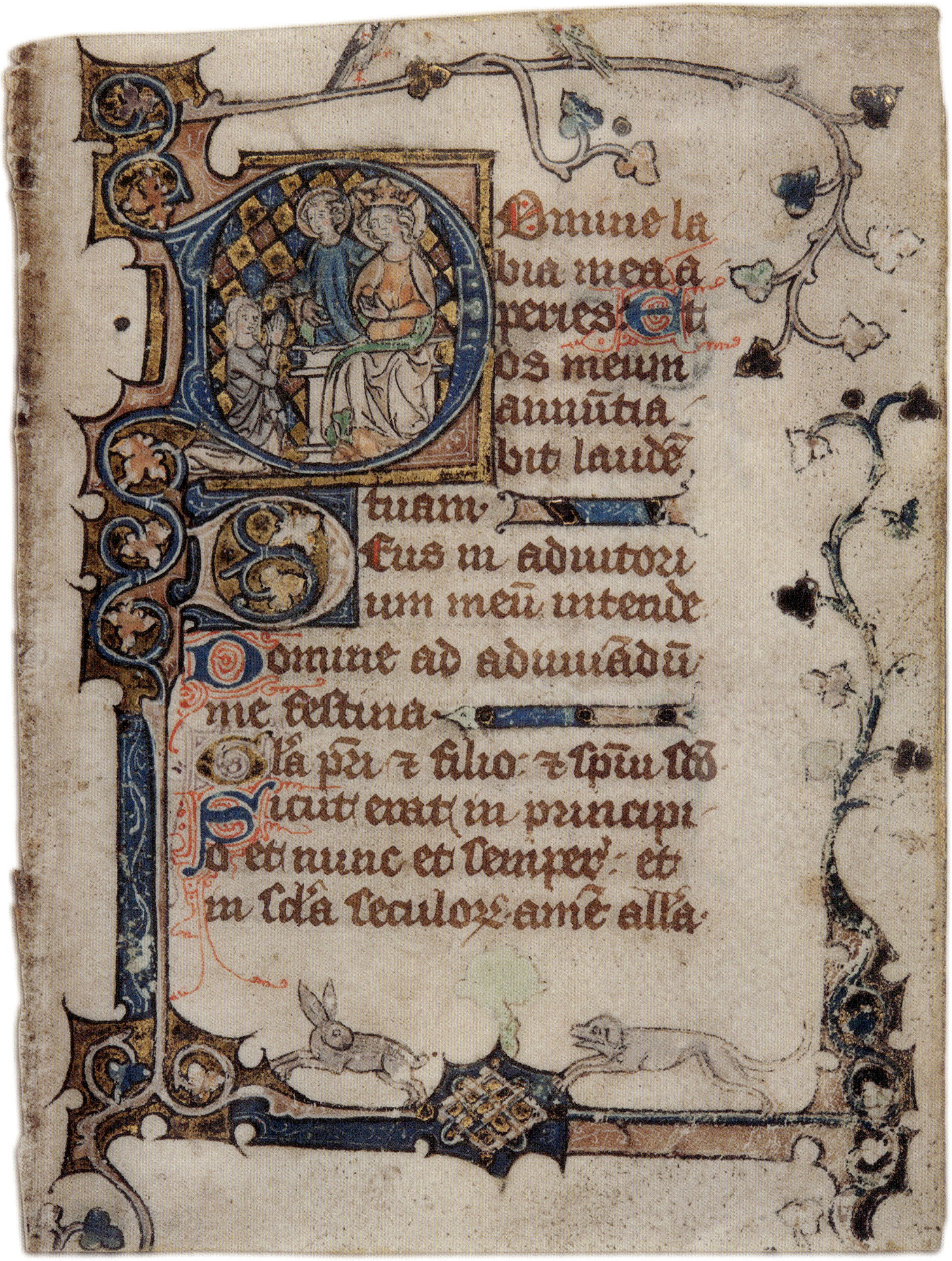

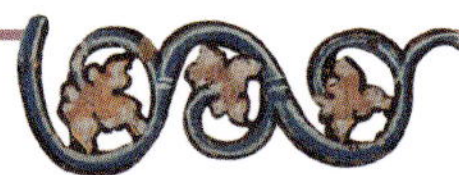

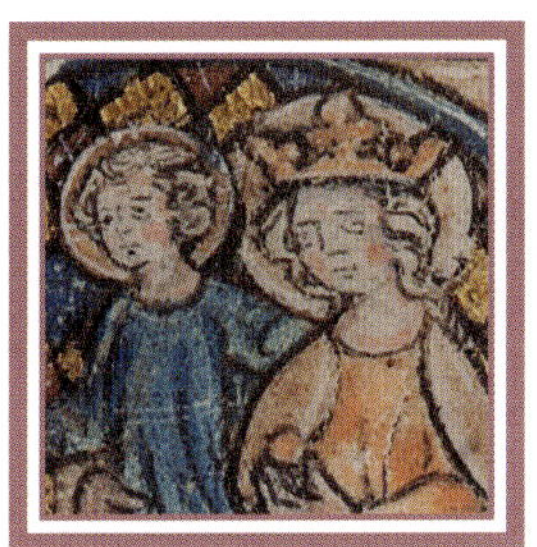

Cat. 14 | Reference 參考編號: BM 1163

Leaf from a Psalter or Book of Hours Depicting a *Female Donor before the Virgin and Child* and a Historiated Initial "D"
《聖詠經》或《時禱書》書頁，描繪「聖母與聖嬰前的女奉獻者」，佔行大寫首字母「D」經中世紀傳統出版風格修飾與變形

Anonymous
Northern France, c.1325
Tempera, gold and ink on vellum
H. 100 mm W. 72 mm

This leaf, most likely from a psalter, was illuminated for a female patron. The depiction completely fills the volume of the 6-line decorated initial "D" with a woman kneeling in prayer on the left before the Virgin and Christ Child, who are enthroned on the right. The text identifies this leaf as the beginning of the Matins Hour of the Virgin ("Domine labia mea aperies" [recto], Psalm 94, "Venite exultemus domino" [verso]). It is written in dark brown ink in a small gothic book hand, in a single column, on 15 lines. The rubrics are in red with illuminated line endings in red, blue and gold, and versal initials alternating in blue and gold with contrasting penwork in red and purple. The leaf also features 2-line initials of burnished gold on pink and blue ground with white tracery fill, and a 3-line decorated initial in pink and blue with white tracery on a burnished gold ground with pink and blue ivy leaf decoration. The borders show ivy vines painted with polychrome leaves, and the lower end of the page illustrates a dog chasing a hare.

This leaf was illuminated and written in northern France, as it is similar to the illustration and script work of two prominent manuscripts: an Hours in Baltimore (MS W.90) and the broken Ghistelles Hours (see Randall 1966, figs. 274 and 489; Walters 1949, no. 51, p. 21, pl. XXVIII). The Ghistelles Hours was written in 1299 or 1300 for a member of a family named Ghistelles in northern France or Flanders, and the Baltimore Hours was written in either 1323 or 1334 for a woman, perhaps in the region of Thérouanne (see cat. no. 9a–c).

匿名
製作於法國北部，約一三二五年
蛋彩、泥金與墨水，犢皮紙
高100公釐，寬72公釐

此書頁是為一位女奉獻者而繪，最可能取自一本《聖詠經》。微繪完全佔據了佔六行大寫首字母「D」內的空間，其中左側有一位向著右邊寶座上的聖母與聖子跪地祈禱的女性。頁中可識別的文字表明此書頁為《聖母晨禱書》的開始（「Domine labia mea aperies」【正頁】，《詩篇》九十四篇，「Venite exultemus domino」【背頁】）。文字處於單列十五行中，為深褐色的哥德體。首題字為紅色，行尾結束符號由紅色、藍色與金色修飾，整個首字母交替為藍色與金色，配以對比強烈的紅色與紫色筆繪裝飾。書頁中還以拋光泥金料的佔兩行大寫首字母為特點，粉色與藍色底，其中填滿白色窗格；以及一個粉色與藍色的佔三行大寫首字母，配以拋光泥金料底之上的粉色與藍色常春藤葉裝飾與白色窗格。邊框為粉色與藍色的常春藤裝飾，配有彩色葉片，頁面底端有一隻狗在追逐一隻野兔。

可以推定此書頁的抄寫與繪插圖完成於法國北部，因為其與兩部著名的泥金插畫手繪卷本類似：《巴爾的摩時禱書》（編號：MS W.90）與破損的《希斯特爾斯時禱書》（見Randall 1966, figs. 274 and 489; Walters 1949, no. 51, p. 21, pl. XXVIII）。《希斯特爾斯時禱書》製作於一二九九年或一三零零年，乃是為法國北部或法蘭德斯的希斯特爾斯家族中的一位成員而製，《巴爾的摩時禱書》於一三二三年或一三三四年為了一位女性而製作，可能在泰魯阿訥地區（見圖錄編號9a–c）。

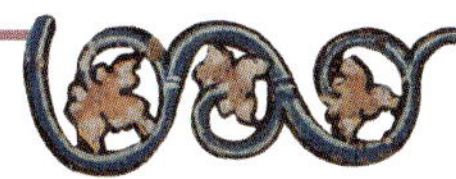

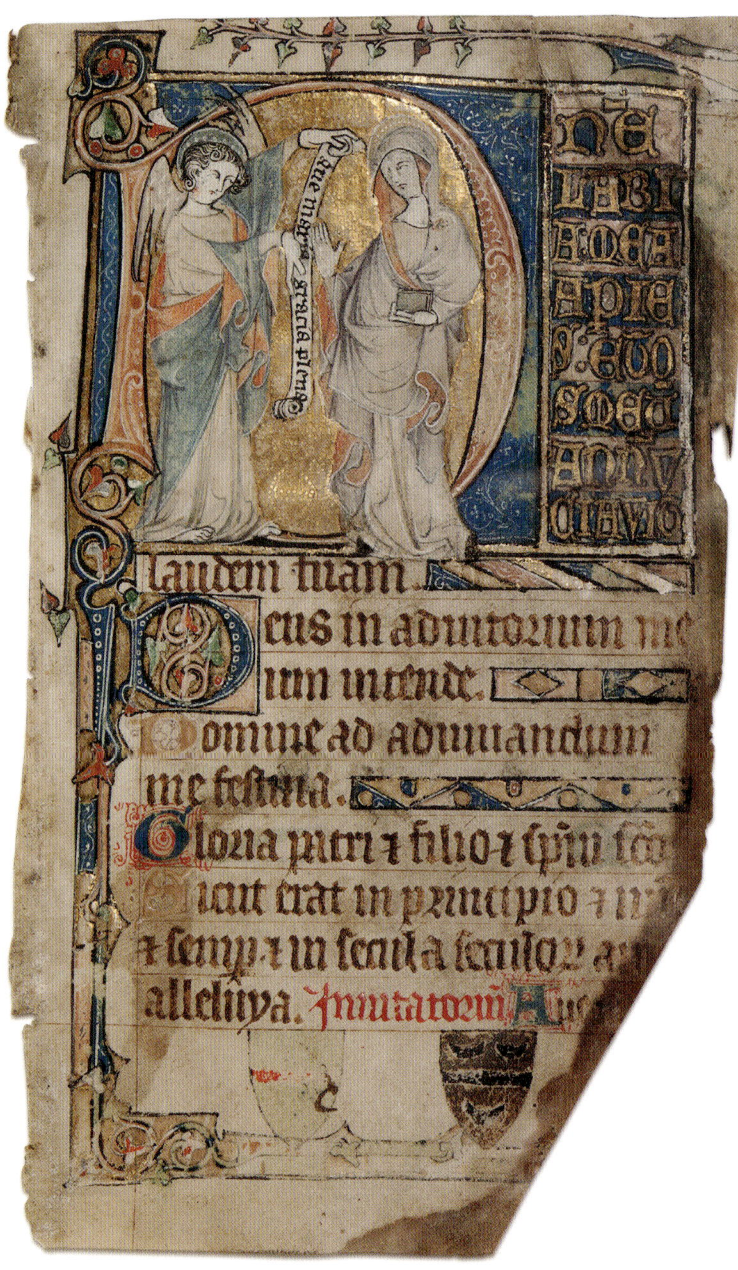

(actual size 原大)

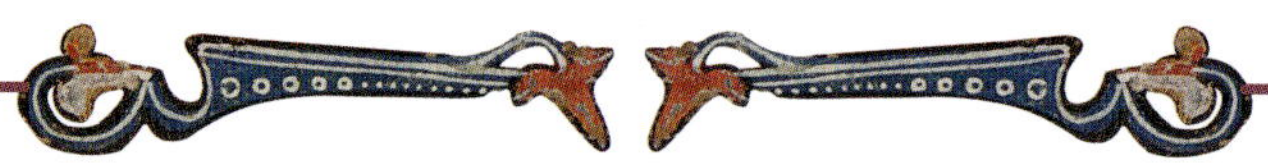

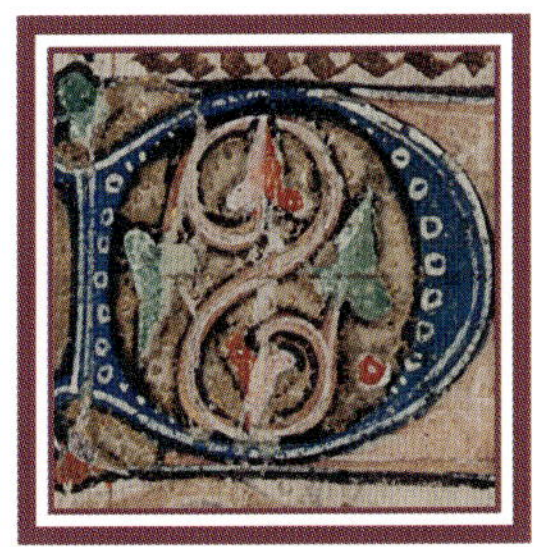

Cat. 15 | Reference 參考編號: BM 1066; SF 3238

Leaf from the Hungerford Book of Hours Depicting *The Annunciation* and a Historiated Initial "D"
《亨格福德時禱書》書頁，描繪「聖母領報」，佔行大寫首字母「D」經中世紀傳統出版風格修飾與變形

Anonymous
East Anglia, England, c.1330
Tempera, gold and ink on vellum
H. 165 mm W. 108 mm

This leaf displays the Pentecost Miniature of the Hungerford Hours, which includes text written in Latin and French in brown ink in a square Gothic script on 17 ruled lines within a 125 mm x 72 mm surface. Details include one 1-line initial, in blue with red penwork, and two 2-line initials, one on each side. A blue "S" on a red ground on the recto, and a red "D" on a blue ground on the verso (illustrated here), both utilize white and gold and bar-and-tendril ivy leaf extenders. The historiated "D" illustrates the Angel Gabriel delivering his written message to the Virgin Mary. Both are depicted on a fine gold ground. A blue "D" on a red recto ground is decorated with white tracery, within which Mary and a group of seven disciples witness the descent of the Holy Spirit. The inner edge is nearly intact, whereas the outer edge has been cropped to the edge of the text.

This is a leaf of the Hungerford Hours, an important English book of hours, one leaf of which bears a damaged coat of arms of the original owner, which has been tentatively identified with those of Sir John de Pateshulle, Lord of Pattishall, Northamptonshire (1292–1349).

Literature: Michael 1990, volume 2, pp. 33–108.

匿名
製作於東盎格利亞，英格蘭，約一三三零年
蛋彩、泥金與墨水，犢皮紙
高165公釐，寬108公釐

此書頁展示了《亨格福德時禱書》中的聖靈降臨日微繪，其拉丁文與法文文字以褐色墨水，寫於125公釐 x 72公釐方形表面的哥德式手本之上，共十七行直紋線。其中細節包括：一個藍色的佔一行大寫首字母，配以紅色的筆繪裝飾，以及兩個佔兩行大寫首字母。正頁有一個紅底的藍色字母「S」，背頁（見圖）有一個藍底的紅色「D」，兩者皆利用了白色與金色、直條與捲曲的常春藤葉延伸裝飾。大寫首字母「D」以精細的泥金料為底，其上描繪了天使加百列正向聖母傳達書寫信息的場景。正頁的紅底藍字母「D」有白色窗格修飾，其中聖母與七位門徒正見證聖靈的降臨。內緣幾乎原封不動，外緣被裁減至文字的邊緣。

此書頁取自《亨格福德時禱書》，一本重要的英國《時禱書》，其上有一層屬於原主的盾徽型破損，暫且被鑒定為約翰・迪・帕特舒爾爵士，帕蒂紹爾王，北安普敦郡（一二九二年至一三四九年）。

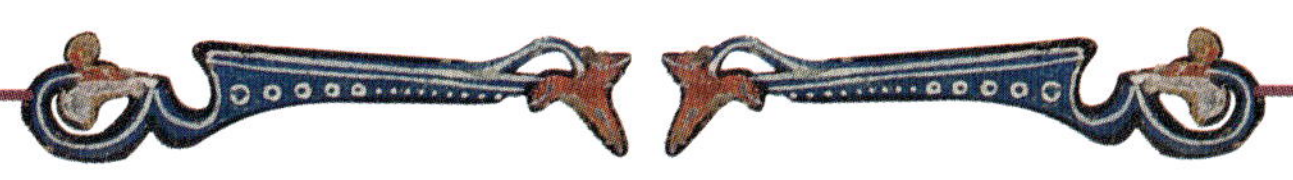

(detail 局部)

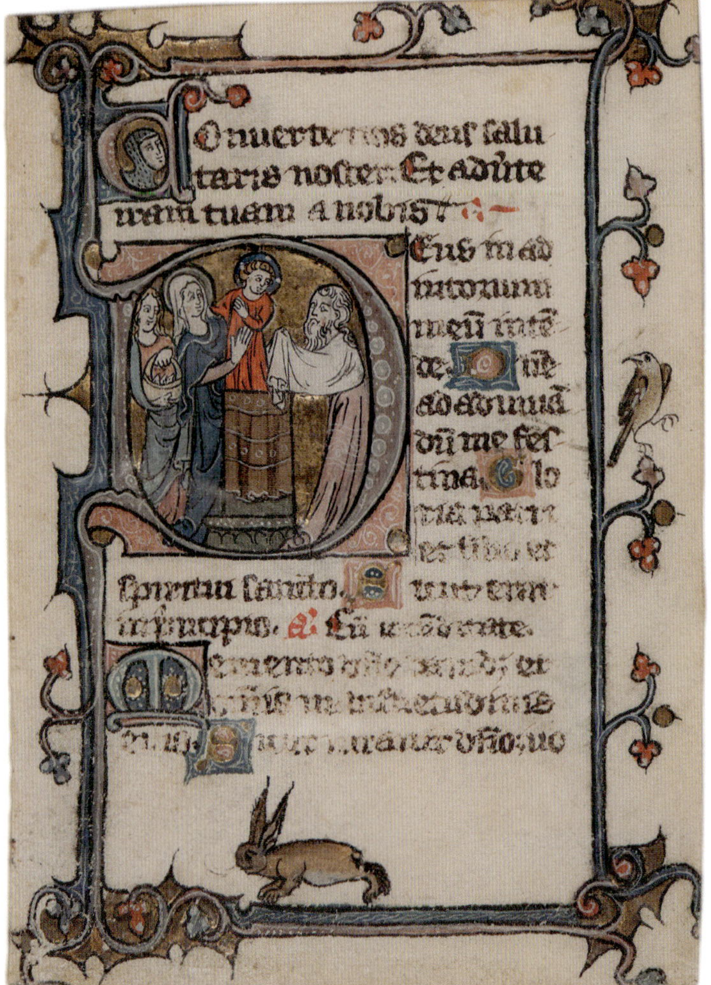

(actual size 原大)

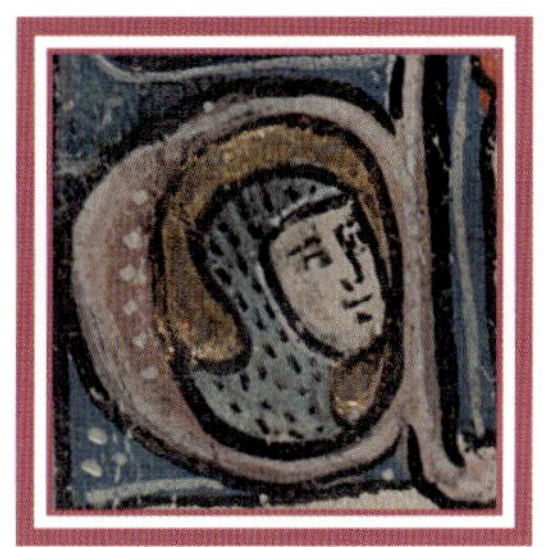

Cat. 16 | Reference 參考編號: BM 2428

Leaf from a Book of Hours Depicting *The Presentation in the Temple* and a Historiated Initial "D"
《時禱書》書頁，描繪「獻主於聖殿」，佔行大寫首字母「D」經中世紀傳統出版風格修飾與變形

Workshop of the Master of the Boethius of Montpellier
Metz, France, c.1340
Tempera, gold and ink on vellum
H. 130 mm W. 94 mm

This leaf from a book of hours shows a 9-line historiated initial "D" enclosing a depiction of *The Presentation in the Temple*. The full text frame terminates in foliage and ivy leaves in orange, light pink, blue and gold bezants that enclose a running hare and bird. 17 lines in black ink are in an early Gothic bookhand. The rubrics have been rendered in red, the capitals are touched in red, and the 1-line initials appear in gold on coloured grounds. The 2-line initials are in pink or blue on contrasting grounds, and one includes the head of a clean-shaven knight in his chainmail.

Literature: Avril 1981, no. 256; Plotzek 1987, no. 11.

蒙特利埃的波愛修斯大師工作坊
製作於梅斯，法國，約一三四零年
蛋彩、泥金與墨水，犢皮紙
高130公釐，寬94公釐

此張書頁取自一本早期《時禱書》，其中「獻主於聖殿」場景，框入一個佔九行大寫首字母「D」中。邊框終止於橙色、淡粉色、藍色與拜占庭古金幣式樣的枝蔓紋飾，另有一隻奔跑的野兔與一隻鳥。十七行文字為黑墨水的早期哥德體，首題字經紅色渲染，金色的佔一行大寫首字母以彩色為底，粉色或藍色的佔兩行大寫首字母出現於強烈對比的底上，其中包括有一個身著鏈甲的不蓄鬚騎士頭像。

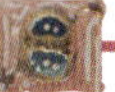
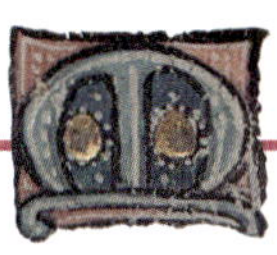
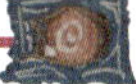

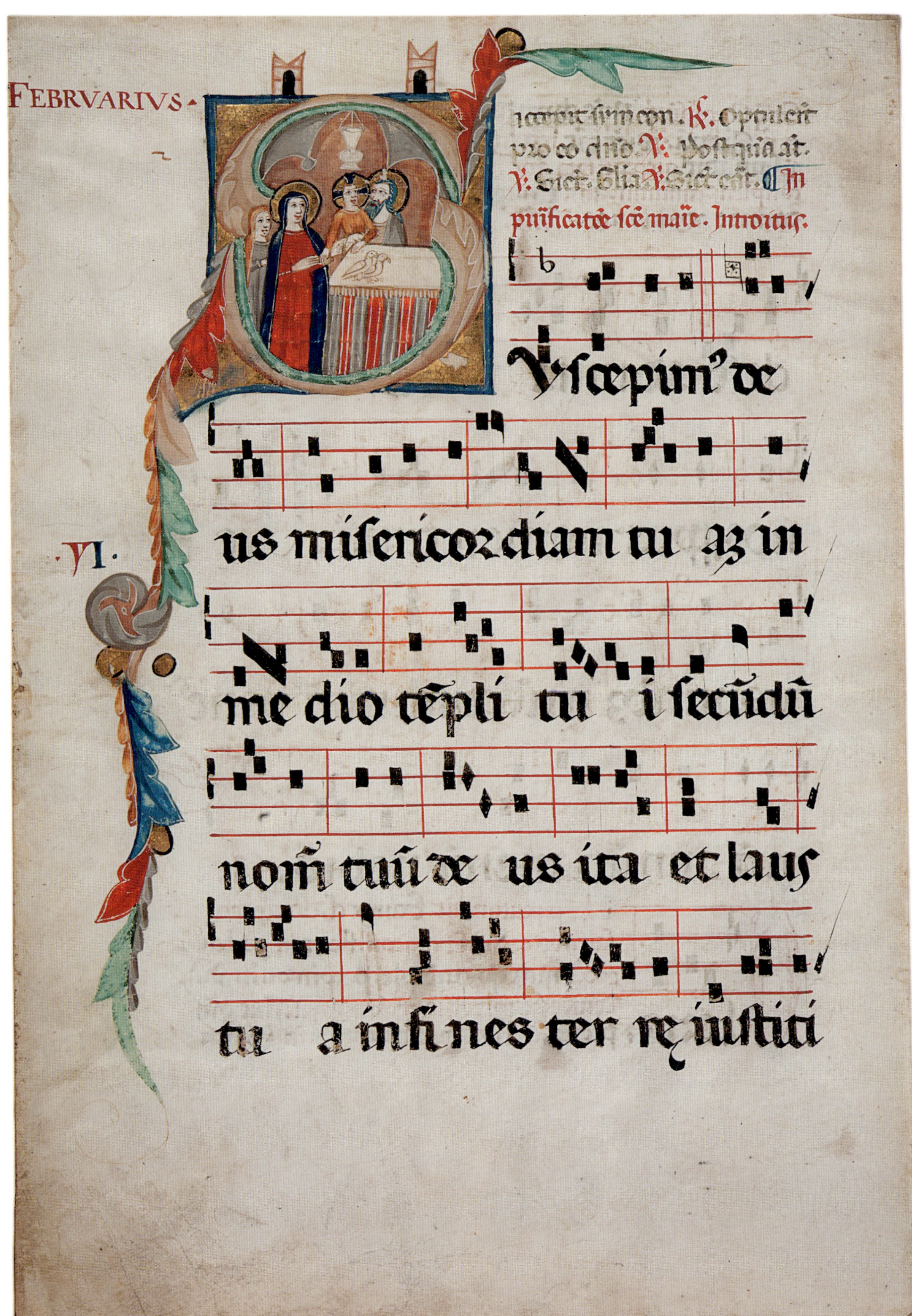
FEBRVARIVS
VI.
us misericordiam

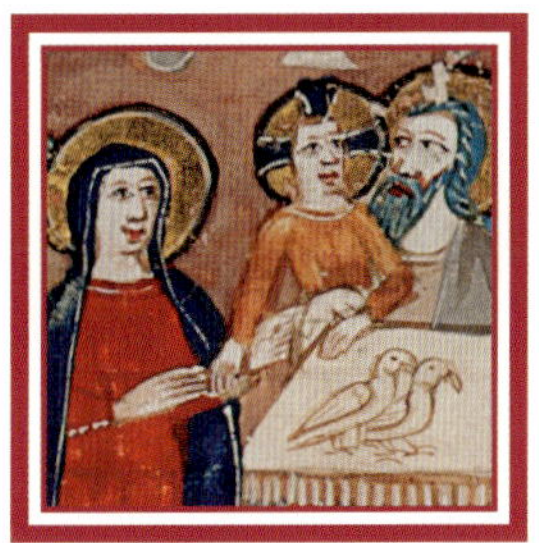

Cat. 17 | Reference 參考編號: BM 2316; SF 517

Leaf from a Choir Book Depicting *The Presentation in the Temple* and a Historiated Initial "S"

《聖詩集》書頁，描繪「獻主於聖殿」，佑行大寫首字母「S」經中世紀傳統出版風格修飾與變形

Anonymous
Umbria or Tuscany, Italy, c.1340
Ink and paint on vellum
H. 530 mm W. 370 mm

This leaf illustrates *The Presentation in the Temple* with Christ being held by Zacharias and touching hands with the Virgin Mary. It was possibly illuminated by a master from the Marches who had also executed the decoration of an antiphonary that is now preserved at the Museo Diocesano Albani in Urbino (Corale 10). His style is quite archaic, which implies that he was based outside the centres of book illumination at that time. The initial "S" marks the beginning of the feast of Candlemas (2nd of February) *Suscepimus deus misericordiam tuam in medio temple . . .*

The miniature measures 123 mm x 118 mm, and the written space extends to 380 mm x 252 mm. The height of the stave is 34 mm. Five staves occupy the recto page and six are present on the verso. There are tetragrams ruled in red and the music is subdivided by bar lines. On the verso three initals are painted in red and blue with decoration in pen. The text is written in brown ink in a *Southern Textualis* (Rotunda). In the upper left in red capital letters: *FEBRVARIUS*. Below on the left margin the number VI in red and blue marks the page or liturgical section. Black script ink on the illuminated face of the page has been partly retouched, probably at an early date, while the script of the present verso is untouched.

匿名
製作於溫布利亞或托斯卡尼，意大利
約一三四零年
墨水與彩漆，犢皮紙
高530公釐，寬370公釐

書頁內的「獻主於聖殿」場景中，基督被撒迦利亞托住，並與聖母牽手。書頁的插畫家可能是來自馬爾凱的大師，他也曾負責裝飾現存於烏比諾的阿爾巴尼教區博物館中（Corale 10） 的《啟應輪唱詩歌集》。他的藝術頗具古韻，這意味著他的風格是在當時的插畫藝術核心地帶之外孕育成形的。佑行大寫首字母「S」標記了聖燭節（二月二日）的開始（原文：*Suscepimus deus misericordiam tuam in medio temple . . .*）。

微繪高123公釐，寬118公釐，文字區域擴展至高380公釐，寬252公釐。四線樂譜高34公釐。正頁共五行四線樂譜，背頁則有六行。四字符以紅色標示，音樂由小節線分節。正頁中三個首字母被繪上紅色與藍色，由筆體裝飾。文字為褐色墨水的「南部書寫」字體（又名Rotunda）。左上大寫文字為「*FEBRVARIUS*」。左下邊緣是紅色與藍色的數字「VI」（六），標記了頁數或禮儀的章節。書頁表面的部分黑字可能在不久之前經過修整，而背頁的字則未經修整。

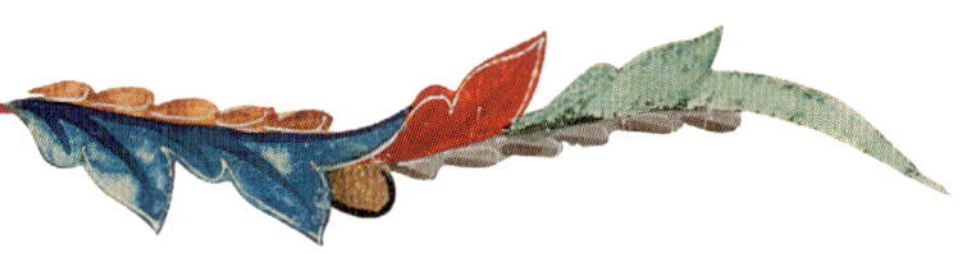

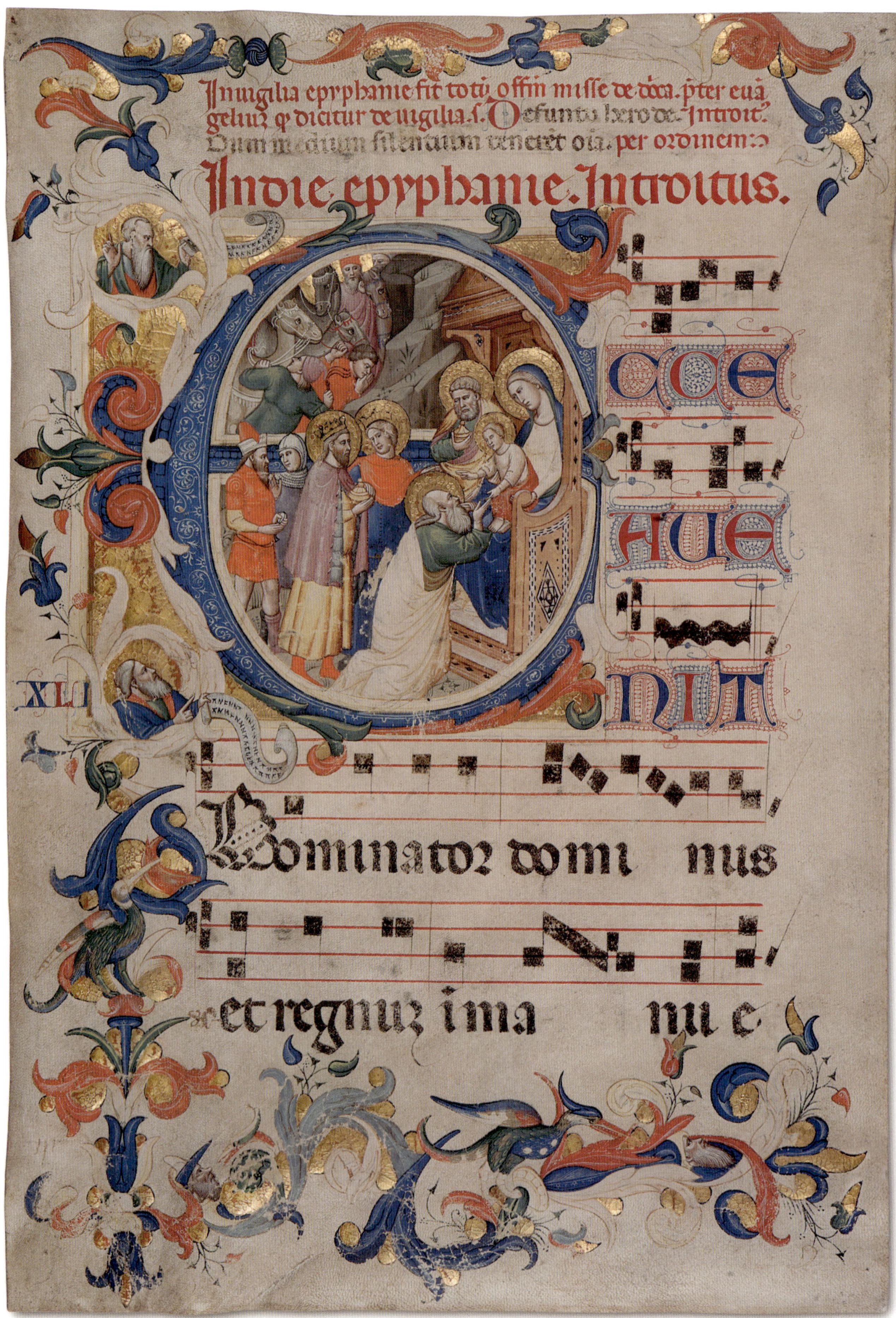
Indie epyphanie. Introitus.
ominator domi nus
et regnu ima nu e

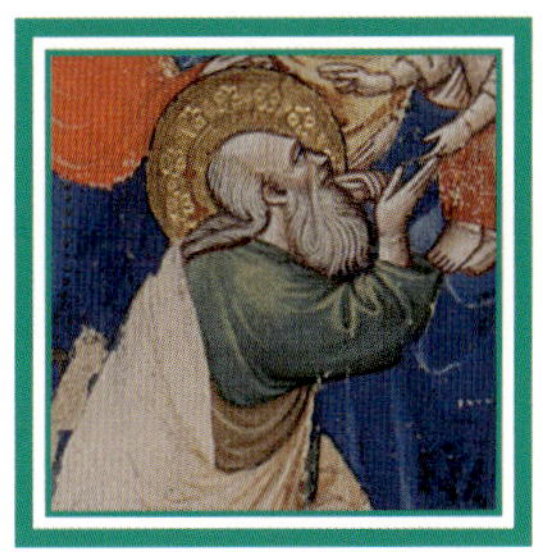

Cat. 18 | Reference 參考編號: BM 1444; SF 9480

Leaf from a Gradual Depicting *The Adoration of the Magi* and a Historiated Initial "E" ("*Ecce avenit*")
《階台經》書頁，描繪「博士來朝」，其中「Ecce avenit」的佔行大寫首字母「E」經中世紀傳統出版風格修飾與變形

Don Simone Camaldolese (active 1375–1398) and workshop
Florence, Italy, c.1380–1390
Tempera, gold and ink on vellum
H. 592 mm W. 415 mm

嘉瑪道理會士唐．施蒙尼（活躍於一三七五年至一三九八年）及其工作室
製作於佛羅倫斯，意大利
約一三八零年至一三九零年
蛋彩、泥金與墨水，犢皮紙
高592公釐，寬415公釐

This leaf originates with an antiphonary. It depicts *The Adoration of the Magi* set within an initial "E" (ECCE AVENIT). It was illuminated by Don Simone, a Camaldolese monk of Santa Maria degli Angeli, Florence, the scriptorium of which was an important centre of manuscript production. Don Simone was originally from Siena but was primarily active in Florence. The text is written in black and red ink, and at the left of the historiated initial is a floral decoration and two medallions of prophets holding scrolls with pseudo-Hebrew inscriptions. An unusual number of signed, documented or dated works attributable to him have survived, demonstrating the course of his career illuminating manuscripts—predominantly choir books—for various Florentine monasteries and churches. The simplicity of his forms and the stylized appearance of his figures distinguishes his style from that of his fellow Camaldolese illuminators—Don Silvestro dei Gherarducci and Lorenzo Monaco—who were fellow residents of S. Maria degli Angeli.

此書頁起源自一本《啟應輪唱詩歌集》，「博士來朝」場景框於佔行大寫首字母「E」（ECCE AVENIT看吶吾王來臨）中。製作者為唐．施蒙尼，一位於佛羅倫斯的天使聖母堂侍奉的嘉瑪道理修士，此堂的繕寫室乃是手繪本製作的重要中心。唐．施蒙尼最初來自錫耶納，但主要活躍於佛羅倫斯。書頁文字以黑色與紅色墨水寫成，大寫首字母「E」的左邊有花飾，以及兩個繪有手持捲軸（題有偽希伯來文）的先知徽章像。相當數量的存世作品經簽署、存檔，並且標有日期，皆歸在他的名下，這例解了他的繪製插圖職業生涯——主要是為許多佛羅倫斯的修道院與教堂製作《聖詩集》。他的簡約藝術形式，以及他風格鮮明的人物造型，皆與他的嘉瑪道理插畫師同僚們不同，這包括後來居住於天使聖母堂的唐．希爾維斯特羅．代．格阿爾杜希以及洛倫佐．摩納哥。

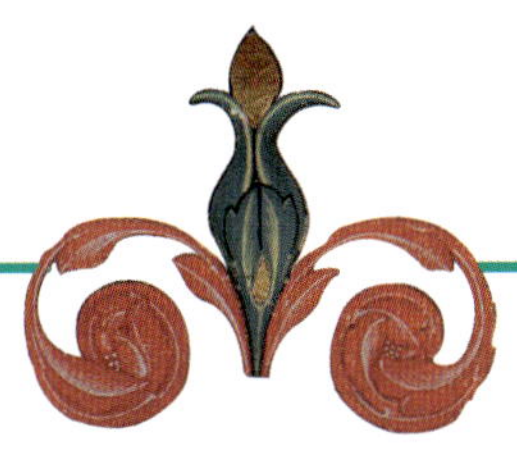

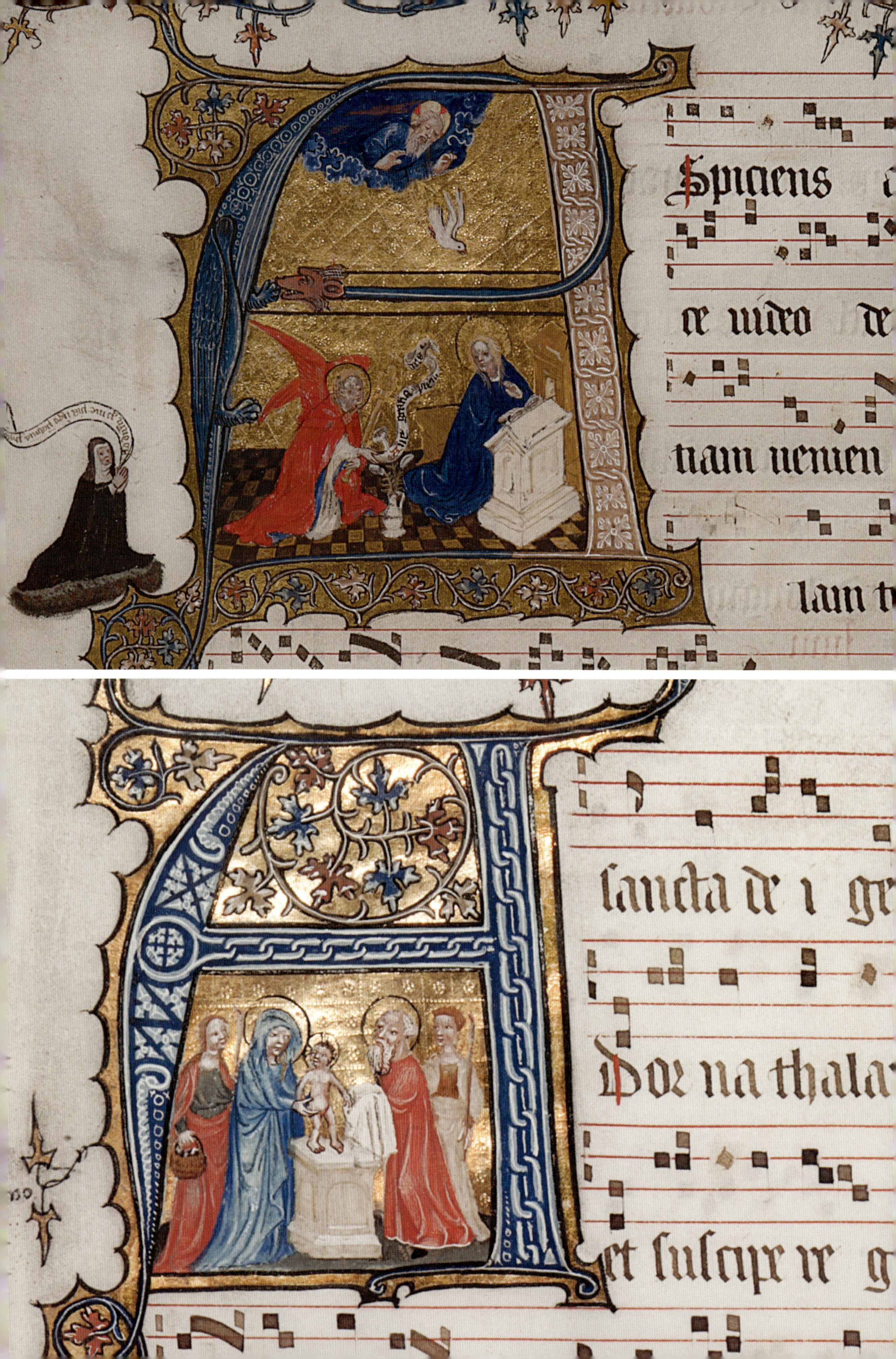

Spiciens
ce uideo
tiam uenien
sancta dei ge
Doz na thala
et suscipe re

The Tournai Antiphonary
圖爾奈啟應輪唱詩歌集

Cat. 19a–b

Two of twenty-four known leaves with historiated initials have come from an antiphonary made in Tournai (c.1400–1410) for a Benedictine convent, as indicated by the nun kneeling by *The Annunciation*. The rubric is written in Dutch, suggesting that this manuscript was executed in the Northern or, more likely, the Southern Netherlands. An origin in Tournai is supported by the instructions to the illuminator in French beside six of the small initials of saints. More significantly, the decoration is typical of Tournai: the striking bar borders, the bold initials with delicately pounced gold ground and the beaded flourishing are all paralleled in manuscripts illuminated by Jean Semont (active c.1385–1414). There are, however, distinctive features, such as the ebullient dragons and the chain forming the initial around *The Presentation in the Temple*. The historiated initials also reveal a distinct and more talented artistic personality. Compared to Semont, the present illuminator has a more detailed and painterly technique, carefully modelling the faces and drapery of his elegant figures to a more expressive and three-dimensional effect. This is reinforced by his greater mastery of perspective. Through this mastery he emulates the innovations associated with Early Netherlandish painters in oil.

此兩張書頁取自一本《啟應輪唱詩歌集》的二十四張書頁(約於一四零零年至一四一零年)，製作於圖爾奈，由「聖母領報」場景中跪拜的修女形象可知此書乃是為一個本篤會女修道院而製。首題字為荷蘭文，故可推測此書應該製作於北尼德蘭，或更像出自南尼德蘭。插畫師以法語寫就的說明以及六個小型首字母中的聖人更證明了此書的確起源於圖爾奈。尤為明顯的是，畫中的裝飾是典型的圖爾奈風格：突出的直條形邊框，粗黑首字母和精緻製作的亮眼的金色，以及鑲珠式的繁華紋飾也相同出現於讓·賽蒙特(活躍於約一三八五年至一四一四年)的泥金裝飾手抄本中。然而，其中也有許多與眾不同的特徵，比如動感十足的龍以及在「獻主於聖殿」場景周圍以鏈條式環繞的大寫字母。經修飾變形的佔行大寫首字母展現了一種更傑出及更有天份的藝術人格魅力。與賽蒙特相比，此處展示的插畫家有著更為精妙和繪圖式的技巧，通過賦予筆下優雅的人物形象以細緻的臨摹面容和衣褶，實現了一種更具有表現力和三維立體的效果。他對透視的精準把握更加強了這一點。此乃他對許多早期尼德蘭畫家油畫創新的效法並應用。

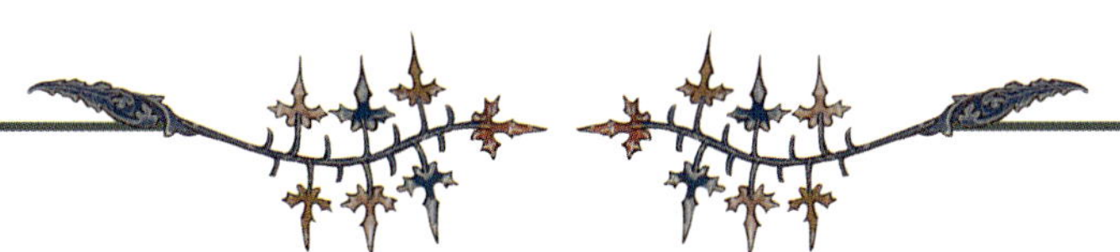

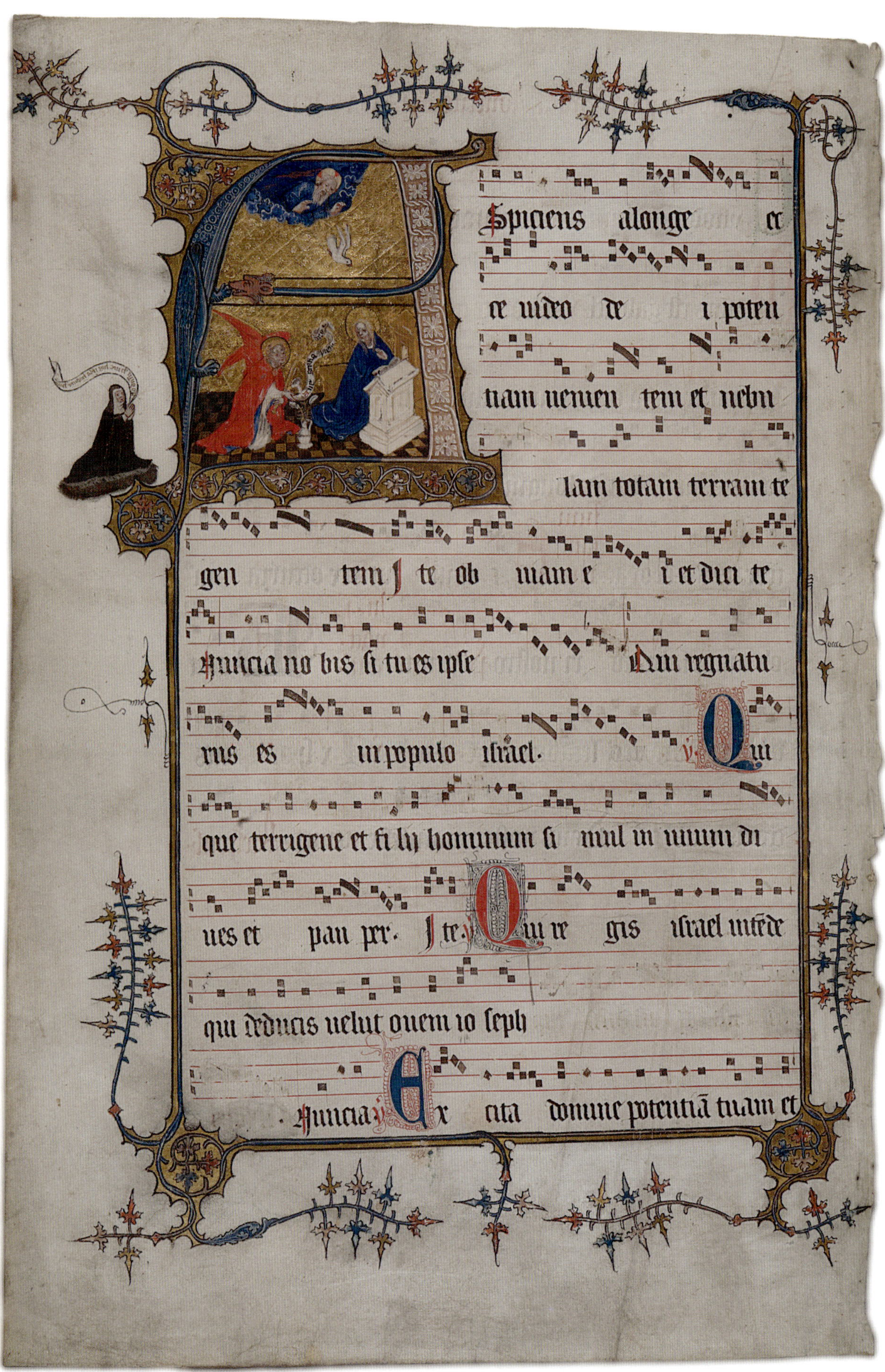
Spiciens alonge ec
ce uideo dei poten
tiam uenientem et nebu
lam totam terram te
gentem Ite obuiam ei et dicite
Nuncia nobis si tu es ipse Qui regnatu
rus es in populo israel. Qui
que terrigene et filii hominum simul in unum di
ues et pauper. Ite. Qui regis israel intende
qui deducis uelut ouem ioseph
Nuncia. Excita domine potentiā tuam et

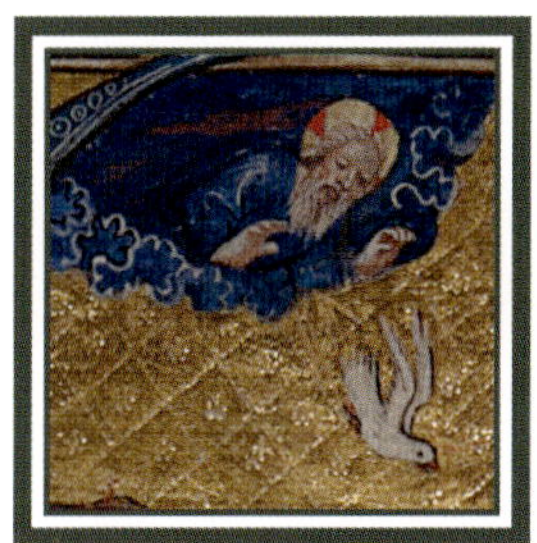

Cat. 19a | Reference 參考編號: BM 2406; SF 16

Leaf from a Temporal Depicting *The Annunciation* and a Historiated Initial "A"
《基督在世時序》書頁，描繪「聖母領報」，佔行大寫首字母「A」經中世紀傳統出版風格修飾與變形

Anonymous
Tournai, Flanders, c.1400–1410
Ink and paint on vellum
H. 500 mm W. 340 mm

匿名
製作於圖爾奈，法蘭德斯
約一四零零年至一四一零年
墨水與彩漆，犢皮紙
高500公釐，寬340公釐

This temporal leaf illustrates *The Annunciation*, here depicted within the initial "A". A nun kneels in prayer in the left margin, while holding a scroll that includes the text "Ad dominum pro me pia virgo precamina prome" (a common enough sentiment, although the exact sequence is only found in a Latin poem by a certain Godefridus [de Thenis?] in a 14th-century codex at Lübeck). The initial opens the responsory for the First Sunday in Advent, "Aspiciens a longe".

Tournai was central to the extraordinary artistic developments evident in the work of Robert Campin (identfied with the Master of Flémalle, active 1406–1444), his pupil Rogier van der Weyden (1399/1400–1464) and the Van Eycks. The initial of *The Annunciation* is closely related in design to Campin's only documented work, the damaged mural of 1406 from St-Brice, Tournai (Musée d'Art et d'Archéologie). The exceptionally thorough iconoclasm in Tournai in the 15th century means that little is known of the artistic context of Campin's mature achievements, or Van der Weyden's youth. The Tournai manuscript illumination is increasingly appreciated for its importance within the history of art, as well as for its inherent qualities (see Vanwijnsberghe 2007, pp. 194–199, 272, 284, 352 [cat. XXVI]).

《基督在世時序》書頁內的「聖母領報」場景，框於佔行大寫首字母「A」(「Aspiciens a longe」)中，這開始了將臨期第一主日的啟應輪唱。圖中一位修女於左側跪地祈禱，手持寫有「Ad dominum pro me pia virgo precamina prome」的捲軸。

圖爾奈對非凡的藝術發展極為重要，這體現於羅伯特．坎平(與弗萊馬勒的大師為同一人，活躍於一四零六年至一四四四年)、其學生羅希爾．范德魏登(一三九九年/一四零零年至一四六四年)及范．艾克兄弟的作品中。「聖母領報」在設計上與坎平唯一留存下來的作品息息相關——一四零六年來自圖爾奈的聖布里斯的破損的壁畫(藝術與考古博物館)。十五世紀於圖爾奈發生的特別徹底的破壞偶像主義運動，使得很少人能夠了解坎平作品曾達到的藝術高度，以及范德魏登的青年時期。在藝術史上，圖爾奈的手繪卷本插圖的重要性，及其內在的特性日益得到重視(見Vanwijnsberghe 2007, pp.194–199, 272, 284, 352 [cat. XXVI])。

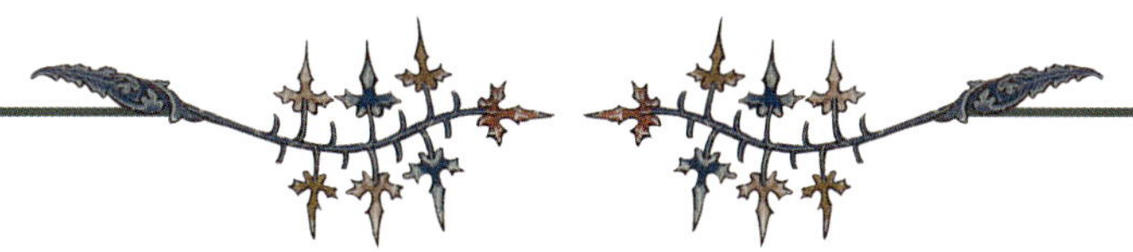

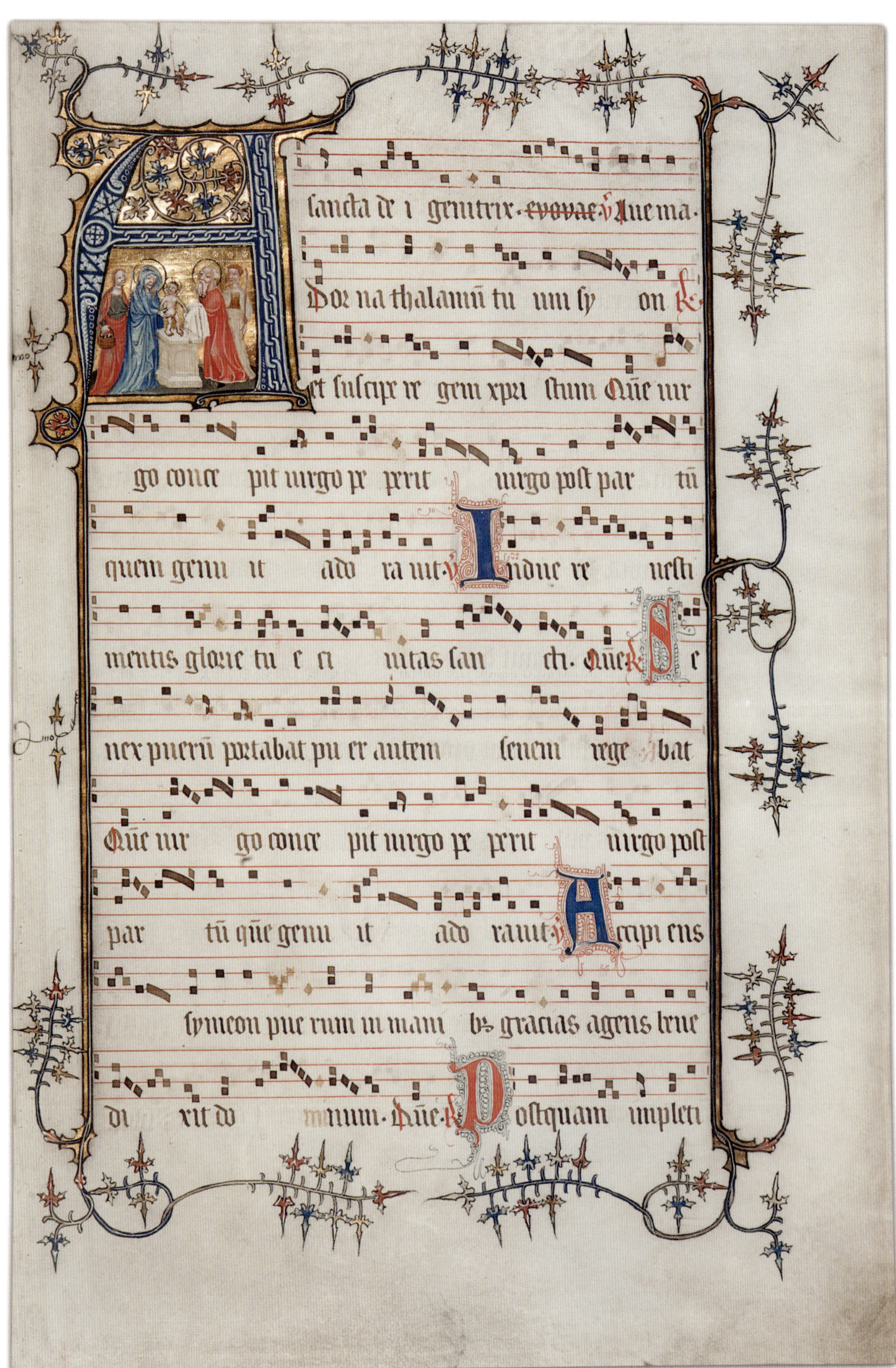

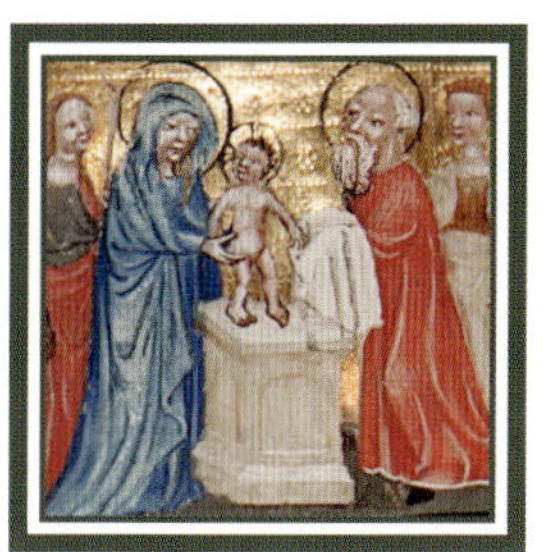

Cat. 19b | Reference 參考編號: BM 2407; SF 19

Leaf from a Sanctoral Depicting *The Presentation in the Temple* and a Historiated Initial "A"
《聖徒紀念時序》書頁，描繪「獻主於聖殿」，佔行大寫首字母「A」經中世紀傳統出版風格修飾與變形

Anonymous
Tounai, Flanders, c.1400–1410
Ink and paint on vellum
H. 504 mm W. 335 mm

匿名
製作於圖爾奈，法蘭德斯
約一四零零年至一四一零年
墨水與彩漆，犢皮紙
高504公釐，寬335公釐

This leaf originated with a sanctoral and represents *The Presentation in the Temple* illustrated inside the initial "A" (106 mm x 90 mm). The initial opens the sixth Antiphon for the Feast of the Purification of the Blessed Virgin, "Adorna thalamum tuum, Sion".

此書頁取自一本《聖徒紀念時序》，「獻主於聖殿」場景框於大寫首字母「A」(Adorna thalamum tuum, Sion)(106公釐 x 90公釐)中，這開啟了聖母取潔日第六輪唱。

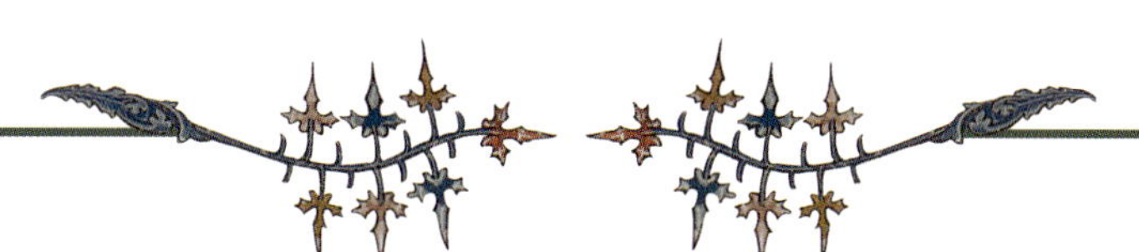

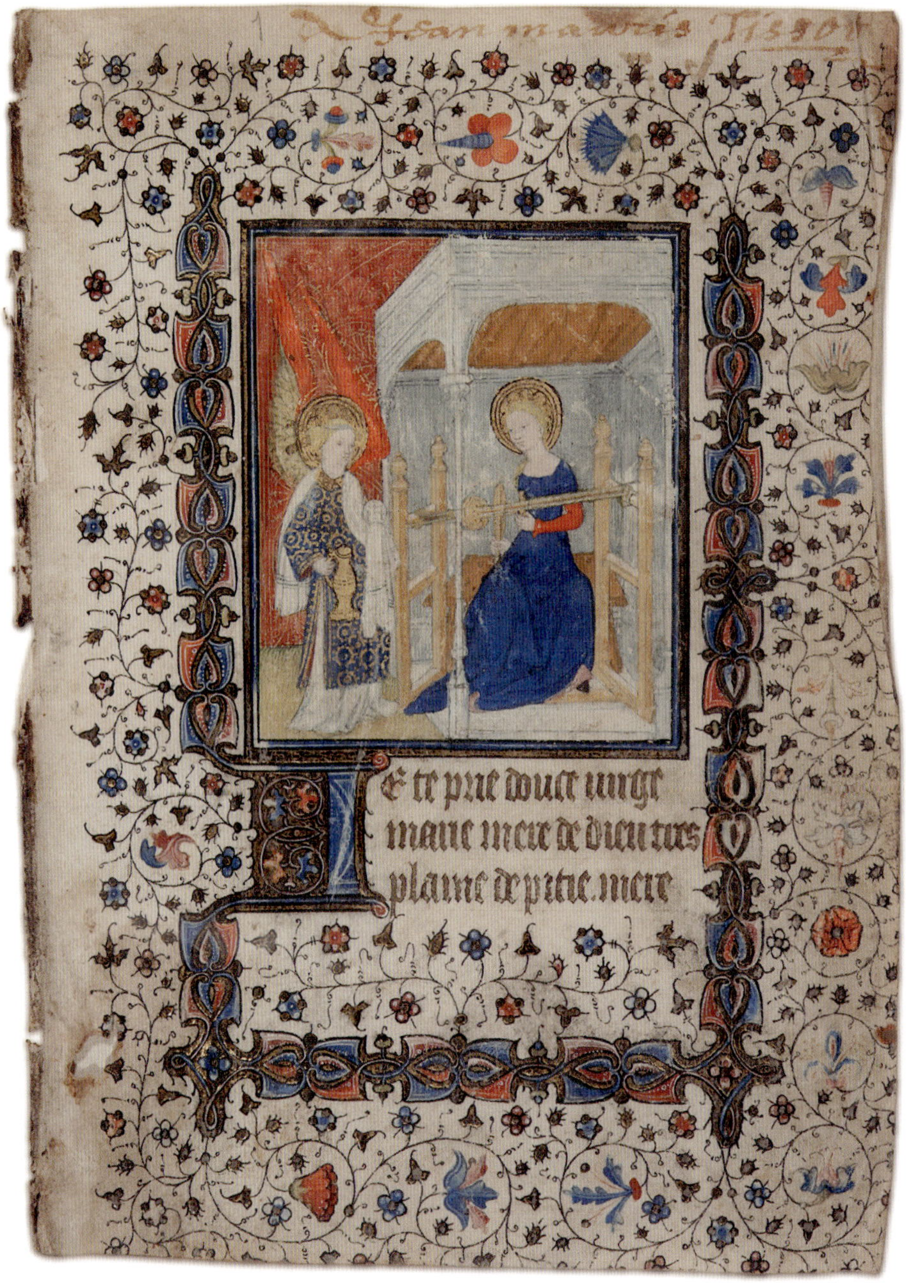

(actual size 原大)

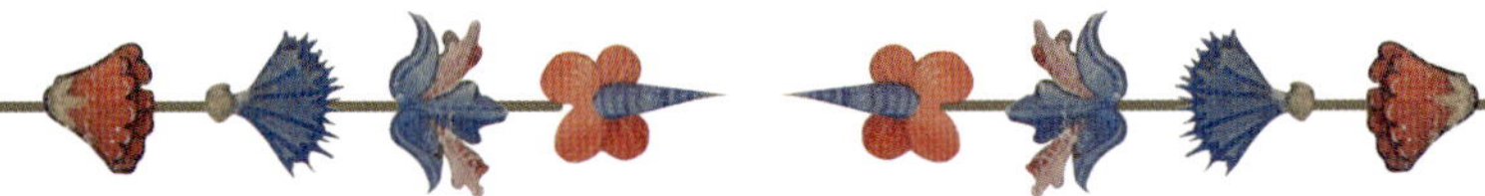

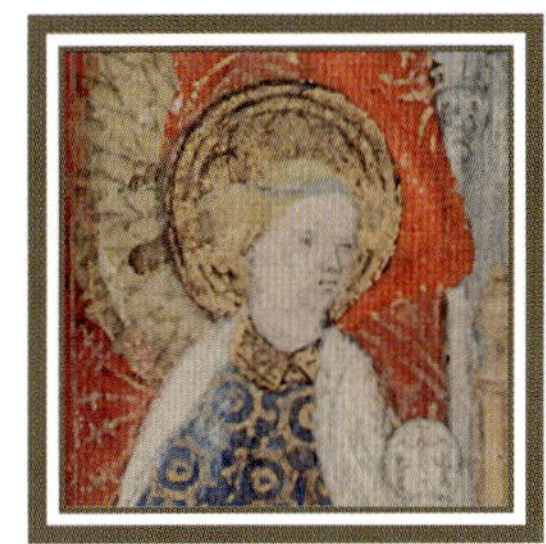

Cat. 20 | Reference 參考編號: BM 1307c; SF 7454

Leaf from a Prayer Book Depicting *The Annunciation*
《祈禱書》書頁，描繪「聖母領報」

Anonymous
Probably Paris, c.1420s
Tempera, gold and ink on vellum
H. 170 mm W. 120 mm

Inscriptions & Markings: inscribed in ink, at the top of the page "[. . . illegible] Tissot"

This leaf depicts *The Annunciation*, in which the Virgin is seen weaving at a loom in a small, open chamber. It originated with a large volume and contains some highly unusual texts, notably the life of the Dominican, Saint Peter Martyr. A large proportion of the text of the volume is in rhyming French verse. It is ruled for 13 lines of text per page, in red ink, with a ruled space of around 90 mm x 60 mm. The text is written in brown ink in a good regular Gothic liturgical script, with rubrics in red. The capitals are stroked with red, and the verse initials are in gold on a blue and red ground with white tracery. Similar line-fillers, more than thirty two- and thirty three-line foliate initials, appear in the same colours on a burnished gold ground. A three-sided border of black ink penwork and tendrils with gold, red and blue leaves accompanies each initial.

The miniature relates stylistically to the work of the Troyes Master, an attribution supported by the text's links to Troyes itself (see Meiss 1974, pp. 406–407). The large-scale treatment of the Virgin at the Loom is unusual; more commonly it appears as a small border vignette (see Randall 1989, p. 277).

匿名
疑似製作於巴黎，約一四二零年代
蛋彩、泥金與墨水，犢皮紙
高170公釐，寬120公釐

題字與標記：書頁上部以墨水刻有「[. . . illegible] Tissot」字樣。

此書頁內的「聖母領報」場景中，聖母在一個開放式的小房間中於織機前織造。書頁源於一本大型卷本，包括一些異常罕見的文字，尤其是關於道明會士維羅納的聖伯鐸的生平，一大部分文字為押韻的法語詩篇。卷本每頁由十三行約90公釐 x 60公釐的紅色橫隔線空間佔據。文字為褐色墨水的常規哥德式禮儀用手寫體，首題字為紅色。聖詩首字母為金色，底為藍色與紅色，另飾以白色窗格式樣。類似的佔行首字母裝飾，三十個佔兩行葉飾首字母及三十個佔三行葉飾首字母以上，在拋光泥金料底上以相同的顏色展現。黑墨水筆繪裝飾的三邊邊框，捲鬚狀的金色、紅色與藍色的葉紋伴隨著每一個大寫首字母。

微繪在風格上與特魯瓦大師的作品相關，因為其中的文字與特魯瓦本人相關（見 Meiss 1974, pp. 406–407）。「在紡織的聖母」場景通常會被作為小的邊框裝飾展現（見 Randall 1989, p. 277），但在此圖中卻不同尋常地得到大規模表現。

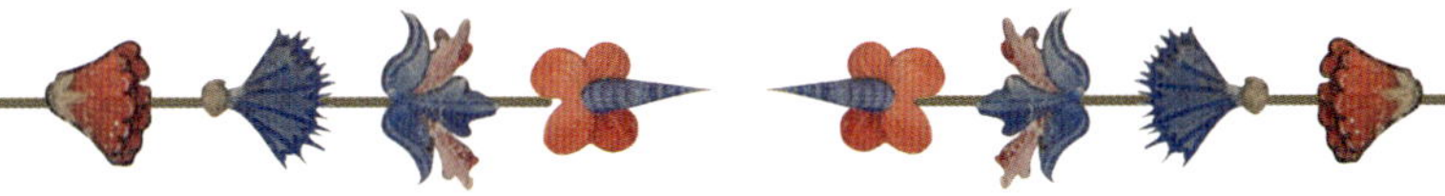

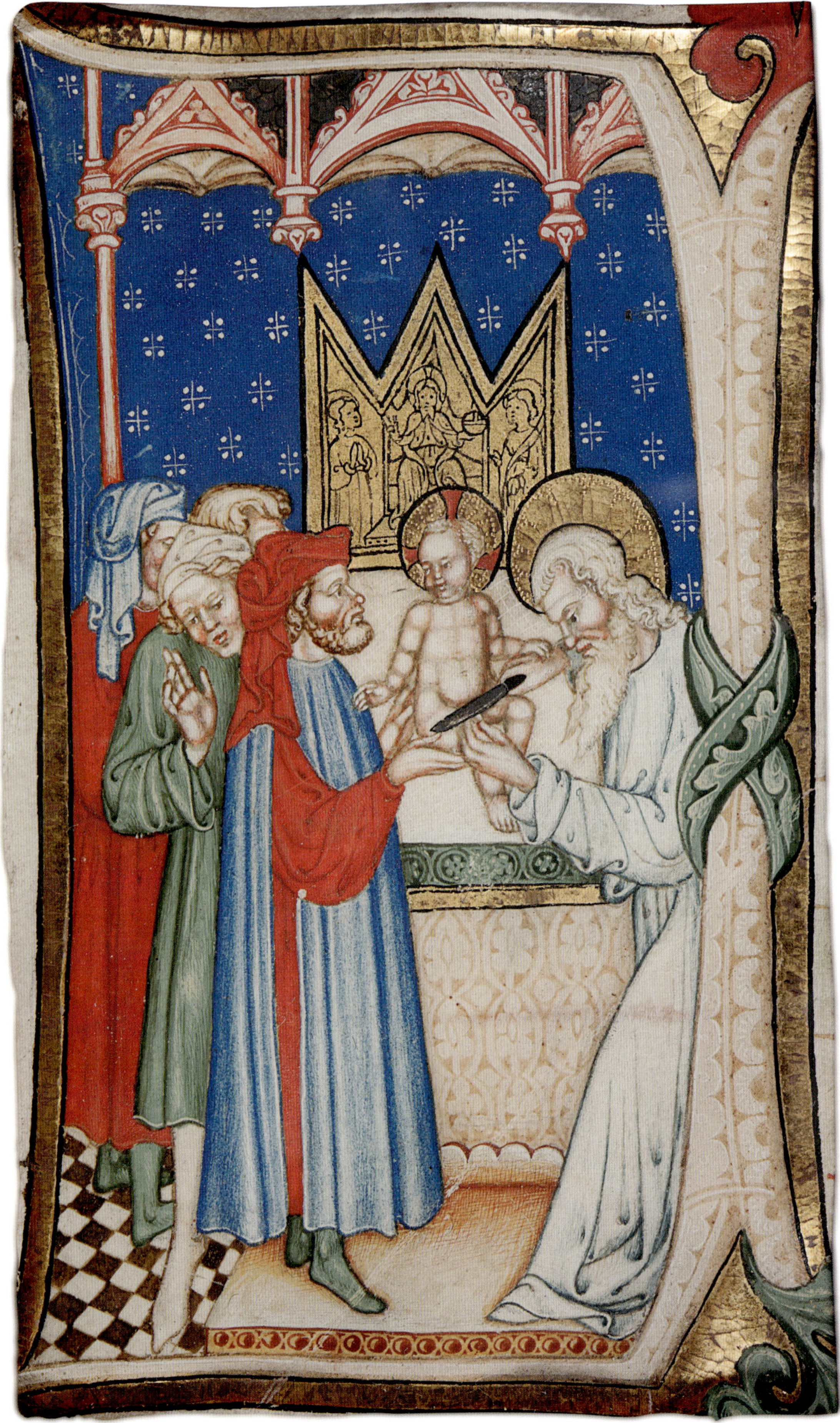

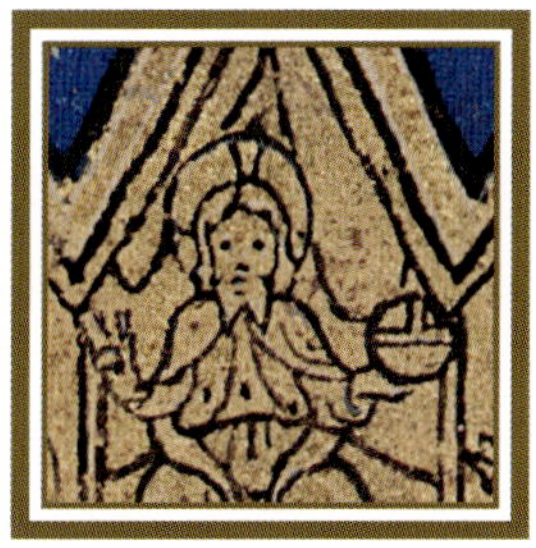

Cat. 21 | Reference 參考編號: BM 1422; SF 9527

Cutting from a Leaf of an Antiphonary Depicting *The Circumcision* and a Historiated Initial "T"
截自《啟應輪唱詩歌集》書頁，描繪「基督割禮」，佑行大寫首字母「T」經中世紀傳統出版風格修飾與變形

Master of the Vitae Imperatorum
Milan, Italy, c.1430s
Tempera, gold and ink on vellum
H. 122 mm W. 75 mm

This leaf depicts *The Circumcision*, illustrated on the side of the initial "T". The scene of the circumcision takes place beneath an elaborate vaulted ceiling with columns and Corinthian capitals. The background is in ultramarine blue with stylized stars. Behind the central figures is an altar with a triptych. Christ is enthroned on the central panel, with a saint on each side panel.

The illumination is attributed to the Master of the Vitae Imperatorum (active 1430–c.1453), an Italian illuminator named after an Italian translation of Suetonius (1430; Paris, Bib. Nat., MS ital.131) made for Filippo Maria Visconti (1392–1447), Duke of Milan, for whom he undertook many commissions. He might possibly have trained with Tomasino da Vimercate (active c.1390–1415) to whom he stylistically relates, although his figures are more carefully executed and his patterns are decorative and ultimately less naturalistic (see Royal Academy 1994).

維塔的因派拉圖倫大師
製作於米蘭，意大利，約一四三零年代
蛋彩、泥金與墨水，犢皮紙
高122公釐，寬75公釐

書頁內描繪的「基督割禮」場景，裝飾於大寫首字母「T」的側邊。畫中的割禮場景發生於華麗的拱形穹頂及有著科林斯柱頭的柱子之下，背景為群青藍色與裝飾星紋，畫面中心是陞座的基督，背後是三聯畫聖壇，兩邊則各一位聖人。

此插畫由維塔的因派拉圖倫大師（Master of the Vitae Imperatorum）（活躍於一四三零年至約一四五三年）製作，他是一位以「Suetonius」的意大利語翻譯為名（1430; Paris, Bib. Nat., MS ital.131）的意大利插畫師，該畫是受米蘭公爵菲利波·馬里亞·維斯康堤（一三九二年至一四四七年）的委託而製。他可能與托瑪西諾·達·維梅爾卡泰（活躍於約一三九零年至一四一五年）一同受訓，他們的藝術風格雖然相關，但是他製作的人物卻更細緻，其藝術模式更具裝飾作用，因此說到底不屬於自然主義風格（見 Royal Academy 1994）。

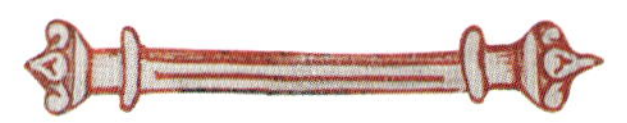
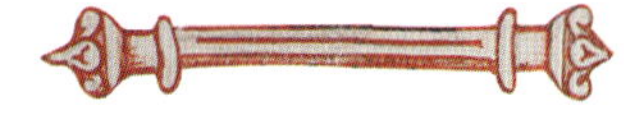

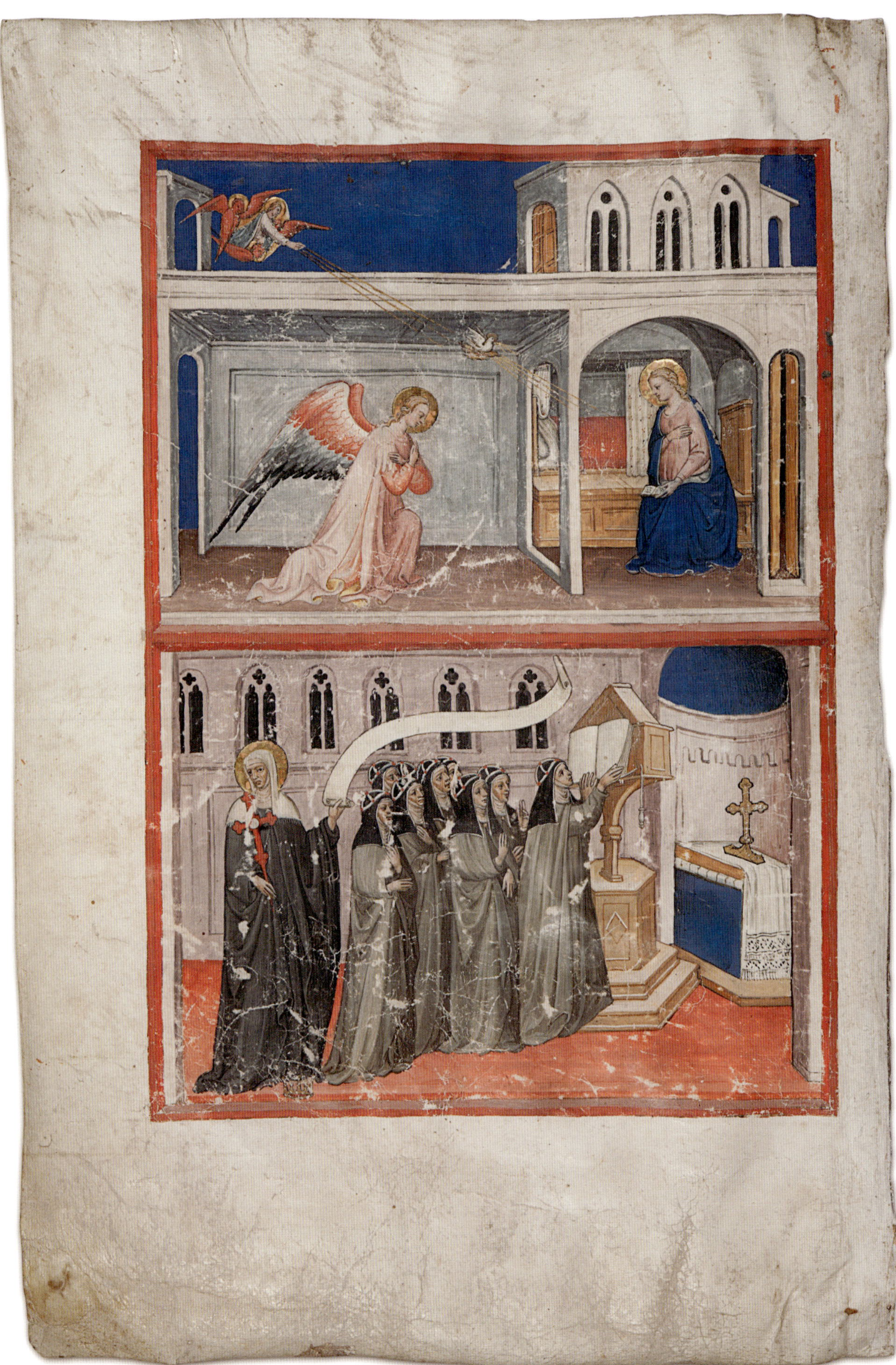

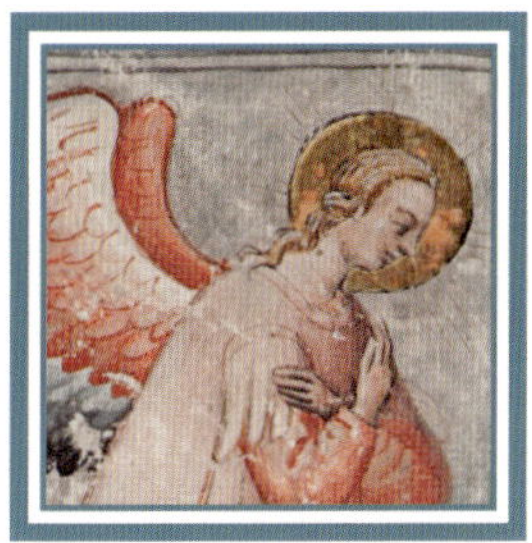

Cat. 22 | Reference 參考編號: BM 1423; SF 9525

Leaf from a Gradual Depicting *The Annunciation* and *The Brigittine Nuns in a Choir*
《階台經》書頁，描繪「聖母領報」與「布雷廷修女們獻詩」

Bicci di Lorenzo (1373–1452)
Florence, Italy, c.1435
Tempera, gold and ink on vellum
H. 555 mm W. 370 mm

This leaf illustrates both *The Annunciation* and *The Brigittine Nuns in a Choir*. It is attributed to Bicci di Lorenzo (1373–1452), and is divided into two registers to accompany both scenes. On the upper register is a scene of *The Annunciation*, with the Virgin on the right and the Angel approaching from the left. The background sky and the Virgin's robe are painted in traditional ultramarine. The lower register depicts a scene from *The Brigittine Nuns in a Choir*, located in front of a lectern and altar. Saint Brigitte is shown on the left, behind the nuns, holding up a scroll that runs above the nuns' heads. Here again ultramarine blue is used for the altar frontal and the dome of the apse.

Bicci di Lorenzo (1373–1452) was a Florentine sculptor and painter famous for full-scale paintings for patrons such as the Medicis. The son of the painter Lorenzo di Bicci, whose workshop he joined, he received, in collaboration with his father, numerous important commissions including a cycle of frescoes of *Illustrious Men* for the Palazzo Medici and Apostles for the Opera del Duomo.

比奇・迪・羅倫佐（一三七三年至一四五二年）
製作於佛羅倫斯，意大利，約一四三五年
蛋彩、泥金與墨水，犢皮紙
高555公釐，寬370公釐

書頁分別描繪了「聖母領報」與「布雷廷修女們獻詩」場景。這幅由比奇・迪・羅倫佐（一三七三年至一四五二年）製作的作品被分置於伴隨兩場景的區塊中。上半部為「聖母領報」，其中聖母在右側，天使由左側趨近，圖畫的背景（天空）與聖母的長袍皆被繪上傳統的群青色。下半部為「布雷廷修女們獻詩」場景，位於經臺與聖壇的前面；聖布里吉特居於左側，修女隊尾之後，手持的捲軸飄浮於修女的頭上；畫中的聖壇前面以及後殿拱頂也使用了群青色。

比奇・迪・羅倫佐是佛羅倫斯的雕塑家與畫家，以其由麥地奇家族等贊助的全尺寸繪畫而出名。他加入了他兒子羅倫佐・迪・比奇創立的工作坊，二人一起接到了許多重要的製作委託，包括為麥地奇宮製作的系列壁畫《傑出的人》與為主教座堂製作的《使徒》。

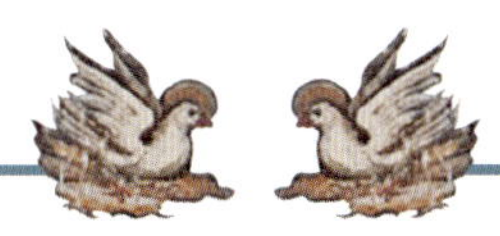

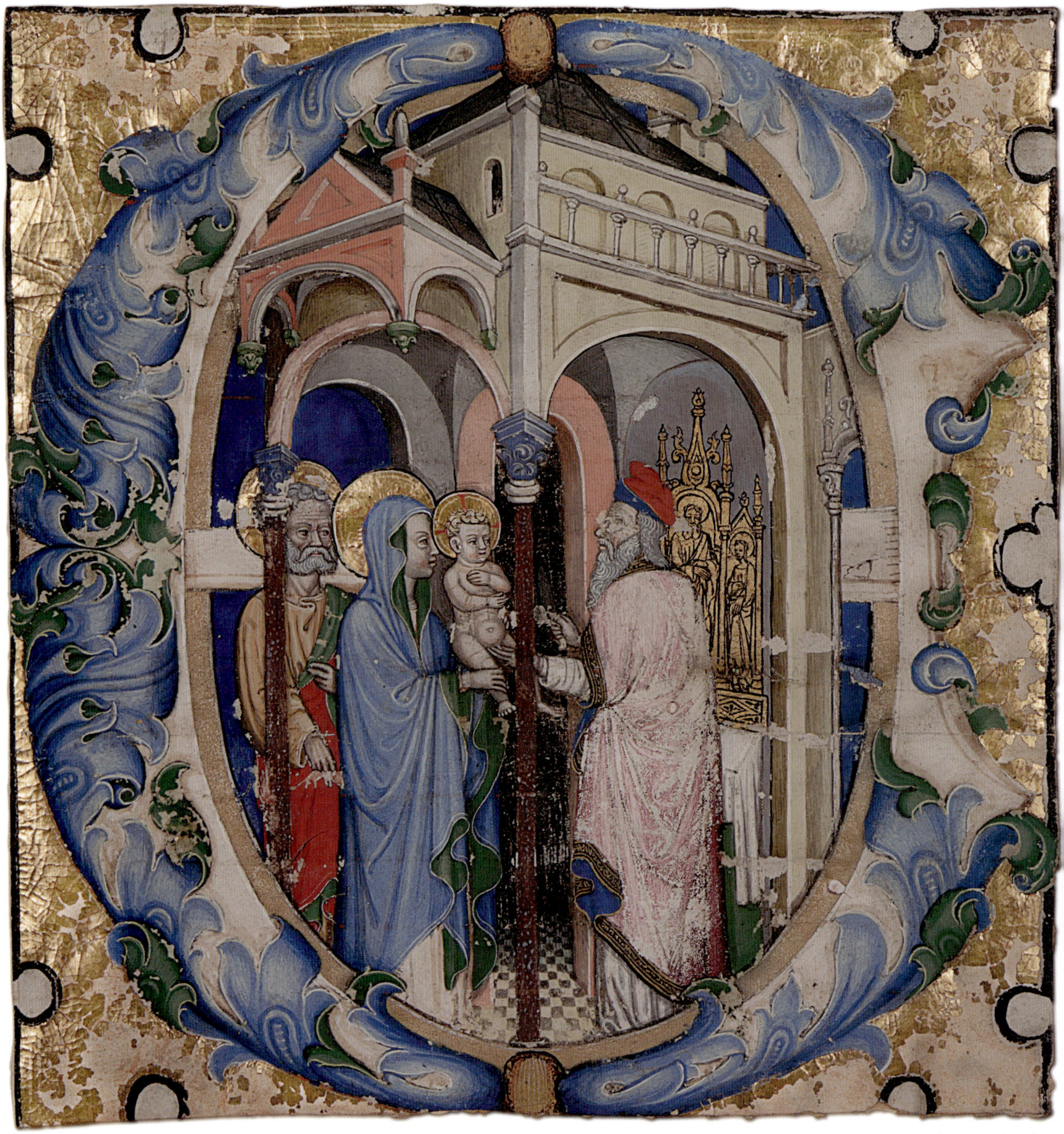

(actual size 原大)

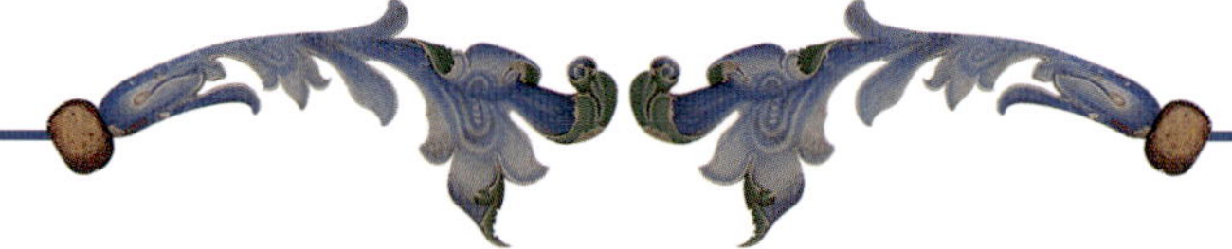

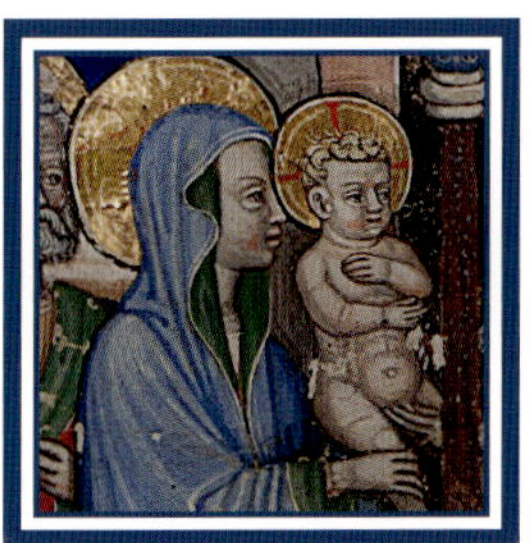

Cat. 23 | Reference 參考編號: BM 1679; SF 10640

Leaf Depicting *The Presentation in the Temple* and a Historiated Initial "E"

書頁，描繪「獻主於聖殿」，佔行大寫首字母「E」經中世紀傳統出版風格修飾與變形

Bologna or Veneto, Italy, c.1430–1440
Tempera and gold on vellum
H.190 mm W. 185 mm

製作於博洛尼亞或威尼托，意大利
約一四三零年至一四四零年
蛋彩與泥金，犢皮紙
高 190 公釐，寬 185 公釐

This leaf illustrates *The Presentation in the Temple* within a scrolling and leafy initial "E", executed in green and blue and set on a burnished gold ground. It likely originates from the antiphonary "Ecce Maria", and the composition is set within the auspices of a Gothic church structure, with tall pillars and multiple vaulting up to a roof with canopies and a balustrade around the attic. The Virgin is passing the Christ Child to the priest, who is standing with his circumcision knife before a magnificent golden Gothic altarpiece. Joseph stands behind the Virgin. The verso preserves Roman choral notation with large square notes on four red lines and a large *Textura*.

The opulent initial is stylistically rooted in north-eastern Italian illumination. The thick foliage of the initials, and other elements are related to the work of Niccolò da Bologna (c.1325–1403), and consequently characterize the work of masters active in Bologna in the first decades of the fifteenth century, such as the so-called Master of the Orsini Missal and the Master of the Servi Missal. Furthermore, the compositional and formal elements are also known from the work of masters in the Veneto working in the wake of Gentile da Fabriano (c.1370–1427), such as Zanino di Pietro (active 1389–1448) and Niccolò di Pietro (doc. 1394–1427).

Literature: Medica 1992; Palladino 2003, cat. 36, pp. 68–69; Zeileis 2004, cat. 13, pp. 48–49.

書頁內的「獻主於聖殿」場景，框於一個捲軸形葉紋裝飾佔行大寫首字母「E」中，為綠色與藍色，並且置於拋光泥金料底之上。書頁有可能起源於輪唱聖詩「Ecce Maria（看吶聖母馬利亞）」，圖畫構圖設置於一座哥德式教堂結構的榮光之中，其中有高聳的柱子與多種拱頂，直延伸至屋頂及欄杆環繞的閣樓。在金碧輝煌的哥德式聖壇之前，聖母正在將聖嬰交給一位手持割禮刀侍立的牧師，若瑟站在聖母身後。背頁保留了羅馬式合唱記譜系統，包括有紅色四線譜上的大方形記號。

此奢華的大寫首字母在風格上起源於意大利東北部的插畫，厚實的葉紋裝飾以及其他元素讓人聯想到尼可洛・達・博洛尼亞（約一三二五年至一四零三年）的作品，因而也表現出十五世紀前十年中活躍於博洛尼亞的一些大師的作品風格，比如所謂的奧爾西尼米薩爾的大師與塞爾維米薩爾的大師。此外，構圖和固定出現的元素也被發現於那些仿效真蒂萊・達・法布里亞諾（約一三七零年至一四二七年）的威尼托的大師們的作品中，比如扎尼諾・迪・彼得羅（活躍於一三八九年至一四四八年）與尼可洛・迪・彼得羅（文獻載於一三九四年至一四二七年）的作品。

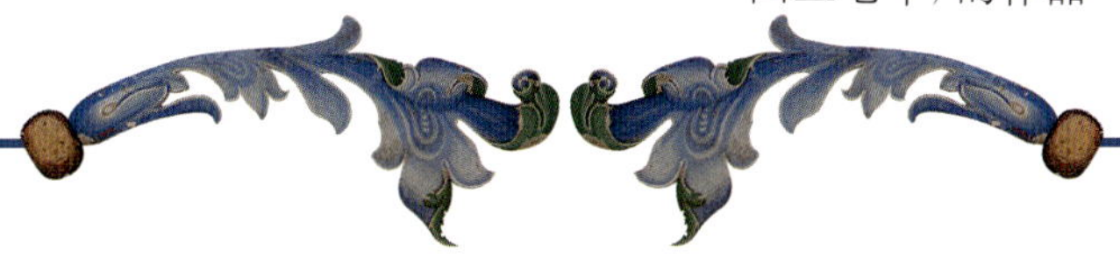

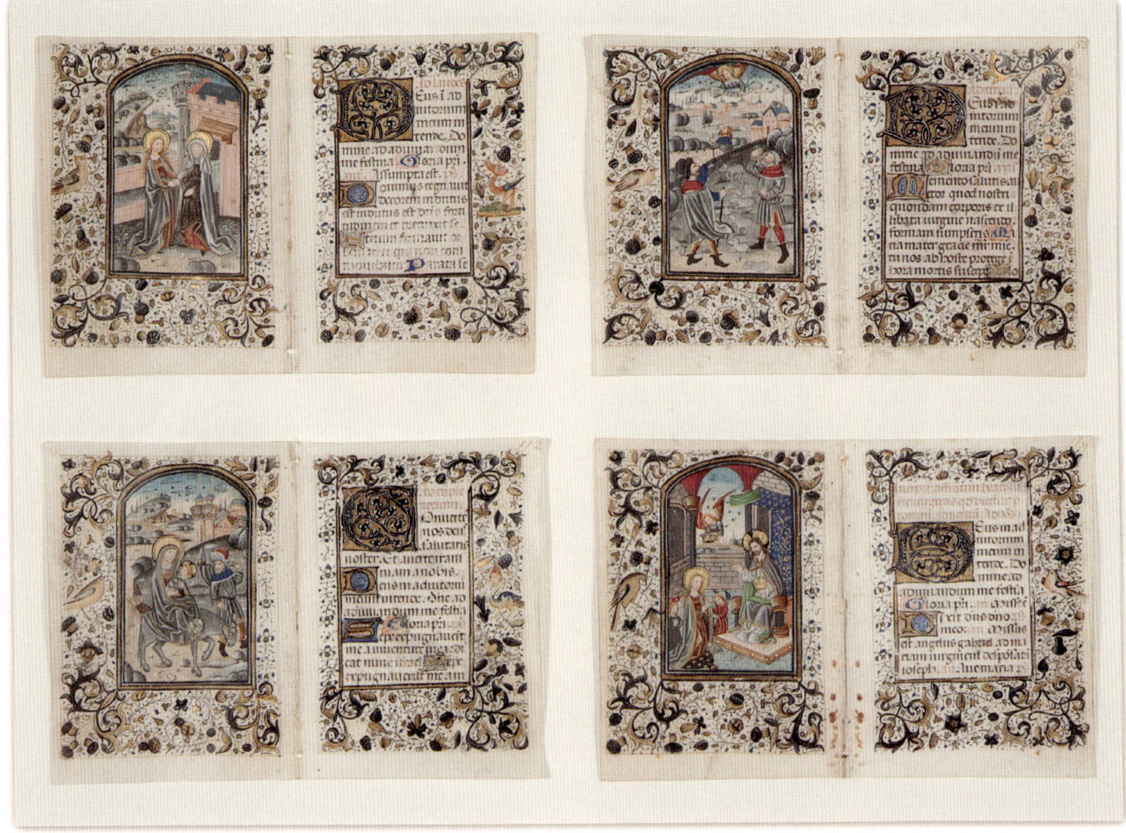

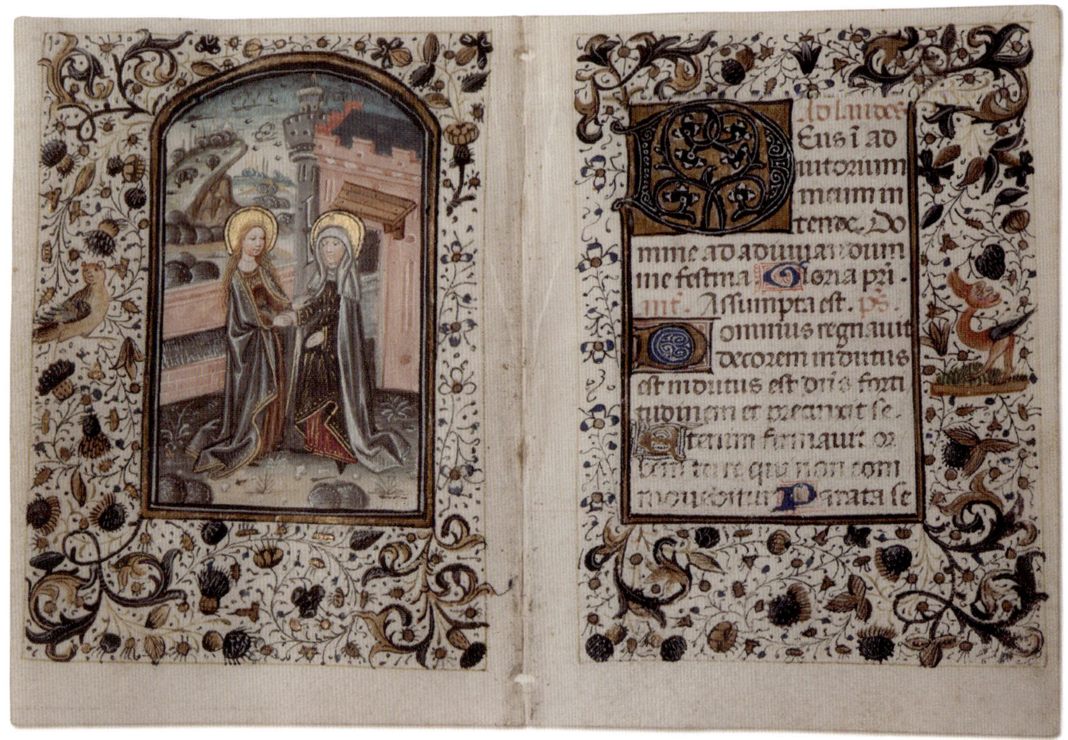

The Visitation「聖母訪親」(actual size 原大)

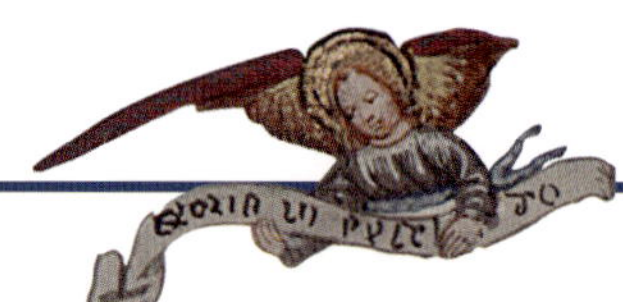

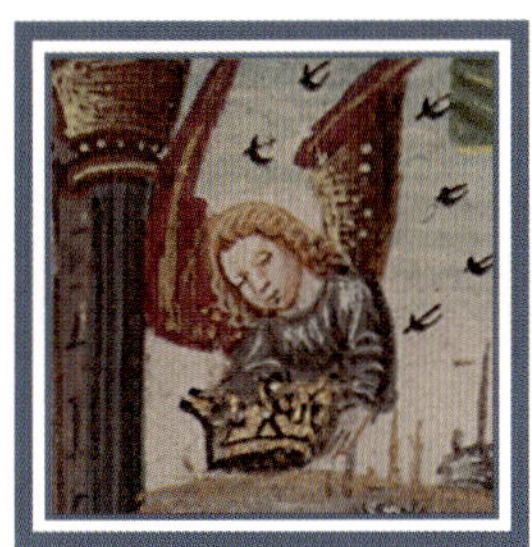

Cat. 24a–d | Reference 參考編號: BM 1120

Four Bifolia Depicting *The Visitation*, *The Annunciation to the Shepherds*, *The Flight into Egypt*, and *The Coronation of the Virgin*
四組跨頁，描繪「聖母訪親」、「天使向牧羊人報喜」、「逃往埃及」與「聖母加冕」

Willem Vrelant's (active 1454–1481) workshop
France, c.1450–1460
Tempera, gold and ink on vellum
H. 95 mm W. 140 mm

威廉．維蘭德（活躍於一四五四年至一四八一年）
工作室，製作於法國
約一四五零年至一四六零年
蛋彩、泥金與墨水，犢皮紙
高 95 公釐，寬 140 公釐

These four leaves depict the *The Visitation*, *The Annunciation to the Shepherds*, *The Flight into Egypt*, and *The Coronation of the Virgin* set in highly decorative borders in grisailles technique. Manuscripts painted in tones of grey (*grisaille*) existed in numerous editions during the 15th century. In as early as the early 14th century, Giotto painted figures of Virtues and Vices in grey in the Scrovegni Chapel in Padua, so that they had the appearance of stone sculpture; and slightly later in the 14th century, grisaille appeared in French manuscript illumination in the spectacular Hours of Jean d'Evreux, painted by Jean Pucelle (c.1300–1355). In the southern Netherlands grisaille painting became popular from about 1425. One of the most influential examples being the figures painted to imitate stone sculptures on the outer panels of the Ghent Altarpiece, by Hubert (c.1385 / 1390–1426) and Jan van Eyck (c.1390–1441). At the time this technique might have been used to demonstrate that the art of painting was superior to that of sculpture. With regards to manuscripts, an important patron was Philip the Good, Duke of Burgundy, who commissioned two grisaille books of hours from the illuminator Jean le Tavernier (active 1450–1462) in the 1450s, and had several other works illuminated in grisaille by Tavernier and Willem Vrelant in the 1450s and 1460s.

四組跨頁中微繪分別描繪「聖母訪親」、「天使向牧羊人報喜」、「逃往埃及」與「聖母加冕」，皆具有極具裝飾效果的邊框，畫中還應用了浮雕式純灰色裝飾畫技巧。以灰色調描繪的手抄本（Grisaille）通常存在於十五世紀的眾多版本中。早在十四世紀早期的時候，喬托在帕多瓦的斯克羅威尼禮拜堂創作的「美德與惡習」人像，以全灰色繪畫，使得他們看上去如同石雕作品；十四世紀稍晚些時候，這種浮雕式純灰色裝飾技巧開始出現於法國裝飾手抄本中，比如讓．皮塞勒（約一三零零年至一三五五年）製作的精美絕倫的《貞德時禱書》。在南尼德蘭地區，浮雕式純灰色裝飾畫約自一四二五年開始流行，最出名的例子是《根特祭壇畫》外層畫板中那仿石雕效果的繪畫形象，此祭壇畫的作者為休伯特．范．艾克（約一三八五或一三九零年至一四二六年）與揚．范．艾克（約一三九零年至一四四一年）。那時，此種技術可能意在表達繪畫藝術高明於雕塑藝術。手抄本的重要贊助人之一是勃艮第公爵菲利普三世，他於一四五零年代委託插畫家讓．勒．塔維涅（活躍於一四五零年至一四六二年）製

Manuscripts are rarely painted in pure grisaille, but typically as “semi-grisaille”, in which some parts of the images are in tones of grey and colour is almost always used. The present manuscript is interesting in that the miniatures are normally painted in full-colour, with the exception of draperies, which are grisaille. The full-page miniatures could be attributed to the workshop of Willem Vrelant, one of the most successful and prolific Flemish illuminators of the mid-fifhteeth century.

Literature: Osterstrom Renger 1983; Cockshaw 1986; Bousmanne 1997; Plonka–Balus 2001; Bousmanne–Delcourt 2011, pp. 238–258.

作了兩本浮雕式純灰色裝飾《時禱書》，還有一些其他的由塔維涅與威廉．維蘭德於一四五零及六零年代製作的浮雕式純灰色裝飾書。

手繪本很少單獨使用浮雕式純灰色裝飾畫，而是「半式」的，在這些作品中灰色調往往只是局部使用，但是彩色幾乎隨處可見。有趣的是，此處四張微繪為正常的彩色，只有所描繪的布料為浮雕式純灰色裝飾技巧。這些微繪可能是由威廉．維蘭德的工作坊製作，他是十五世紀中葉最成功最多產的佛拉芒插畫家之一。

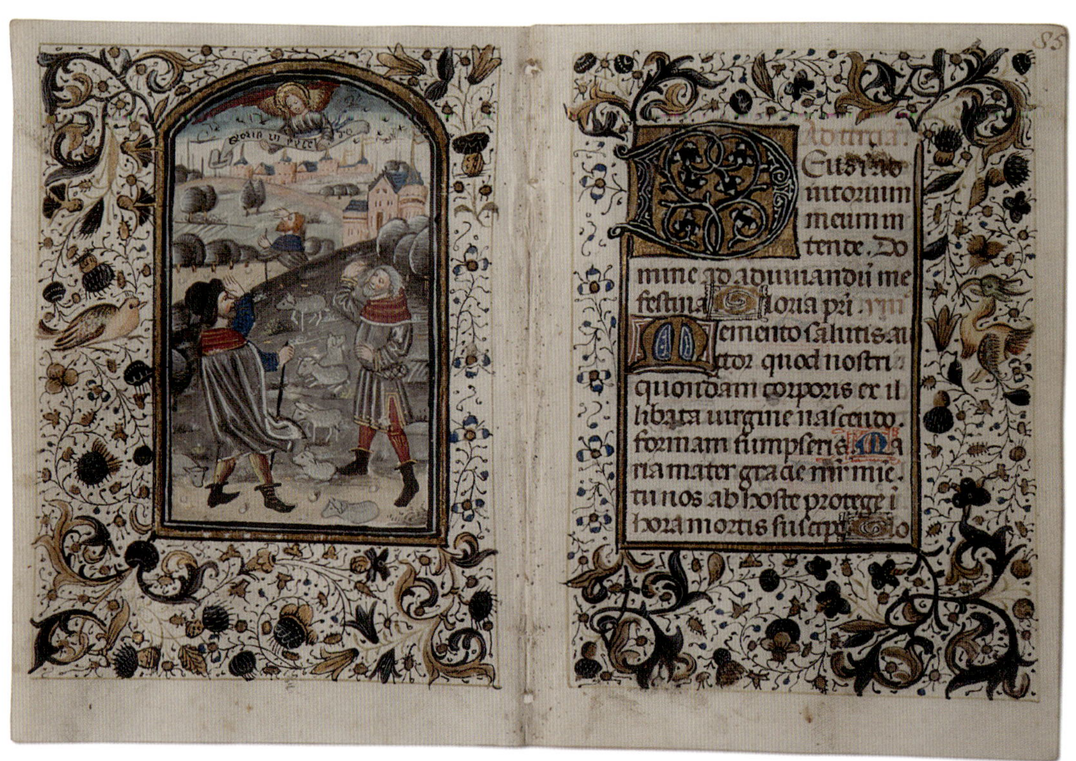

The Annunciation「天使向牧羊人報喜」(actual size 原大)

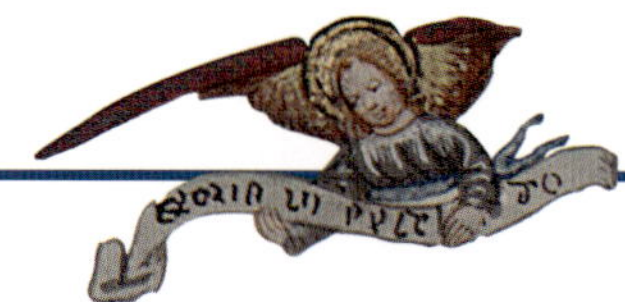

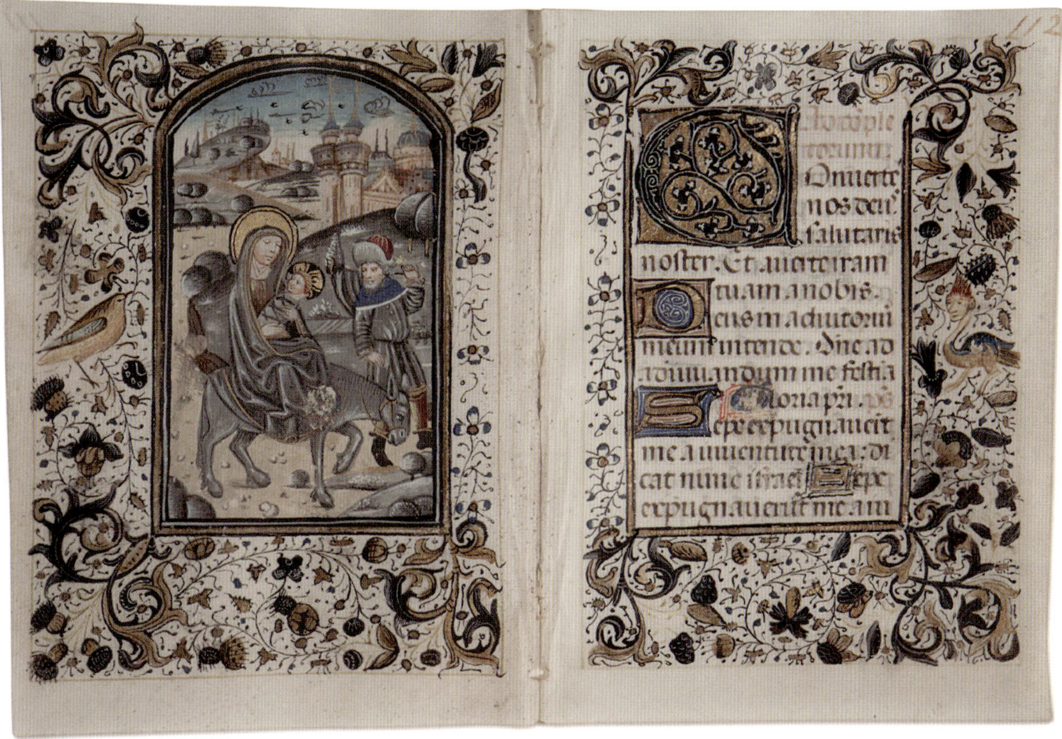

The Flight into Egypt「逃往埃及」(actual size 原大)

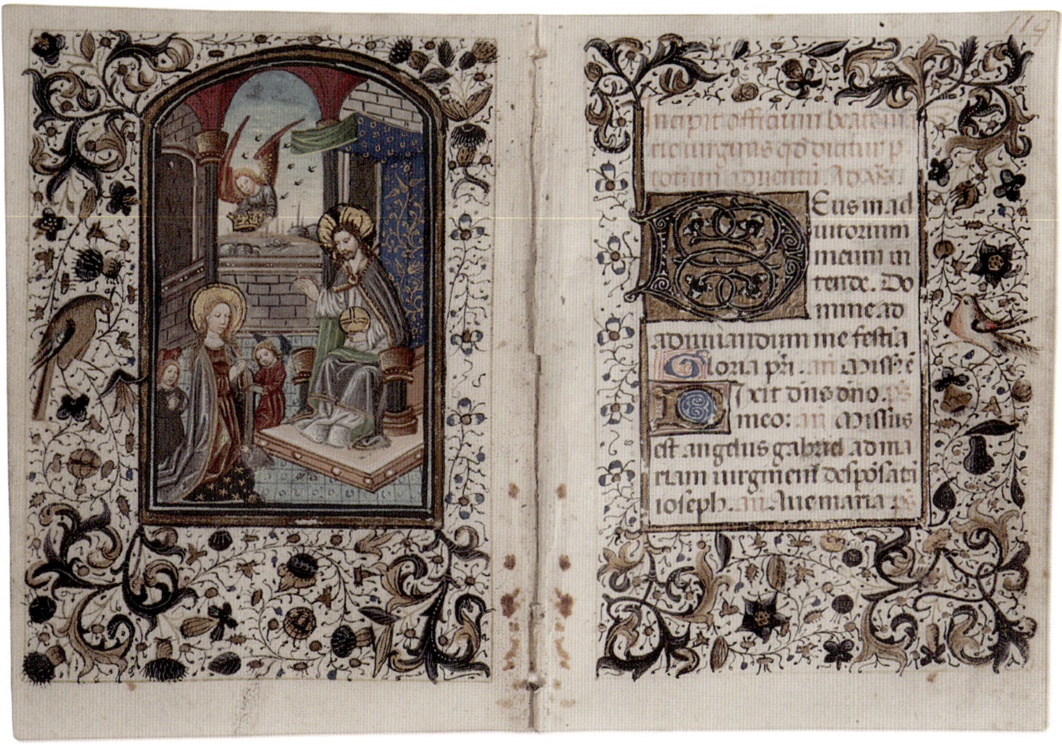

The Coronation of the Virgin「聖母加冕」(actual size 原大)

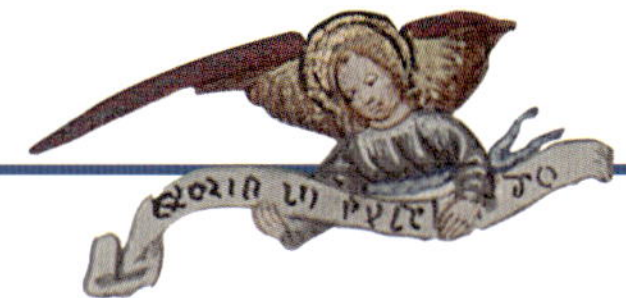

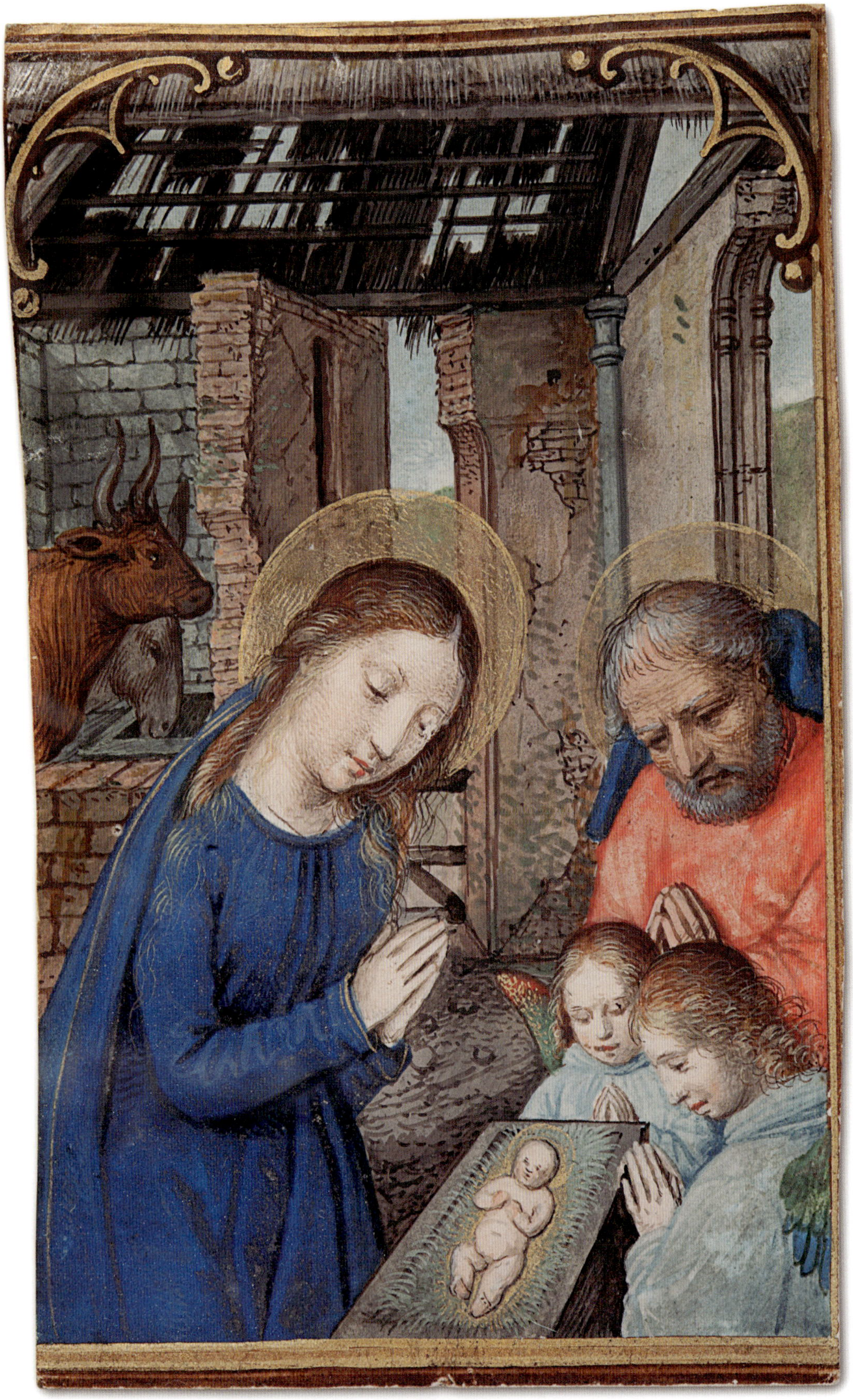

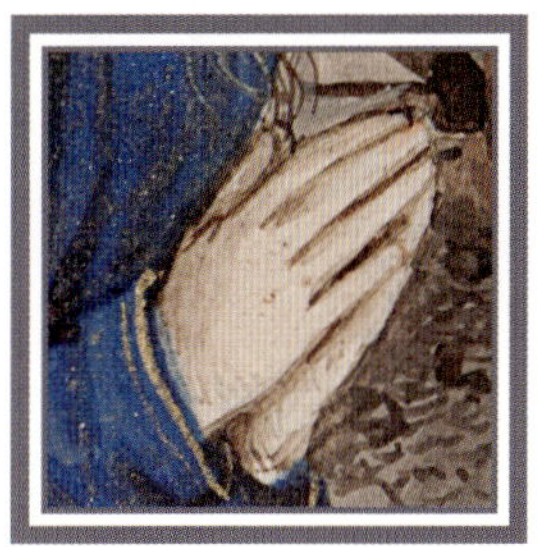

Cat. 25 | Reference 參考編號: BM 2394

Leaf from a Rosarium Depicting *The Nativity*
《玫瑰經》書頁，描繪「耶穌降生」

Simon Bening (Bruges, 1483–1561)
Bruges, Southern Netherlands, c.1520–1530
Tempera and gold on vellum
H. 76 mm W. 45 mm

This leaf depicts *The Nativity*, showing the Virgin Mary and Joseph with hands joined, gazing down at the newborn Christ Child who is shining rays from his body, in the foreground, set within a gold bar border with brackets at the upper corners. Two angels witness the scene while an ox and an ass appear in the background inside ruins of a barn.

This illuminated manuscript was executed by Simon Bening (1483–1561) who was the celebrated master of a number of miniature suites for use in small-scale books of hours, rosariums, and other devotional manuscripts. One of Bening's most significant artistic achievements was his development of the "close-up narrative," used in the so-called Chester Beatty Rosarium, the Stein Quadriptych, and miniatures in books of hours.

In this Nativity scene, Mary, Joseph and the Christ Child occupy the foreground of the miniature. Several stylistic elements present in this depiction relate to the Chester Beatty miniatures of the *The Nativity* and *The Adoration of the Magi*. The neglected stable with remnants of a thatched roof and brick walls is closely comparable, as are the models for the angels, the ox and the ass. The pillar, which dominates and divides the Chester Beatty scene, is now moved to the back resting in the corner. Joseph is undoubtedly the same facial model and his blue cowl curls around his neck in exactly the same way as in the Chester Beatty miniatures.

施蒙．貝寧（布魯日，一四八三年至一五六一年）
製作於布魯日，南尼德蘭地區
約一五二零年至一五三零年
蛋彩與泥金，犢皮紙
高76公釐，寬45公釐

書頁內的「耶穌降生」場景中，聖母與若瑟皆雙手合十致禮，俯視著閃射出光芒的新生聖嬰；前景中有直條型金色邊框，其上兩角為托架；兩位天使也現身此景；後景的廢舊穀倉中出現一頭牛與一頭驢。

此插畫由施蒙．貝寧（一四八三年至一五六一年）製作，他是為《時禱書》、《玫瑰經》及其他虔修敬拜用書繪製微型插畫的著名大師。貝寧最知名的藝術成果是對「特寫敘事」的發展，這應用於所謂的《切斯特．比替玫瑰經》、《斯泰因四聯幅》與《時禱書》中的微繪。

此「耶穌降生」場景中，聖母、若瑟與聖嬰佔據了微繪的前景。其中的一些風格元素與切斯特．比替的「耶穌降生」與「博士來朝」微繪相關。荒廢的畜棚及其殘破不堪的茅草棚頂與磚牆形成強烈的對比，天使、牛與驢的模板亦然。切斯特．比替畫作中用以支配並分隔場景的柱子，在此處被閒置於背景的牆角。毫無疑問，若瑟的面部模板以及捲曲環繞在其脖頸的藍色斗篷，皆同切斯特．比替的微繪完全一致。

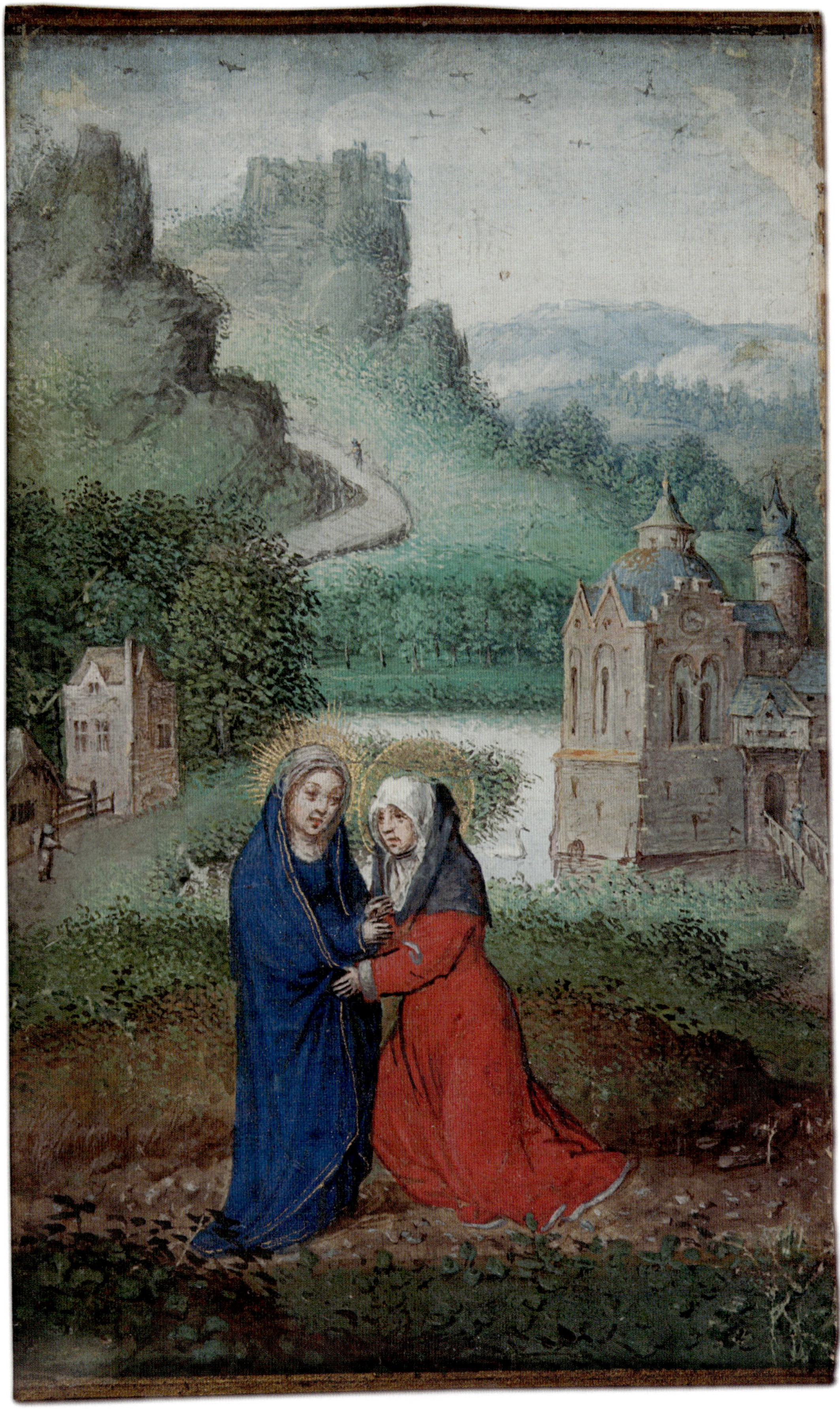

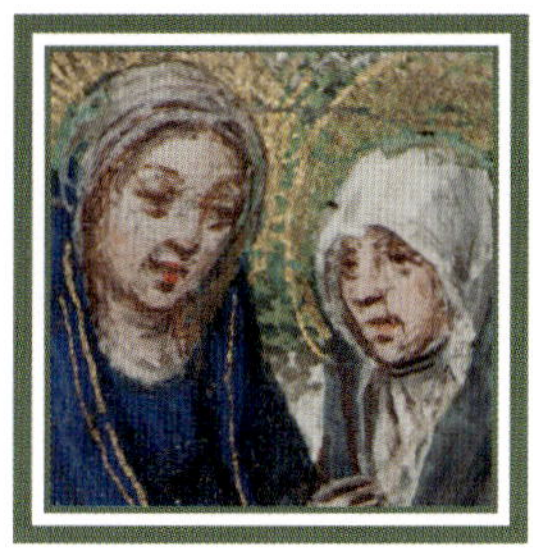

Cat. 26a | Reference 參考編號: BM 1456; SF 9458

Leaf from a Book of Hours Depicting *The Visitation*
《時禱書》書頁，描繪「聖母訪親」

Simon Bening (Bruges, 1483–1561)
Bruges, Southern Netherlands, c.1540
Tempera and gold on vellum
H. 75 mm W. 48 mm

施蒙．貝寧（布魯日，一四八三年至一五六一年）
製作於布魯日，南尼德蘭地區
約一五四零年
蛋彩與泥金，犢皮紙
高75公釐，寬48公釐

This leaf illustrates *The Visitation*, in which the Virgin Mary is wearing a blue coat (a traditional representation), whereas Elizabeth is clothed in red. Both figures are placed in an elaborate mountain landscape background with a castle and a house. This miniature shows unusually fine detail and vibrant colours, a technique and style attributed to Simon Bening. Born in Antwerp or Ghent, Bening was employed by the Elector of Mainz and the King of Portugal, and was the only northern illuminator mentioned in Vasari's *Lives of the Artists*, in which Vasari praised him for his ability to paint landscapes on the smallest scale. Bening's miniatures depict biblical scenes set in his contemporary surroundings of 16th-century Flanders. The origin of this leaf remains unknown. Stylistically it relates to The Capricorn Book of Hours, which Simon Bening illuminated in Bruges around 1530.

書頁內的「聖母訪親」場景中，聖母身穿藍色外衣（傳統上指向馬利亞的符號），而以利沙伯則穿著紅色衣服，兩人皆置身於細緻精美且點綴有城堡與房屋的風景圖之中。該微繪有著非比尋常的細節捕捉與節奏明快的顏色，這種技巧與風格被認為是施蒙．貝寧的特色。施蒙．貝寧，出生於安特衛普或根特，曾受僱於美茵茨選帝侯與葡萄牙國王，而且也是唯一一位出現於瓦薩里的《藝苑名人傳》中的北方插畫家，書中瓦薩里讚美了他那在微繪中表現風景的能力。貝寧從他身處的十六世紀法蘭德斯的周遭環境中取材，來創作聖經故事場景的微繪。此書頁的出處至今未知，其創作風格與貝寧一五三零年左右製作於布魯日的《摩羯宮時禱書》相關。

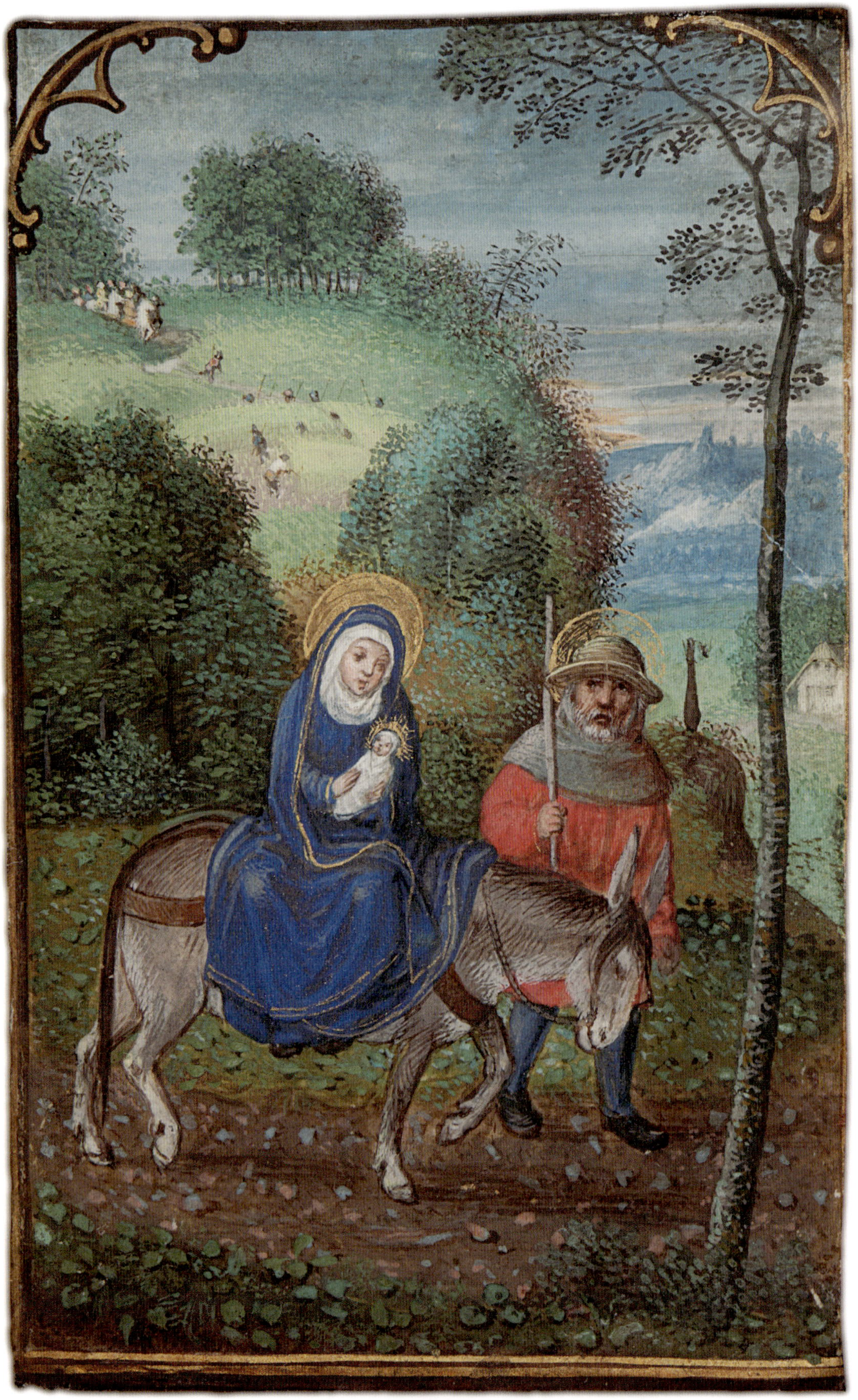

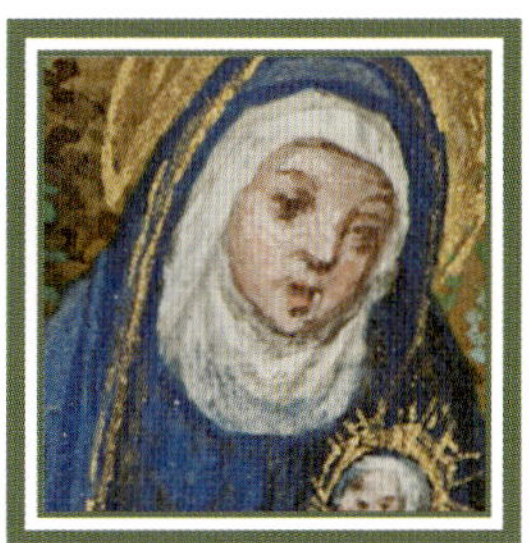

Cat. 26b | Reference 參考編號: BM 1457; SF 9460

Leaf from a Book of Hours Depicting *The Flight into Egypt*
《時禱書》書頁，描繪「逃往埃及」

Simon Bening (Bruges, 1483–1561)
Bruges, Southern Netherlands, c.1540
Tempera and gold on vellum
H. 73 mm W. 46 mm

施蒙・貝寧（布魯日，一四八三年至一五六一年）
製作於布魯日，南尼德蘭地區
約一五四零年
蛋彩與泥金，犢皮紙
高73公釐，寬46公釐

Possibly originating from the same book of hours as the depiction of *The Visitation* (cat. no. 26a), this leaf illustrates *The Flight into Egypt*, depicting the Virgin riding on a donkey holding the Christ Child, as Joseph walks slightly ahead. In the background, Roman soldiers are descending the slope of the hills in pursuit. This composition is particularly deep, offering a wide perspective into the faraway background. The three-dimensionality is increased by the brilliant highlights and shading. The detail of this miniature is very fine and its colours are well preserved.

可能與描繪「聖母訪親」的微繪（圖錄編號26a）一樣，皆出自同一本《時禱書》。書頁內的「逃往埃及」場景中，聖母抱著聖嬰，騎在驢背，若瑟則稍稍走在前邊。背景中，羅馬士兵正順山坡向下搜尋。此幅作品構圖深邃，提供了一種頗具景深的透視效果。這種三維立體的觀感又因著藝術家對高光與陰影的絕妙描繪技巧而進一步加強。此幅微繪具有精緻的細節，顏色得到很好保存。

Bibliography 參考書目

Alexander 1977: Jonathan J. G. Alexander, *Italian Renaissance Illuminations*, New York, 1977.

Alexander 1992: Jonathan J. G. Alexander, *Medieval Illuminators and Their Methods of Work*, New Haven, 1992.

Alexander 1994: Jonathan J. G. Alexander (ed.), *The Painted Page: Italian Renaissance Book Illumination, 1450–1550*, Munich, 1994.

Alexander 2002: Jonathan J. G. Alexander, *Studies in Italian Manuscript Illumination*, London, 2002.

Avril 1981: François Avril, Françoise Baron and Danielle Gaborit-Chopin, *Les Fastes du gothique: le siècle de Charles V*, exh. cat., Paris, 1981.

Backhouse 2004: Janet Backhouse, *Illumination from Books of Hours*, London, 2004.

Bland 1958: David Bland, *A History of Book Illustration: The Illuminated Manuscript and The Printed Book*, London, 1958.

Boskovits 1997: Miklos Boskovits, Giovanni Valagussa, Milvia Bollati and Biblioteca nazionale braidense, *Miniature a Brera, 1100–1422: manoscritti dalla Biblioteca nazionale braidense e da collezioni private*, Milan, 1997.

Bousmanne 1997: Bernard Bousmanne, 'Item a Guillaume Wyelant aussi enlumineur', in *Willem Vrelant: un aspect de l'enluminure dans les Pays-Bas méridionaux sous le mécénat des ducs de Bourgogne, Philippe le Bon et Charles le Téméraire*, Turnhout, 1997.

Bousmanne–Delcourt 2011: Bernard Bousmanne and T. Delcourt (eds.), *Miniatures flamandes, 1404–1482*, exh. cat., Paris and Brussels, 2011.

Branner 1977: Robert Branner, *Manuscript Painting in Paris During the Reign of St. Louis*, Berkeley, 1977.

Büttner 2004: Frank Olaf Büttner (ed.), *The Illuminated Psalter. Studies in the Content, Purpose and Placement of its Images*, Turnhout, 2004.

Calkins 1978: Robert G. Calkins, 'Stages of Execution: Procedures of Illumination as Revealed in an Unfinished Book of Hours', in *Gesta*, vol. 17, no. 1 (1978), pp. 61–70.

Calkins 1983: Robert G. Calkins, *Illuminated Books of the Middle Ages*, Ithaca, 1983.

Canova 1978: Giordana Mariani Canova, *Miniature dell'Italia Settentrionale nella Fondazione Giorgio Cini*, Vicenza, 1978.

Canova 1979: Giordana Mariani Canova, 'Nuovi contributi alla serie liturgica degli antifonari di San Domenico in Bologna', in *La miniatura italiana in età romanica e gotica. Atti del I congresso di storia della miniatura italiana, Florence*, 1979.

Cockshaw 1986: P. Cockshaw, *Miniatures en grisaille*, exh. cat., Brussels, 1986.

Coleman–Cruse–Smith 2013: Joyce Coleman, Mark Cruse, and Kathryn A. Smith (eds.), *The Social Life of Illumination: Manuscripts, Images, and Communities in the Late Middle Ages*, (series: Medieval Texts and Cultures in Northern Europe, vol. 21), Turnhout, 2013.

De Hamel 1986: Christopher De Hamel, *A History of Illuminated Manuscripts*, London, 1986.

De Hamel 1992: Christopher De Hamel, *Medieval Craftsmen: Scribes and Illuminations*, Buffalo, 1992.

De Hamel 2001: Christopher De Hamel, *The British Library Guide to Manuscript Illumination: History and Techniques*, Toronto, 2001.

De Ricci 1937: Seymour De Ricci (with W. J. Wilson), *Census of Medieval and Renaissance Manuscripts in the United States and Canada*, New York, 1937.

Euw–Plotzek 1979: Anton von Euw and Joachim M. Plotzek, *Die Handschriften der Sammlung Ludwig*, Cologne, 1979.

Ferrini 1987: Bruce P. Ferrini, *Important Western Medieval Illuminated Manuscripts and Illuminated Leaves*, cat. I, Akron, 1987.

Freuler 2004: Gaudenz Freuler, Studi recenti sulla miniatura medievale (soprattutto) emiliana. Appunti intorno ad una recente mostra americana (part I), in *Arte Cristiana*, vol. XCII, 2004.

Freuler 2013: Gaudenz Freuler, *Italian Miniatures from the Twelfth to the Sixteenth Centuries*, Milan, 2013.

Forrer 1902: Robert Forrer, *Unedierte Federzeichnungen Miniaturen und Initialen des Mittelalters*, Strassburg, 1902.

Gibbs 1994: Robert Gibbs, 'Towards a History of Earlier 14th-Century Bolognese Illumination: Little-Known Manuscripts by Nerio Bolognese and the Hungarian Master', in *Wiener Jahrbuch für Kunstgeschichte*, vol. 46–47, no. 1 (Dec 1994), pp. 211–222.

Günther 1993: Jörn Günther, *Mittelalterliche Handschriften und Miniaturen*, Hamburg, 1993.

Holcomb 2009: Melanie Holcomb, *Pen and Parchment: Drawing in the Middle Ages,* exh. cat., New York, 2009.

Kanter 1994: Laurence B. Kanter, Barbara Drake Boehm, Carl Brandon Strelhke, Gaudenz Freuler, Christa C. Mayer Thurman, and Pia Palladino, *Painting and Illumination in Early Renaissance Florence, 1300–1450*, exh. cat., New York, 1994.

Kelly–Thompson 2005: Stephen Kelly and John J. Thompson (eds.), *Imagining the Book*, Turnhout, 2005.

Lazaris 2010: Stavros Lazaris, *Art et science vétérinaire à Byzance: Formes et fonctions de l'image hippiatrique*, Turnhout, 2010.

Lazaris 2010: Stavros Lazaris, 'L'illustration des disciplines médicales dans l'Antiquité : hypothèses, enjeux, nouvelles interprétations', in M. Bernabò (ed.), *La Collezione di testi chirurgici di Niceta, Rome*, 2010, pp. 99–109.

Lazaris 2013: Stavros Lazaris, 'L'image paradigmatique: des Schémas anatomiques d'Aristote au De materia medica de Dioscoride', in *Pallas*, vol. 93 (2013), pp. 131–164.

Manion–Fines–De Hamel 1989: Margaret M. Manion, Vera F. Vines and Christopher De Hamel, *Medieval and Renaissance Manuscripts in New Zealand Collections*, London, 1989.

Michael 1990: Michael A. Michael, 'Destruction, Reconstruction and Invention: The Hungersford Hours and English Manuscript Illumination of the early fourteenth Century', in *English Manuscript Studies: 1100–1700*, vol. 2 (January 1990), pp. 33–108.

Medica 1992: Massimo Medica, 'Aggiunte al Maestro del Messale Orsini e ad altri miniatori bolognesi tardogotici', *Arte a Bologna*, vol. 2 (1992), pp. 11–30.

Medica 1997: Massimo Medica, *Libri Miniati del Museo medievale*, Bologna, 1997.

Medica 2000: Massimo Medica, *Duecento. Forme e colori del medioevo a Bologna*, exh. cat., Bologna, 2000.

Meiss 1974: Millard Meiss, *The Limbourgs and their Contemporaries*, New York, 1974.

Mickenberg 1985: David Mickenberg, *Songs of Glory: Medieval Art from 900–1500*, Oklahoma City, 1985.

Nordenfalk 1979: Carl Nordenfalk, *Bokmalningar fran medeltid och renässans i Nationalmusei samlingar*, Stockholm, 1979.

Oliver 2004: Judith H. Oliver, 'A Primer of Thirteenth-Century German Convent Life. The Psalter as Office and Mass Book (London, British Library, MS. Add 60629)', in *Büttner*, 2004, pp. 259–270.

Osterstrom Renger 1983: M. Osterstrom Renger, 'The Netherlandish Grisaille Miniatures: Some Unexplored Aspects', in *Wallraf-Richartz-Jahrbuch*, vol. 44 (1983), pp.145–173.

Palladino 2003: Pia Palladino, *Treasures of a Lost Art: Italian Manuscript Painting of the Middle Ages and Renaissance*, Metropolitan Museum of Art, New York, 2003.

Plonka-Balus 2001: K. Plonka-Balus, 'Grisailles in the Illuminated Manuscripts in the Time of Dirk Bouts: Technique, Function and Meaning', in *Bouts Studies* (Leuven, 2001), pp. 151–159.

Plotzek 1987: Joachim M. Plotzek, *Andachtsbücher des Mittelalters aus Privatbesitz*, Cologne, 1987.

Pächt 1986: Otto Pächt, *Book Illumination in the Middle Ages*, Oxford, 1986.

Randall 1966: L.M.C. Randall, *Images in the Margins of Gothic Manuscripts*, 1966.

Randall 1989: L. M. C. Randall, *Medieval and Renaissance Manuscripts*, cat. vol. I, France, 875–1420 (in the Walters Art Gallery), Baltimore, 1989.

Riches 2000: John Riches, *The Bible: A Very Short Introduction*, Oxford 2000.

Royal Academy 1994: Royal Academy and Pierpont Morgan Library, *The Painted Page: Italian Renaissance Book Illumination 1450–1550*, exh. cat., London and New York, 1994.

Stork 1992: H. W. Stork, Die Wienerfranzösische Bible Moralisie, *Codex 2554 der Österreichischen Nationalbibliothek*, Vienna 1992.

Stokstad 2005: Marilyn Stokstad, *Art History*, Upper Saddle River, 2005.

Swarzenski 1936: Hans Swarzenski, *Die Deutsche Buchmalerei des 13. Jahrhunderts. Die lateinischen illuminierten Handschriften den 13. Jahrhunderts in den Ländern an Rhein, Main und Donau*, 2 vols., Berlin, 1936.

Vanwijnsberghe 2007: Dominique Vanwijnsberghe, *'Moult bons et notables': L'enluminure tournaisienne à l'époque de Robert Campin (1380–1430)*, Leuven, 2007.

Voelkle–Wieck 1992: William M. Voelkle and Roger S. Wieck, *The Bernard H. Breslauer Collection of Manuscript Illuminations*, The Pierpont Morgan Library, New York, 1992.

Walters 1949: Walters Art Gallery, *Illuminated Books of the Middle Ages and Renaissance*, Baltimore, 1949.

Walther–Wolf 2005: Ingo F. Walther and Norbert Wolf, *Masterpieces of Illumination (Codices Illustres)*, Cologne, 2005.

Watson 2003: Rowan Watson, *Illuminated Manuscripts and their Makers*, London, 2003.

Wieck 1996: Roger Wieck, 'Folia Fugitiva: The Pursuit of the Illuminated Manuscript Leaf', in *The Journal of the Walters Art Gallery*, vol. 54 (1996), pp. 233–254.

Zeileis 2004: Friedrich Georg Zeileis, *Più ridon le carte: Buchmalerei aus Mittelalter und Renaissance: Katalog einer Privatsammlung von illuminierten Einzelblättern*, Gallspach, 2004.